Benjamin Penhallow Shillaber

Partingtonian Patchwork

ISBN/EAN: 9783337143602

Printed in Europe, USA, Canada, Australia, Japan

Cover: Foto ©ninafisch / pixelio.de

More available books at **www.hansebooks.com**

PARTINGTONIAN PATCHWORK.

BLIFKINS THE MARTYR:

THE DOMESTIC TRIALS OF A MODEL HUSBAND.

THE MODERN SYNTAX:

DR. SPOONER'S EXPERIENCES IN SEARCH OF THE DELECTABLE.

PARTINGTON PAPERS:

STRIPPINGS OF THE WARM MILK OF HUMAN KINDNESS.

NEW AND OLD DIPS

FROM AN UNAMBITIOUS INKSTAND.

HUMOROUS, ECCENTRIC, RHYTHMICAL.

BY B. P. SHILLABER.

" 'Tis not so deep as a well, nor so wide as a church-door;
but 'tis enough."

BOSTON
LEE AND SHEPARD, PUBLISHERS.
NEW YORK:
LEE, SHEPARD, AND DILLINGHAM.
1873.

TO

JOHN H. EASTBURN, Esq.,

THE PRINTER AND THE PRINTER'S FRIEND,

𝕮𝖍𝖎𝖘 𝕭𝖔𝖔𝖐,

BY ONE OF THE CRAFT,

IS CORDIALLY DEDICATED.

PUBLISHERS' PREFACE.

THE great fire which destroyed the business-por-
tion of Boston spared, for the benefit of the world,
a few sheets of Mrs. Partington's new book, and the
plates; upon which the publishers congratulated themselves, and the expectant public took heart. Arrangements were made to reproduce the work in
season for the holidays: but the second fire, at Rand,
Avery, & Co.'s, swept away both sheets and plates;
and expectations, like those of the wicked, were "cut
off." The book at this time makes a fresh appeal,
trusting that the interest has not abated, and that the
present issue may be spared any more fiery trial than
the kind stricture of friends, or the honest opinions
of critics.

While contemplating the republication, during the
icy season in December, we received a visit from Mrs.
Partington, and enjoyed a refreshing season of wise
impartation, that like dew in summer, which cheers

and invigorates, gave hope and promise to our enterprise. "You rise," we said, laboring with a new idea that just then enlightened us, "like the phœnix from its ashes." She turned as we spoke, and attempted to brush something from the skirts of her outer garment. "I don't know about the phœnix," she replied; "but I do wish people that put ashes on their sidewalks would dispense with 'em more judicially. I declare, I felt like an ambulance, for the ashes were as thin as human virtue, and I expect I am covered with confusion." We called her attention to our proposition to reprint. "Well," she replied, with the unselfishness that distinguishes her, while a gleam from her spectacles shot like sunlight around the room, "I hope it may be successive, and that the people may cry for it as the children used to for Gen. Sherman's Lozenges, and that everybody may buy it for your sake." Could any thing be more disinterested? In return for this, our wish is, that the dame may be the gainer, and never urge her friends to give it the patronage she wishes for us; trusting that, between us both, a large sale may be the result.

JANUARY, 1873.

LUBRICATORY.

IT is a necessity, with ship-builders, that, before they attempt to put the vessel they have built into the water, they liberally grease the ways, on which it rests in its cradle, in order that it may slide off easily into its "native element," as I have known enthusiastic reporters term the water in describing a launch. Well, an author's book is something like the ship. It is a structure that he has builded, as well as he knew how, to sail out on the waves of literature, to meet with a fate similar to that of the bark; for it may be favored with excellent weather, and sail over gentle seas, or be dashed about, and be wrecked, even, by adverse winds and angry elements. Therefore a preparatory lubrication may not be amiss, through which the fabric may glide down on its mission — to find its way to favor, or be as speedily forgotten as may be. In presenting his book, the author has three objects in view: To offer a claim for continued remembrance by his friends; to amuse the reader who may be attracted; to secure a little of that benefit for which the best of people make books. The author makes no very strong pretence to immaculateness in his book, either in style or quality; he has not, as he conceives, any grand leading moral idea in it; but he deems that if it succeed in making the reader for a moment forget his worldly cares and pains, and awakens a smile at eccentricities of thought or speech, it will have done as much good as though it made more pretension. No one, perhaps, who reads the author's name will purchase the volume with any expectation of finding aught beyond this; for though doubtless capable of writing books on abstruse subjects, he is content to let the Bacons of the age write them, and reserve to himself the humbler and more popular field of humor. In his pages, Dr. Spooner, the martyr Blifkins, and Mrs. Partington hold place, while there are many things, new and old, that are submitted in the form of stories, in some considerable variety, and sketches and rhythmical efforts that the author commends. He has taken for his motto, as being very fit, the remark of Mr. Mercutio regarding his wound, and satisfied that it is " enough," and will " serve," he leaves his book in the hands of his friends — and of his enemies, likewise, if he have any, to bide the result.

CONTENTS.

NEW AND OLD DIPS FROM MY INKSTAND:

PARTINGTONIAN PATCHWORK.

THE BLIFKINS PAPERS.

THOMAS MOORE, in a note to one of his satirical songs, wherein he alludes disparagingly to the marriage state, repudiates the sentiment of his Muse, and declares himself the happiest of men in the relation which he affects to deride. In these papers there may appear a degree of levity where they touch upon the domestic relations of Mr. and Mrs. Blifkins, and some may see an invidious rule, for general application, in the little acerbities depicted, that are, however, merely the momentary obscurations of the sun, rather than the blotting of it out entirely — like those shadows that flit above a pleasant landscape in summer, rendering the scene more bright because of the interruption. It wouldn't be a blessing to have it fair weather all the time, in a meteorological point of view, and in matrimony, the acid, though antagonistic to the saccharine, if admitted in slight proportion, makes the latter more positive, and secures keener enjoyment. Therefore this element in the Blifkins economy renders the life of that estimable pair happy, plus. The eccentricities and fickleness of Blifkins that will appear in these pages, tend measurably to keep the acid in active readiness, but they are really mere spots upon the sun, which, while we speculate upon them, disappear and leave his affection to shine in unclouded splendor upon his own fireside. The editor of these papers, therefore, as he publishes the idiosyncrasies of his friend, and lays his faults open to criticism, points to his virtues, as the Yankee enthusiast pointed out Bunker Hill Monument to an English visitor, without saying a word, leaving them to speak for themselves. It was the remark of a distinguished jurist that every tub should stand on its own bottom, and Blifkins must stand or fall by the verdict upon his own merits. Our acquaintance with him began during the war, when we received a letter from him detailing his experience in country quarters, through the reprinting of which we introduce him to our readers. This we entitle —

I.

BLIFKINS'S SUMMER RETREAT.

HARDSCRABBLE VILLAGE, September 1, 1861.

I CAME here to enjoy my *opium cum digitalis* amid Hardscrabble scenery. In front of us a cranberry meadow stretches away into the interminable distance. A fine view is presented, because there is no tree or bush to break off the prospect; in the rear the awful hills arise in their sublime grandeur, which, the people here say, can be seen with the naked eye on a clear day, being but seventy-five miles away. Between me and the hills a fine growth of huckleberry meets the desire for swamp scenery, and on nights the song of the buttermonk and bull-frog gratifies the primitive musical taste that delights not in Strauss and Chopin. The stage road runs by the west end of the house, beyond which a precipitous hill shuts out the last rays of the descending sun, that are called "unhealthy" by local science. The stage affords an unending interest, as it passes three times a day to and from the depot, raising a cloud of dust, and awakens lively anxiety for the fate of the children who may be lying round loose, and for the furniture, which is sure to receive a plentiful supply of the insidious particles. A preventive is supplied, however, in closing the doors, which keeps the children inside and the dust out. On the east, beyond a potato patch, is more cranberry meadow, and a small pond full of impracticable pond lilies and mud turtles.

Mrs. Blifkins heard of this place as one delightfully retired, where board could be had cheap; and she said to me one day, when I came home from a hard day's work, — I had devoted the whole day to collecting a bill of three dollars, —

"Mr. Blifkins, the Joneses have gone into the country."

"Well, my dear," said I, "I cannot conceive how that concerns us in any way."

"No, I suppose not," said that charming woman, rather sharply; "it doesn't concern us at all — Oh, no! and it doesn't concern us, nor the children either, I suppose, that this hot weather is making us miserable here, or that the vacation is passing with no recreation for the little dears. It doesn't concern us at all — Oh, no!"

"But the Joneses are able," I said; "Mr. Jones has just got a large contract for furnishing clothes-pins for the army, and is in first-rate business besides. A trip to Saratoga or the White Mountains would ruin me."

She saw, blessed woman, where the shoe pinched, and came at once to my relief and her own triumph.

"Blifkins," said she, "don't be ridiculous; how many more times do you want me to tell you so? Who wanted to go to Saratoga? But you are always jumping at conclusions from the most absurd premises. I have a trip to the country in my mind, where we can rusticate for a fortnight, and come back healthy and strong, from pure air and wholesome food. I have just the place in my eye."

" Is it painful ? " I asked.

" That's just the way with you," she said. " I never say a thing that you don't make light of it. Oh, go on, and laugh! my feelings are of no consequence."

" My dear," said I, penitently, " pardon me. I am now all attention, from the crown of my head to the sole of my feet. Drive on."

This " drive on " expression is a favorite with me, because I am naturally of a jockeylar turn.

She then told me that an old friend of the family, Polly Simonds by name, had married a well-to-do farmer in Hardscrabble, and that Polly's sister had that afternoon called to inform her that Mrs. Doolittle — the Polly aforesaid — would take a few boarders at one dollar per week, provided that the family were not to be " put out any," but take such food as they indulged in, and be, in fact, as members of the family.

" Now I know," said Mrs. Blifkins, tapering off her story with an emphatic period, " that Polly is a good soul, and she knows what good living is, too, and her sister says she is so nicely situated ; and, Blifkins, we can't do better than shut up the house and go and enjoy a week in the country. Poor little Bub looks very spindling, and Melinda Ann is a mere shadder. It makes my heart ache to look at them."

" Not another word," said I ; " your logic is forcible, your reasoning unanswerable. But hold on a bit. Smith's note must be attended to the first of next week, and I have an engagement for Thursday. Now, if you can trust your devoted Blifkins till Friday, — a week from to-day, — and go on yourself with the children, I will rejoin you at that time."

She thought it over, apparently meditating all the chances, when she brightened up and said, as Rebekah said to the servant of Abraham, "I'll go." I had a letter from her, telling me of her arrival; but it was very brief. I got ready, and the next Thursday saw me on my way to Hardscrabble.

"Do you want to go to Hardscrabble Taown Haouse or to Doolittle's Misery?" asked the driver of the conveyance labelled "Hardscrabble Stage," at the depot. It was a cast-off omnibus, of the "Governor Brooks" pattern, that had done duty in the city in former years, and was in the last stage of dilapidation.

"I don't know," I said, affecting pleasantness. "I want to find a man called Derastus Doolittle, who resides in these parts, and you'll do much for Doolittle, if you will take me to his pleasant mansion."

I wondered to myself if "Doolittle's Misery" could be the place of rest that was to recuperate our enervated powers, and felt assured that it was, a moment thereafter, by hearing a fat-looking man, with a surly face, say, —

"Yas, that's it; the're 'specting somebody from daown below. Drop him at Misery."

"Well," I thought, "this is a cheerful prospect. Here I have run away from tribulation to find an abiding-place in Misery. How much I have made by the operation remains to be seen."

After a jolting ride of about five miles, the only passenger in the old omnibus, the wheels screeching and screaming as though they were fiends laughing at and deriding me, the vehicle came to a stand still, and I was told that this was the Misery. There was no sign of a house in sight, and, upon asking the driver where Mr. Doolittle lived, he said, —

"Half a dollar, squire," holding out his hand; "take that

'ere path — thankee — that runs down by the barn yender, and that'll lead you into the old stage road that goes right by his house. 'Taint mor'n a mile there."

He left me at this, standing in the road, with my carpet-bag in my hand. The sun was well nigh down, and the long shadows were stretching away out over the landscape. And this was Misery. I had but one thing to do — follow the man's directions, which I did. Arriving at the old stage road, I felt that it was all right, and trudged on like a volunteer. By and by two hogs, quietly reposing beneath a broken hay-cart by the wayside, and a crowd of turkeys roosting on a fence near by and on the trees overhead, assured me of my approach to a farmhouse, and stepping towards a very rickety looking gate, I was about entering to inquire for Doolittle, when a dog came at me furiously, which made me beat a hasty retreat. I heard a mustering of somebody inside, and immediately afterwards I heard the dog yelp as if kicked, and a man's voice say, "Git aout!"

"Can you tell me," said I, timidly drawing nigh a pair of white shirt-sleeves that I saw, amid the gloom, resting upon the gate, "where Derastus Doolittle lives?"

"Come from Boston?" was the question in response.

"Yes, sir; but it is important that I find Mr. Doolittle; and if you will direct me" —

"What's the latest news of the war? Have they caught Jeff Davis yet? I tell 'em I don't believe they ever will ketch him. He's a mighty smart critter, and I tell 'em so."

"But, my dear sir, will you be so kind as to direct me to Doolittle's, for my coat is thin, and I am getting chilled?"

"This tax'll be hard to bear just naow, but I s'pose we must pay it, — cuss 'em."

I construed the anathema as applying to the rebels, and

though I doubted not the man was a patriot tried and true, I wished he would abate enough of it, for the sake of hospitality, to tell me where Derastus Doolittle lived.

"Is that you, Mr. Blifkins?" said a voice coming from beyond the gate on which the arms were leaning; and in a moment the arms dropped from their position, my wife rushed at me with a ferocity almost equal to that of the dog, and I received a volley of kisses that really were refreshing, indicating a return of feeling that I had supposed long ago dulled by domestic care, convincing me, besides, of the truth of the idea of T. H. Bailey's, that "absence makes the heart grow fonder."

"Where is Doolittle's? said I, "and who is the fellow that I've been talking to?"

"That is he," she replied, in a whisper: "hush! don't say a word; he is a queer man, but he means well."

Saying this, she opened the gate and we went in. Polly was at the door, and received me with the air of a sentry-box on parade, and was as rigid as the big churn in the corner, which she much resembled in shape. She wore no hoops, however, and the churn did. She was about forty, and her face was as sharp and blue as faces look that have been running against a severe wind in winter. Her eyes were small and cunning gray, her lips firm and determined, and her hair twisted up on an old-fashioned high-backed comb, which made her look like an antique picture of Queen Elizabeth, lacking the ruff, though the rough was evidently there in other guise.

Mrs. Blifkins introduced me, and she deigned me a hand; but it was as cold as a toad, and as expressionless in its feeling as a hand of tobacco. There was no light in the room we entered, except a badly-burning tallow candle, in a tin candlestick, which was eclipsed by Mr. Doolittle in an effort to light a clay pipe by it. My wife intro-

2

duced me to Mr. Doolittle, who made no reply, but puffed out a cloud of extra smoke, and, as he deposited the candle on the table, reached out a hand slippery with tallow, for me to shake. After several whiffs, he asked, —

"Bring up any papers?"

Handing him an "Extra," that I bought in the cars, he retired to a corner, where he monopolized the light, and became with it obscured by the paper held before him.

"Now, Mrs. Doolittle," said I, "the long ride and the long walk have provoked my appetite; and if you will have the kindness to give me a bite of something, I will bestow on you my warmest blessing."

"There wan't nothing left over," said she, with a slight touch, I thought, of mustard in her tone; "But if you'd like some milk, you can hev it."

"Certainly," said I; "any thing. Your good, sweet country bread and new milk are fit for a prince. Let's have the milk, by all means."

She went to fetch the milk, and I asked my wife about the children. All well. Then I asked how she was, and she said she was very well, excepting a little headache. "The result, my dear," said I, "of excessive indulgence in country luxuries, I fear. Prudence should attend you here as well as at home. I shall have to look after you."

The re-appearance of Polly silenced the conversation. She placed on the pine table that stood in the middle of the floor a small pewter plate, not very bright, with a small bannock of bread. and a bowl containing about a pint of milk.

"It's sweet milk, though it's skimmed," said she; "we let the new milk stand for cream."

"Excellent economist!" said I, drawing up to the table with a feeling far from happy, for I thought I detected a leak in the commissariat; and a lean larder in a country of plenty is an evil not to be endured. Some one has said that we should always rise from the table yet hungry, and be sure in this way to save ourselves from the sin of gluttony. I certainly was more hungry when I arose than when I sat down.

It was now about nine o'clock; and, as I sat at the window admiring the moon as it came up behind a skeleton pine in the distance, Mr. Doolittle arose, folded his paper, and passed out of the room, leaving the candle on the table.

"We all go to bed at nine o'clock," said Mrs. Doolittle, gathering herself up; "it's the rules of aour haouse."

She stood a moment to see if her shot had taken effect on me. I felt strongly opposed to moving; but Mrs. Blifkins arose with wonderful humility, I thought, and bore me from the room. A door slammed, and then another, a few smothered words came from a chamber adjoining that we were to occupy, and the house was still. Not so around the house. A flock of geese held a noisy council beneath our window, and a horse in an invisible barn had the St. Vitus' dance; a pig was indulging in a swinish soliloquy; a calf, ambitious of being veal, was mournfully eloquent; and the dog, which had rushed at me, amused himself with a prescription of bark every half hour. There was no sleep for my eyes or slumber for my eyelids all that night.

By daylight, startled from a cat-nap that had seized me in despite of untoward circumstances, I looked from the window, and saw Doolittle hauling a load of muck from the meadow. A more uncouth figure I never saw. Of course I didn't expect to see a man dressed in his best while hauling muck, and as certainly I had never expected to see a man look so badly. His properties would be invaluable to an actor whose *rôle* was the desperate loafer.

No one part seemed to belong to the other part. At first I thought it some ponderous scarecrow that had walked away from the field in a fit of eccentricity, and was disposed to try its terrifying properties in other quarters. But Doolittle's voice, in pleasant rebuke of the cattle, that seemed a little contrary at being called so early, satisfied me of his identity.

"Stan' still, cuss ye!" said the voice; and there was no doubting Doolittle.

I went down stairs, and joined him. He greeted me with a surly "good morning," and immediately began about the war, taking up the contents of the "Extra" I had given him, which he had apparently learned by heart. I took advantage of the first pause, and ran faster than the congressmen from Bull Run. I took all the bearings of the landscape, and found it as I have described at the outset of this letter. At about six o'clock, the blast of a tin horn signified to me that breakfast was ready; and I was prepared by my early exercise to do justice to it. I was picturing to myself aldermanic biscuits, ham and eggs, sweet butter, creamy cheese, fried trout, new potatoes, a bit of fowl, served up on a snowy table. The misgiving of the night previous, however, crossed my mind, I must confess. What business had it there at such a time? I entered the house to prepare for breakfast, but found all at table, — wife, children, all, — including Mr. Doolittle in his muck rig! I looked at Mrs. B. She colored some, but said nothing.

"Come, fall to," said Mr. Doolittle. "Folks in the country don't stand on no ceremony. Good appetites don't want no long graces. 'Eat and be filled' is our motter."

I looked along the board for that which was to fill us. A plate of hard-baked corn bread stood near the centre of the table, flanked on one side by a dish of fried pork swimming in fat, on the other by a dish of potatoes; and this was all.

"Lord, what a wretched land is this, that yields us no supply!" came into my mind, but I didn't say it.

"Will you have some dip?" said Mrs. Doolittle.

I was a little perplexed to know what she meant; but as she tipped the dish with one hand, and held a spoon with the other, as if to bale out some of the fat, I guessed what it was, and declined, asking at the same time for a little butter. I found I had got my foot in a hornet's nest.

The Doolittles looked at each other, and then Mrs. Doolittle spoke for both, saying, that butter was a cash article that they couldn't afford to indulge in themselves, and their boarders were to be as "one of the family." For her part, she thought pork was a great deal more "healthy" than butter, and was sorry I didn't like their fare. I could have done better, she dared say, at the hotel, where they charged more.

I felt humbled, and confess that I came down to "dip," as the Israelites came down to the pool of Siloam. I said no more, but thought it would be made up at dinner. I spent the morning with my children, and it seemed as long as three days in one. Dinner time came, and I looked for the summons very eagerly. Judge of my horror to find boiled pork for dinner, with the addition of potatoes and the cold bread! At supper we had some preserved barberries, black tea, with brown sugar, and underdone saleratus bread.

The next day was Sunday; and now, thought I, there must be a change in the bill of fare: then I can make up for the losses of yesterday. The breakfast was delayed till near eight o'clock, and, when summoned to it, the inevitable "dip" was there, and the corn bread! I felt that I was a doomed man, and imagined myself an Edson, a living skeleton, going round the country, showing myself at so much per sight. But I still hoped for dinner. There were fowls in the yard, whose magnificent proportions I had marked, and indulged in anticipatory images of pot-pies; and, as I came from the church with Doolittle, I fancied which of them had become a sacrifice to my epicurean taste, rather lamenting his fate. Needless thought. I was told by Mrs. Doolittle that she always cooked enough on Saturday for Sunday's dinner; therefore she had boiled double rations of pork, which we were to eat cold. At supper we had the half-baked bread and the sour barberries, and the black tea, sweetened with brown sugar, repeated.

I told Mrs. Blifkins this morning, in a domestic council in chambers, that she and the children may enjoy this felicity to their hearts' content, — live on pork till, like Jeshurun, they wax fat and kick, or squeal like pigs, — but that I am no individual to surrender myself in this way, and as soon as the "dip" is disposed of this morning, I shall start on an excursion to Hominy Ridge, about three miles from this, where there is a hotel, and shall not come back to dinner.

I leave this letter with her to send to you by the stage, as I haven't got strength to carry it to the post-office.

II.

BLIFKINS THE HOUSEHOLDER.

The situation of Blifkins's house is a very singular one, as, by some combination of circumstances, the snow always drifts in front of his door. His next-door neighbors, on both sides of him, are not troubled in this way; but when the snow before his house is piled as high as his chin, before theirs it is as bare as one's hand. Let the wind blow east, west, north, or south, it is the same. The compass is not made that has a point to favor him, so he says. It may be imagined, in this state of things, that he has considerable to do to keep shovelled off in a snow-storm, so that those gentlemen in blue coats and bright buttons shall have no hold upon him; and the sums that he has paid in dimes for the performance of this work has amounted, in the course of a winter, to a snug little fortune, let us tell you.

It was the morning after a great snow-storm that Blifkins called upon us. He looked, we saw at a glance, agitated and unhappy. Seating himself in our only spare chair, and holding his feet before our blazing fire as unconcernedly as though the words, "Busy Day — Short Calls," were not hung outside the door, he said, —

"Tough storm — wasn't it?"

We expressed to him in brief that we thought it was, and uttered the remark, with considerable confidence, that we should have more snow before the winter was out. He looked at us very seriously a moment, and then asked, —

"Do you have to shovel off in front?"

"Of course," we told him, "whenever we have occasion for it."

"Yes," said he, sardonically, "that's what you all say, 'whenever there's occasion for it,' which implies that there may be storms when there are no occasions for it. With me, now, if so little snow falls that an old woman could carry it off in her apron, there comes a drift before my door as high as my head. Queer — isn't it?"

We made further inquiries, and learned the facts.

"I bought the house in August," said he, "and not a word was said about snow-drifts; but the winter assured me of the reason why the one I bought of was so anxious to sell. The drifts arose to my window-sills. I tried to get my taxes abated last year on account of it, but couldn't. I've tried to sell out, but nobody'll buy. Every snow-storm four policemen stand looking round the corners near my house, to pounce upon me in case I should fail to shovel off. It'll cost me a fortune to hire it done."

"Why don't you do it yourself?" we asked.

"That's just what my wife said," replied he. "I got up yesterday morning, and, just as I expected, there was the drift as high as my head. 'Mr. Blifkins,' said my wife, 'why don't you go out, now, and shovel it off yourself?' Said I, in reply, 'Your counsel is excellent, and I think I will.' I at once proceeded to prepare myself for the task; but before I could get ready, there were five applications for the job, and five refusals. I pulled on a pair of long boots, tied a comforter round my ears, and went out. 'You're going to pitch into it, I see,' said a voice, as I began. 'Twas one of the policemen, and he looked, I thought, rather disappointed. 'You don't catch me this time,' said I. I commenced vigorously, throwing the snow aside with 'heart of controversy.' But I began too fast. The fifth shovelful assured me that I had reckoned without my host; and I was almost tempted to abandon my undertaking by the offer of a deluding Hibernian gentleman, who insinuated that he might shovel it 'off for a quartier of a dolliar.' But an incidental remark seemed to reflect on my ability to perform the task, and I bade him depart. 'Are you almost done?' said my wife from the upper window. How unreasonable these women are! I pitched in, not deigning a reply. I grew very hot, realizing the philosophical fact of there being heat in snow; strange I never noticed it before! 'Don't shovel the snow against the house!' said my wife from the upper window. At that instant an avalanche came from the roof, burying me in the snowy grave I had just been digging. 'Did it hurt you much?' asked my wife from her upper point of observation. I replied to her, as soon as I could free myself, that it did not, and playfully essayed to throw a shovelful of snow at her. It fell short of its mark; but the shovel found its way through three squares of my parlor window. 'Save the pieces!' said my wife in an ironical tone. I looked at my damaged property with bitterness of spirit. It occurred to me that my neighbor's snow-shovel was better than mine, and I went to borrow it. When I returned, I found that some one had stolen my own shovel in my absence. In a rage I smote the pave with the borrowed one, and broke it short off in the handle, with a remark that sounded something like profanity. At this I withdrew from the field, determined to employ the first one who came along who wished to shovel me out. I waited all the forenoon, but no one came. It was wonderful how they managed to keep away. In the afternoon I received a summons to appear before the police court by the hands of one of my watchful policemen, and have just returned from that august tribunal, where I have paid three dollars, without costs. So, reckoning my labor, the lost time, the stolen shovel, the broken one, the smashed window, the three dollars, and the aggravation, I think it don't pay."

He ceased, and looked to us for sympathy. He misconstrued our smile of pity for one of derision, and went off as mad as a percussion cap.

3

III.

BLIFKINS THE MECHANIC.

"Mr. Blifkins," said my wife, on the morning of washing day, "Bridget complains that something is the matter with the soft-water pump."

"Well, my dear," I replied, — I am very careful to put in all the little tender terms on washing days, having found them serve admirably as mollifiers at such times, — "I will see about it."

I had not quite finished reading my morning paper, and sat a moment to conclude the account of the last fearful casualty, when Bridget's face was thrust into the door, as red and bright as an old-fashioned brass warming-pan.

"Indade, mem," said she, "the pump's gone again."

"I wish you was," arose to my lips, but I didn't speak it.

"Well," replied my wife, "I've done all I could about it, unless *I* am expected to draw the box and fix it. I expect every day when I shall have to do such work. A woman's life is hard enough at the best, but a little additional service would not hurt her, I dare say. Perhaps, in the intervals of household duties, she might take in jobs of pump-mending."

I said nothing.

"Mr. Blifkins," said my wife, "will you see to the pump?"

This was said in a tone that completely overcame the horror awakened by the casualty, and throwing the paper aside, I proceeded to the kitchen. I tried the handle of the pump, and, sure enough, the water refused to flow. A few drops only oozed from the nose, and, as I plied the handle, the pump gave forth a rumbling sound, as though it were surly in its refusal to yield the accustomed supply.

"This is a pretty state of things for washing day!" said my wife.

"Well, my dear," said I, "I don't see how you can blame me for it. 'Thou canst not say I did it.'"

I immediately essayed to take out the box. The screws that secured the top were rusty, and refused to turn.

"Mrs. Blifkins," said I, "where is the hammer?"

"How should I know where the hammer is?" she replied. "It is probably where you used it last. You leave every thing for me to take care of. My father used to say, 'A place for every thing and every thing in its place.' I wish *all* men were as particular."

I remembered that I had used the hammer to repair a chicken-coop some weeks before, and, proceeding to the spot, I found it, rusty and dirty, lying just where I had left it. A system like this, closely followed, would prove of immense advantage; for a memory of where an article was used would immediately suggest the spot where it was to be found. Returning to the kitchen, I commenced work. The rusty threads of the screws refused persistently to yield; but patience wins; and after a half hour's sweating and fretting, I had the top removed, and the pump-box in my hand. There were evident signs of decay in the leather; and bringing my natural ingenuity to bear upon it, I hammered, and tacked, and cut, and pulled, until I fancied that I had attained perfection in my effort.

"Mrs. Blifkins," says I, in my momentary satisfaction, "can you tell me the difference betwixt a man who mends pumps and a prune?"

Of course she couldn't; and I told her that one was a plum and the other was a plumber; whereat she was pleased to smile, though, I thought, rather derisively.

"Now we shall see," says I, putting in the box, "the triumph of genius. Pour in some water, Bridget, and as I pump, you shall see the water flow."

I manned the brakes; but in vain my effort. No effect was produced but the most painful sound — a sort of asthmatic wheezing, like that of a porcine quadruped just expiring under the effect of a surgical operation upon his neck. My triumph changed, and my chipper notes partook of a more tempestuous character, as I muttered an expression that nothing but the immediate circumstances could justify.

"That's right," said my wife; "I would talk in that way. It will help the matter, I dare say, very much. Men have got no patience. If they had to bear as much as women do, I don't know what would become of them."

"I will bring mechanics," said I, a little subdued, "and they shall bring the pump."

I immediately sought Lumb.

"Send workmen," said I, "O man of lead pipe and solder, and mend that without which washing day becomes a Sabbath without a sermon — for what were washing day without water?"

Two men accompanied me to my home — philanthropists, with disposition and ability to relieve the difficulty under which I labored.

"Now, my boys," said I, as I introduced them to the field of their operations, "put her through."

The term "her" struck Mrs. Blifkins as irrelevant, and somewhat personal, as I judged from her looks. No barometer could be more exact than was her countenance to my experienced vision.

"Look here, sir," said one of the men, trying the handle; "there ain't nothing the matter with the pump."

"Then what is the bother with the infernal thing?" I asked, excitedly.

"The principal reason is, I think, sir, that the cistern has gin out."

I looked at the man wonderingly; but his honest eye convinced me that he was sincere, and after examination proved the truth of what he said.

"My friend," said I, "here is a trifle for you, and I will settle with Lumb. Don't say any thing about it."

I never knew how the matter came out, but always thought Mrs. Blifkins must have told of it.

IV.

BLIFKINS AND THE CAT.

"Care killed a cat," the old adage runs; and Blifkins held care responsible for a feline corpus found in his front yard one morning. His experience in the premises being very trying, we essay its impartation as he told it to us, as nearly in his own words as possible. Reader, imagine Blifkins seated before you, telling the following: —

"Mr. Blifkins!" cried my wife from the kitchen on Sunday morning, the morning of all the week on which I like least to be disturbed. I rose on my elbow, before answering, and looked at my watch. It was only seven o'clock.

"Mr. Blifkins!" the voice said again. It was wonderful how sleepy I was, and so I made no reply. What can call her up so early? I asked myself. It can't be breakfast yet, for that's an eight o'clock matter. I nestled down in the pillows once more, and stretched myself diagonally across the bed, drawing my thousand nerves and sinews — more or less — out to their proper tension. What a luxury this is, to be sure!

"Mr. Blifkins!" said the voice, louder than before; and immediately after a severe pinch on my bare arm assured me that my wife had come up stairs. I started up in affected surprise, and rubbing my eyes open, asked her if that was a proper expression of the regard she felt for the one she had vowed to love, cherish, and nourish, and all that. She replied by calling me a fool, in her most winning way, and told me that there was a dead cat in our front yard.

"A dead cat!" cried I, tragically, jumping out of bed in a style quite melodramatic, though not very well costumed.

"Yes," said my wife; "it is right under the window, and is as big as a cow."

I looked at her face, where womanly truth was wont to shine, and repeated her remark, —

"As big as a cow!"

"I mean," said she, "that it is a very large one comparatively."

"Oh!" said I, completing my toilet by thrusting my right foot into my only slipper, and proceeded down stairs. There, sure enough, was one of the most monstrous cats I had ever seen. It was old and very gray, and there was a rigidness in its form that seemed to say, "I've come to stay with you;" speaking in dumb show as plainly as the big trunk and many bandboxes that the stage drops at our door on anniversary week. I looked at it horror-struck.

"Throw it into the street," said my wife, with that promptness which eminently fits her to be the captain of a company.

"Can't do it, my love," said I; "for I should render myself liable by so doing; if not to the law, at least to my own conscience; for why should I offend the sight of my neighbors by the unseemly thing?"

"Bury it in the yard," said my wife.

Now, considering that she has got every inch of our territory so closely planted with flowers that one can, in the season of them, measure odor and bloom by the cubic inch, that was impossible. I told her so.

"I do wish, Mr. Blifkins," said my wife, "that you had a little more energy; you are not nearly so smart as you were twenty years ago."

"True, my love," replied I; "and in this respect there is a great difference between you and I, for I think your *smartness* has increased." I meant it for irony, but she took it as a compliment, and smiled upon me with that heavenly expression which resembles somewhat a slumbering hurricane.

"Mr. Blifkins," said my wife, "throw it on the vacant lot round the corner."

"What!" replied I, "and poison the air of my neighbors? Never."

"What's the row?" said my friend Wagg, going by.

I told him in a few words my difficulty, to which my wife added a few soothing remarks of her own about "stupid husbands" and "never knowing how to do any thing."

"I'll tell you how to get rid of it," he said; "*draw* it away."

"Draw it?" I queried.

"Yes," said he, poking me under the ribs; "draw it away with a cataplasm."

He passed along laughing. My wife likewise indulged in a little cachinnation at my expense, which quite overturned my little remaining resolution.

"This morning air is too much for you, my dear," said I; "you had better retire to the house, and if you wish to take further part in the inquest, I'll bring the carrion in."

She saw that I was moved, and went.

There are, I know by actual count, a thousand boys in our neighborhood. My peace by day and night is disturbed by them. Their whistling and howling awake me the first thing in the morning, and I am kept awake by them till late in the night.

"Eureka!" said I, slapping my knee; "I'll have a boy."

I don't know what my wife, who was surveying the scene from an upper window, thought of the remark; but she drew in her head suddenly, like a clam.

I looked up and down the street for a boy, and round the corners, and over into yards, and into all sorts of places; but they had strangely disappeared, all but a little boy who was studying his lesson for Sunday school, whose meditations I would not disturb. How welcome would have sounded the familiar yell, usually so annoying! Thus I stood walking sentry over the remains for one hour, looking out as anxiously for a boy as a shipwrecked sailor for rescue. At last relief came. A boy appeared upon the scene, dragging along the limb of a tree, and making a wonderful dust. I beckoned to him. He stood still, with evident distrust, as I had threatened him many times with vengeful visitings for juvenile misdemeanors.

"My little man," said I, "do you wish to earn some pennies for the Fourth?" at the same time shaking some coppers at him, as they shake corn in a sieve in order to catch a horse.

"Yes, sir," said he, with great alacrity.

"Don't give him more than two cents," said my wife from the window.

I put twelve into his hand, — six more than I had intended, — and told him to take that offensive object down to the river and throw it in. He started to do so with a grin that looked as if he had thrown it in the yard himself; and I half suspected he did, for before he had gone a dozen yards from my house he was joined by ten others, who laughed so loudly that I heard them where I stood. But I was happy in being rid of my torment.

Going into the house, the thought of the adventure assailed me, and thinking how similar the scene was to that wherein Burns turned up the mouse-nest with his plough, I sat down and wrote this.

Blifkins took a paper from his pocket, and adjusting his spectacles, read as follows : —

TO A CAT,

*On finding one turned up in a corner of my front yard very **dead**.*

Thou howling, yowling, growling pussy,
Thou night and day disturbing hussy,
No more thou'lt wake the feeling fussy
    With thy fierce clamor,
Driving 'the quietest to curse thee,
    Like tongs and hammer.

Full many a night thou'st kept me waking,
My nerves like aspen leaflets shaking,
Till, some convenient missile taking, —
    A jug or boot, —
I've dashed it in among ye, raking,
    And made ye scoot.

Thy voice I knew, when fiercely bawling,
'Bove all thy brothers' notes appalling,
There, 'mid my flowers, pulling and hauling,
    And mischief making ;
But thou hast stopped thy caterwauling,
    And no mistaking.

And yet I'm sad to see thee lying,
Though long my patience thou'st been trying;
I look upon thee, no denying,
    With feeling sickening,
And wonder how thou felt'st when dying
    Of sudden strychnine.

Didst thou look back with thought regretful
At making people vexed and fretful,
Or that thy horn of joy, not yet full,
    Should be capsizen ? *
Or grieve that thou wert such a great fool
    As eat the pizen ?

Alas ! like many a fool that's human, —
Seen every day. or man or woman,
Who grasp at pleasures fair and bloomin', —
    Thou'st reckless bitten,
And found too soon that sin's consumin'
    To man and kitten.

He ceased reading, and after a moment's pause, asked us what we thought of it. We candidly told him that it was barely respectable, and by no means to be compared to Burns's Mouse " on turning one up." He smiled faintly, saying, " That's just what my wife said," and went out.

    * " Capsizen hisn porritch dishe." — *Canterbury Tales.*

V.

BLIFKINS THE SUFFERER.

One warm morning we met Blifkins with a patch over one of his eyes, and supposed it might be another attack of the amaurosis with which he had been troubled. He looked anxious and care-worn, and in response to our morning salutation merely nodded as he attempted to go by.

"What!" said we, "going by without one word or one shake of the hand?"

He stopped, and extended his dexter digits with a feint at cheerfulness, but failing very signally. "What's the matter with your eye?" we inquired, in a tone very sympathetic; "fell down, eh, and trod on it?"

He lifted up the patch without saying a word, and pointed to his eye that looked — not exactly looked, either, because it was nearly closed, and had a wide, dark circle around it, as though from a severe blow — very badly.

"What did it?" we said, much shocked.

He opened his mouth, and slowly said, "Mosquitoes!"

"For Heaven's sake! what!" we said, greatly shocked; "mosquitoes did that?"

He nodded.

"We adjure you, then, O Blifkins! in the name of friendship, to tell us how," we cried in great agitation; and dragging the unfortunate fellow into a place where sedatives could be procured if needed, we bade him tell his story.

"My wife," said he, lifting the patch and wiping his eye with the corner of his silk handkerchief, "is very much afraid of mosquitoes. They are the pest of her life; her worriment by night and by day. There cannot be a mosquito anywhere in the neighborhood that does not find her, and they manifest their partiality by biting her, deeming her good to eat. They bite her face and hands, and neck and ankles, and — not to be further explicit — are generally fond of her as the New Zealanders are of missionaries. During the warm evenings they pursue her unrelentingly. She shuts herself in darkness, that they may not see her, like the foolish partridge, that puts its head beneath a leaf, fancying that it is hidden. Comparatively like, you understand, for Mrs. Blifkins would do no such ridiculous thing as that. Mosquito bars are no hinderance, for if the bars are put up at the windows, the persistent things will come in through the open doors; and she declares, on her honor as a veracious woman, that she has known them to push up a window in order to get where she was. At any rate, she could not account for the window's being up on any other hypothesis. They do not allow her to sleep, and though I dose her freely with anodynes, and she thus slumbers, she has dreams of mosquitoes that render sleep unrefreshing.

"Last night we had retired, as usual, and I was fast going towards dreamland — had, indeed, become unconscious of surroundings in a dim twilight of sense, — when her voice aroused me.

"'Mr. Blifkins,' said my wife, 'there he is!'

"I started up, and reached to the corner where for twenty years the big cane has stood with which I am sometime going to make myself wretched by braining a burglar, should one be so unfortunate as to enter my sanctuary.

"'Where is he?' said I, seizing the cane, and jumping out of bed; 'where is the marauding villain?'

"'Mr. Blifkins,' said my wife, as she has a good many

times, 'don't make a fool of yourself. I don't mean a burglar — 'tis a mosquito. He has bit me on my hand. Can't you hear him ?'

"I listened. The big ear of Dionysius could not have done more in the listening line than I did for fully five minutes, and then answered, 'No.'

"'Do *you* hear him ?' said I, carrying the war into Africa. There was no answer to my question, and her deep breathing assured me that she was asleep. I didn't believe there was a mosquito within a quarter of a mile of the house, and went to bed again breathing orisons more profound than pious.

"I had got once more in a comfortable state ; was, indeed, dreaming that a Houri, in a short striped dress, was presenting me with a bushel basket full of peaches, each of which would weigh a pound, when I felt a sharp nudge in the side, that I deemed, in my obliviousness, to be a stab given by some dark assassin who was my rival. I was just going to perform some act of valor that might have eclipsed the braining of the burglar, when —

"'Mr. Blifkins !' said my wife.

"'Foul caitiff !' I cried, 'down, down to '—

"'Mr. Blifkins !' repeated my wife, with another nudge sharper than the first, and I was awake.

"'What is the matter ?' said I ; 'are you sick ?' There had been a bad case of the cholera in the neighborhood that day, and I feared its epidemic character, as I had seen some watermelon rinds in the sink the evening before.

"'No,' she replied ; 'but hear them mosquitoes.'

"I raised myself on my elbow and listened, but could not catch a sound. It was near midnight, and every thing was still as death.

"'I don't hear them,' I said, vexed at being disturbed, and was about lying down again.

4

"'There!' cried she; 'there they are, plain enough.'

"I listened again, and heard a faint, murmuring sound, that at first I could not define. At last it came more distinctly.

"'That,' said I, 'is the Brigade Band, serenading the newly-married couple over in Confederation Square.'

"I was malicious in my triumph, I know. She said nothing in reply; and after looking out of the window and hearing the distant music, as I could do distinctly through the open window, and, seeing a light still burning in a house far off, wondering whether somebody wasn't sick there, or was only being troubled with mosquitoes, I went to bed again.

"How sweetly sleep comes to one after being thus disturbed! I realized it, to its full extent, and almost ere my head touched the pillow the most delicious stupor seized me, in which I seemed to be borne away somewhere on invisible wings, breathing airs blown over multitudes of opening roses and everlasting beds of clover. I had just bidden farewell to earth, resolved on making a settlement in the beautiful region where I found myself and becoming a squatter sovereign on celestial territory, and had begun a speech appropriate to the occasion to a crowd of angelic beings who stood around, when a voice, that I knew to be my wife's, said, —

"'Mr. Blifkins! Mr. Blifkins! there they are again.'

"'Let them stay there, then,' said I, 'and we'll stay here.'

"The perfume of the roses, and the clover, and the heavenly scenery vanished under the influence of my wife's elbow, and I immediately knew I was anywhere but in heaven.

"'What is it?' said I, as pettishly as a child cutting its teeth; and mine always have been cutting their teeth, if pettishness is any sign.

" ' Hear the plaguy mosquitoes,' replied my wife, threshing the air as if she were frantic.

" I listened again, this time to detect that the sound was the complaint of a dog in a neighbor's shed, whose bark was deadened by the intervention of partition walls. Says I, rising up, getting out of bed, and lighting a lamp, —

" ' Mrs. Blifkins, I can stand this no longer, and will not. I *must* sleep; and here I declare to you in the solemnity of this deep midnight, that though mosquitoes come as single spies or in battalions, come in the sonorous tones of a brass band or as the howling of a cur, come in their own natural voice or with no voice at all, " I'll to my couch again, and try to sleep it into morn." '

" I threw myself on the bed, murmuring, ' Come,

> ' Sleep, that knits up the ravelled sleeve of care,
> The death of each day's life, sore labor's bath,
> Balm of hurt minds, great nature's second course,
> Chief nourisher in life's feast.'

Perhaps I mixed the quotation up a little, for before I got well to the end of it I was fast asleep.

" How long I remained thus I don't know; but I was awakened by a violent blow in the eye, that made me see lights enough to supply a whole Fourth of July night with coruscations. The first thought I had was the burglar; the second, that Mrs. Blifkins had been taken suddenly insane, and was making me a sacrifice to her fury. This seemed borne out by the fact: for, upon opening my eyes, she stood over me with a lamp in one hand, and some article of clothing in the other, rolled up like a boxing-glove, with which she had given me one punch in the eye, and from the expression of her face I thought she was just about giving another.

" ' For Heaven's sake,' said I, ' what is the matter ? ' and jumped out of bed with an alacrity that I did not deem myself capable of.

" 'I thought it was a mosquito,' replied she, with great indifference in her tone, as I thought; 'but I see now it was only the mole on your cheek!'

" 'Blast the mosquitoes,' cried I, infuriate; 'and in future, Mrs. Blifkins, before you attempt to kill mosquitoes on my face, be sure they are what you suppose, and be careful of buttons.'

" I pointed out to her the abrasion of the skin that a button on her mosquito exterminator had caused, and she was dutifully sorry; but that wouldn't prevent the black eye I've got this morning, you know, nor restore the sleep lost for the rest of the night.

" Bad — isn't it ? " said he, lifting up the patch again. "Hereafter," continued he, "during the mosquito season, I'm going to sleep down cellar."

We tell the story nearly as he told it us, and leave the world to draw its own moral from it, provided it has one.

VI.

BLIFKINS THE AUTHOR.

"I AM going to write for the press," said Blifkins, as his wife asked him what he had under his arm when he came home one day. He laid upon the table, as he spoke, a half ream of paper, a box of steel pens, a pint bottle of ink, four sheets of blotting-paper, a pot of mucilage, a new inkstand, and a bunch of pen-holders. "I am going to write for the press," he said, "and my name shall hereafter be known as one of its most honored contributors."

He said it gayly, with an assumed light-heartedness that he often put on when met with similar questions as, "Where have you been?" "Who have you seen?" and the like. In this instance, however, there was more of truth than marked his answers at times, because at those other times there was an acerbity in the tone of the questions that caused irritation. and the answers swerved occasionally from the line of honest confession, as the magnetic needle will vary under peculiar influences.

"Yes," continued he, "here, in the quiet of my own home, surrounded by sweet domestic influences, will I build me up a fabric of fame, and place the name of Blifkins among the stars."

Mrs. Blifkins. with the spirit of a true helpmeet, simply said, "Nonsense!" and Blifkins, taking his stationery, moved up stairs to the place which he called his "study." He adopted this room and christened it his study in conformity with a belief he had long held that every one should have a place for retirement, where, the world shut out, the soul could confer with itself and become beatified in the atmosphere of peace. The room was unfortunately located for quiet, as below it was the piano-room, where the elder children took their lessons, above it the nursery, where the younger ones pursued their games, on the right of it the reception-room, on the left of it the sewing-room, provided with a sewing-machine, back of it a broad stairway, and it fronted on the busiest street in town. But Blifkins put a desk in one corner of it, hung up a shelf for the accommodation of Worcester's Dictionary, and a Thesaurus of English Words, stretched a map of Boston on the wall, and called it his "snuggery," his "study," his "sanctum," very pettingly.

Here was to be the field of his trials and his triumphs, and here he brought his stationery preparatory to the intellectual flights he meditated.   He sat down at his desk, and arranged every thing in the most judicious order, and all wore a very literary aspect.   Blifkins looked admiringly upon the work of his hands, which was to be succeeded by the work of his head, and dipped his pen in the inkstand, ready to begin when the inspiration should come.

Artemus Ward says that "every man has his fort." Blifkins knew this, and wondered what his "fort" was. He thought it could not be poetry, for he despised the effeminacy of rhyme; neither could it be history, for he had no sympathy with the ponderous sentences of the historians.   He felt that it was on the field of romance that he was to excel, and he realized a glow of enthusiasm as he reached this conclusion.   Here he would compete with Cobb, and Ingraham, and Murray, and win a fame coeval with that of those stars in the literary firmament.

Every thing depends, of course, upon a title, — all romancers know this, — and the best story the world ever saw, without the sensational prefix, might as well never have been written, so far as popular favor is concerned.   Its perusal must be confined to the interest of a few friends, and then forgotten.   "The Bloody Handspike, or the Pirate of the Coral Reefs," contains a story in the very title; so does "The Eleven Giants of Castile, or the Ghost of the Alhambra;" and so does "The Wolf's Nest of the Pyrenees, or the Doom of Domville."   Blifkins sat there, with his pen between his fingers, thinking of a title.   For full fifteen minutes he sat thus, looking down upon his sheet of paper, which lay in unprofaned purity before him, occasionally running his fingers through his hair, as though endeavoring to harrow a title up from the roots of it.   But the title wouldn't come.   At last, his feelings wrought to their utmost tension, the idea came to him as the shower of gold did to the young spendthrift, who, when reduced to his last penny, essayed to hang himself, agreeably to a pleasant codicil in his father's will recommending such course, and pulled the treasure about his ears that the wily old gentleman had placed behind the fatal beam. The idea came, and Blifkins wrote —

> " *The Cruise of the Seven Pollies :*
> *A Tale of the Sea.*

" At the close of a lovely day in the autumn of 1816, the sun sinking beneath the western wave, leaving behind a trail of effulgent glory, bathing every object in its crimson light, the Seven Pollies came to her moorings in Ossipee Bay. Her captain was a mere youth, but upon his brow were discernible the marks of deep care, and as he gazed earnestly towards the shore, he said to the first officer, who leaned listlessly over the rail " —

" Mr. Blifkins ! "

The sudden call from below startled Blifkins from his meditation, and he forgot what the captain was going to say. It was his wife's voice that had threatened the story of the " Seven Pollies."

" Mr. Blifkins ! "

The cry came louder this time, and Blifkins, opening the door, inquired, in a voice as vehement as a melodramic boatswain's —

" What do you want ? "

" Mr. Blifkins, will you come down and get some coal? The fire is out in the grate, and mercy knows I have to work hard enough without going down cellar after coal, though some men think it is a woman's place to do so, and to do all sorts of drudgery, while they sit down and fold their hands, and have nothing to do."

More was said, but Blifkins closed the door, and the rest subsided to a murmur. He left his story upon the table, and went down to perform the required service. He was an adept in bringing up coal, he had got so used to it. At whatever time of night or day he might be in the house, he was called upon to bring coal. He was chained to an unbending destiny that had coal for its formula. An English friend of the family called him a " hod fellow ; " and it was a pleasant thing for him to say, " Poor Tom's a coaled," which melancholy and sombre joke always elicited a smile. Blifkins was wont to express the belief that if he was at the last mortal strait, his thoughts reaching into the unseen world, he would be recalled by the demand for coal — a forcible but very preposterous idea.

Having discharged this duty, he again retired to commune with the " Seven Pollies." He sat down at his desk, and read what he had written, but he couldn't recall what the youthful captain was going to say. He took out his penknife, and unconsciously whittled away at his penholder, until the floor was covered with chips.

" Mr. Blifkins." said his wife, suddenly breaking upon him from a side door like an avalanche, " aren't you making a pretty mess here ? Look at these chips now. You won't be so ready to gather them up, I dare say. But no matter — it is only another grain added to the burden. 'The Cruise of the Seven Pollies!' So this is what you have been doing? Well, what *did* he say ? "

" Upon my word." said Blifkins, " I haven't the least idea, at present ; it was in my head, but was entirely driven out by a hod of coal."

" That's it, Mr. Blifkins, that's it," said she ; " make me responsible for every thing ; I dare say you will accuse me of destroying your appetite next. Think of a poor woman's duties, and then you will never make so much fuss because you have to get a hodful of coal in a day."

Blifkins groaned, and Mrs. Blifkins went out, slamming the door after her.

—— " He said to the first officer, who leaned listlessly over the rail " —

A bran new pen hovered over the sentence to finish it, and the eyes of Blifkins, in a fine frenzy rolling, stared fixedly upon the page before him. At last he threw the manuscript into his desk, and went out, impressed with the idea that the influences were unfavorable for inspiration, and that a man could not tap himself, like a cider barrel, for thought when he chose ; particularly inveighing, in his own mind, against the coal hod that had smothered his idea.

" What did the captain say ? " Mrs. Blifkins inquired the next day at dinner, with a mischievous twinkle of her eyes.

" Blifkins pushed back his chair, and went up to his " study," remarking before he went that he would show people that some things could be done as well as others — an exceedingly original remark, which went to show the lively nature of Blifkins's fancy.

—— " He said to the first officer, who leaned listlessly over the rail " —

" What the deuse did he say ? " said Blifkins, dipping his pen again and again into the inkstand, as though the word were in there, and he were trying to dig it out. He was in the condition of the man who had ideas enough, but couldn't think of them.

Click ! click ! click ! click !

The sewing-machine in the sewing-room sent up a pleasant note ; Mrs. Blifkins and a neighbor were discussing domestic economy in the sitting-room ; Mary Jane thrummed the piano in the room below ; above, the children " volleyed and thundered ; " the little boy was dragging his trucklecart down stairs; and in the street an alarm of fire made noise enough to drown the crash of the Union when it breaks.

Poor Blifkins seized his hat and rushed out in a condition bordering on despair.

We were in his study a few days since, and as we sat conversing with him he told us his experience, the ambition that had inspired him, and its failure.

"Mr. Blifkins," said a voice on the stairs, "will you come down and bring up some coal?"

He looked at us sadly, and went out like a lamp poorly trimmed. We lifted a sheet of paper from the floor, and upon looking at the writing found it to be —

"The Cruise of the Seven Pollies :
A Tale of the Sea.

"At the close of a lovely day, &c., &c., &c., he said to the first officer, who leaned listlessly over the rail" —

And that is all that the world will ever know of it.

VII.

BLIFKINS THE COASTER.

BLIFKINS paid us a winter morning call, and asked us if we had ever thought of the danger to pedestrians, of "coasting." We told him that we thought, as that practice of the boys was now confined to the Common, and was all the time under the eye of the police, it was not well to say any thing about it, because the boys must play somewhere, and if we could keep them from the streets, that was as much as we might reasonably expect. He gave what seemed a very unwilling assent to this, and said, "Perhaps so."

"What do you mean?" we inquired.

"Nothing," he replied, "of any value to anybody but myself, as the advertisements of lost wallets say. I've been thrown."

"Ah," we said, "that alters the position of things."

"Certainly," he replied, with a sepulchral laugh. "It altered mine."

"How was it?" we asked.

"Why," said he, "as I was passing down the Park Street Mall, indulging in an attempt to call to mind a commission with which Mrs. Blifkins had intrusted me, and was necessarily considerably confused. my ear was assailed by the cry of, 'Ulla, ulla!' which arrested my attention, inasmuch as it brought to memory my early experiences in Constantinople, where the cry, *Allah il Allah* was frequently heard. I was then struck by the sound, and in a moment more was struck by something more tangible, as a boy's head was thrust between my legs, and I was thrown violently on my back, with my legs elevated in the air like the two masts of a schooner. I could not rally my faculties for some time to determine the character of the disaster; but I found myself going onward with great velocity, while a voice beneath me cried out, vehemently, 'Get off o' my back!' The wind was high at the time, and my hat, taking advantage of my position, basely seceded, rolling away on its rim with a frantic exultation, seemingly, at its freedom. I came to the conclusion, before I came to the foot of the hill, that I was a victim of 'coasting;' and, indeed, with my feet elevated, I bore no inapt likeness to a fore-and-after scudding under bare poles. Upon getting on my legs, I found that I had been an object of great interest among the boys, who had regarded my involuntary race as a thing for competition, and gave me three cheers and a tiger, as they gathered round me, at my success; for our sled, from the increased momentum caused by my fall, had come in several lengths ahead. But glancing upon the spectators who had marked my feat, my horror was great to observe one of my female neighbors, who would, I knew, at once convey the news of my discomfiture to Mrs. Blifkins.

" 'Gracious goodness!' said she. 'Mr. Blifkins, who would have thought it? I declare I never saw such a sight before!'

" 'Probably not, ma'am,' I replied, somewhat chagrined, 'because, as I approached you in the manner I did, the sight must have been behind.'

" I was abundantly avenged. She looked at me with a grim smile, and went to tell my wife, which she did with a regard for embellishment that stamped her as an artist of much brilliancy of fancy. My hat was stopped by a friend's putting his foot in it."

He ceased his narration, and asked what we thought of it. We told him that it was another capital illustration of the mutability of earthly things, of our danger of falling even when feeling most secure, and of the ups and downs in life. We still clung to the idea that the boys must have their fun; and made him at last admit that, if he had used proper care, and kept his eyes open, the accident and its attendant mortification could not have occurred.

VIII.

BLIFKINS THE MOURNER.

"Bless my soul!" said Blifkins, as he took up a morning paper; "so poor Whiffletree is dead — thrown out of his carriage, eh?   How suddenly these things do come upon us, to be sure!   Here to-day, and there to-morrow. Heigh-ho!"

It was a deep sigh that Blifkins brought up from the depths of his feelings, and he lighted a fresh cigar, to do full justice to the subject that filled him.

"He was not so old as I am by three years," he ruminated; "seemed likely to live for a great while, and be a blessing to — to — livery stable-keepers; and here he is, now, swept away like the blaze of a candle, or the ashes of a cigar!   Rather rough; but death takes us at any disadvantage, and we are gone before we think of it.   I wonder how much he has left?   Not much, I guess, for he has lived close up to his means, if he hasn't exceeded them, and his wife doesn't know the first step of prudence."

Who may know, beyond conjecture, what tribute he paid to the economical virtues of Mrs. Blifkins in this reflection!   Not a word was uttered; but how natural it was to let his mind revert to the many modes of saving inaugurated by that excellent woman, which, though regarded a bore by himself, nevertheless kept money in his pocket.   Anybody else would have thought of this; but Blifkins, it must be remembered, is a "brute," as Mrs. Blifkins has many times affectionately remarked, and has not those nice perceptions of womanly excellence, it is feared, that he has of cigars.

"Poor Whiffletree!" he continued. "It isn't a week since I played billiards with him. Capital player! Gave me twenty-five, and beat me. Promised to teach me his game; but guess he will have something else to think of. Wonder when he is to be buried? 'To-morrow at three o'clock, from his late residence in Puddle Lane.' Well, 'tis the last I can do for him, and I'll attend his funeral. Poor Whif!"

He concluded his cigar; but he could not banish the accident from his mind. Whiffletree infused himself into all his business. He drew a check payable to Whiffletree. He addressed a telegraph despatch to Whiffletree. He asked his clerk if any letters had been received from Whiffletree. At night he went home dispirited, and told Mrs. Blifkins what had happened. She is a woman of wonderful calmness, and heard it with great placidity, remarking that she was sorry he hadn't been a better man. For her part, she said, she wondered why men of respectable families could associate with such people as he had been, and thought it very strange — she would not say desirable — that the accident hadn't happened years before. This, of course, awakened Blifkins to a defence of his friend, and a few moments were spent in a delightful interchange of sentiment, that ended in deeper contemplativeness on his part, and a more general withdrawal of Mrs. Blifkins into her domestic pursuits, firing an occasional shell, as the turret of her thoughts revolved to a proper bearing, to which Blifkins was oblivious. He was asleep on the sofa.

The next day he adhered to his determination to go to the funeral, though no further remark was made on the subject. Blifkins had found that, as matters became liable to provoke discussion, it was better that they should be dropped; and Whiffletree was banished forever from that precinct. He went down town in a humor not the happiest, and his displeasure was heightened by the fact that the shares bought by his partner in the Universal Washing-machine and Clothes-pin Manufacturing Company had fallen in value five per cent by the last report from the Brokers' Board.

Every one has noticed that when one has an object in view, particularly if he wishes to go away, a thousand things rush in to prevent its accomplishment. Thus it was with Blifkins. As the hour of three arrived, it seemed as if Dame Fortune had taken that moment wherein to ply him with business, and he thought that she had, in her blindness, made a mistake regarding the time of day. He had, as it was, to leave several things to be finished up by the clerks and his partners, and started at the time to attend the funeral.

"Puddle Lane!" said he to himself. "Where the deuse is Puddle Lane?"

"Did you speak to me, sir?" inquired a voice by his side.

"No, sir; I was talking to myself," replied Blifkins, a little sharply.

"Ask pardon, sir," said the owner of the voice. "Congratulate you on having so pleasant a companion."

"Where's Puddle Lane?" Blifkins inquired of a cab-man standing at a corner.

"I'll carry yer there," was the reply. "Can't tell yer, because it would be agin my biz."

"Mercenary wretch!" thought Blifkins; "and I going to poor Whiffletree's funeral!"

"Puddle Lane, sir," said a seedy-looking individual, with a red nose, standing by, "is up to the West End, sir, near the hospital. Take the right hand corner arter you come to the school-house, and then — let me see: one, two, three

— the fourth turn is Puddle Lane. You can't help missing it."

"Thank you," said Blifkins, handing him a specimen of postal currency, which the man, with a slight cough, deposited in his waistcoat pocket.

Blifkins went as directed, but found, when he had arrived at the West End, that he had not got from the man who directed him the name of the street where the school-house was located, nor the name of the school-house itself. He asked a little colored boy if he could tell him where Puddle Lane was, who set up a fearful cry, as though he (Blifkins) had been a slave-catcher; and he scarcely dared inquire again. Going on a block farther, he came to a school-house, and, trusting to luck, he turned the corner, as directed by the man. He went along counting the streets, and, looking down the one corresponding with the direction, he saw a number of carriages standing before a door, and felt that he was right. He went to the door, rung the bell, and was admitted.

The services were nearly concluded, the closing portion of which dwelt with particular earnestness upon the virtues of the deceased, to which he listened with delighted surprise, and thought to himself what a triumphant answer it would be to Mrs. Blifkins's charges, could she hear what was said of his deceased friend, and wondered how he had done so much good without his knowing it. It occurred to him, indeed, that the good man was laying it on a little thick regarding his virtues, and estimated the chances of Whiffletree himself, in shadowy presence, being there, blushing at praise which, at least, appeared rather exaggerated. If such a thing is permitted as "coming back," — and, indeed, do we *go*? — many a ghostly cheek must redden at hyperbole which partial lips express — hardly deserved. But the time prompts to kindness, and this excused, if it did not justify, the eulogy to the mind of Blifkins.

"Do you ride with the mourners?" an attendant asked, with a subdued voice.

"I hardly know," replied Blifkins, in a deep whisper; "but I was one of his most intimate friends."

"What name, sir?" was asked.

"Blifkins," he whispered, "Benjamin Blifkins."

The man left him, and the calling commenced. Very soon he heard his name uttered; and, entering the coach, he found himself *vis-a-vis* with a remarkably fine-looking young woman, — a friend of the family likewise, — whose dark eyes scanned Mr. Blifkins very inquiringly as he entered. Her face was one of the conversational sort that provoke address — bright and sparkling, with an epigram in every line of it. The others in the coach were grave people, — excellent for mourners at anybody's funeral, — with no talk in them. After riding some distance, Blifkins began : —

"'Twas a very sad affair, madam."

"Yes, sir," was the reply; "but it must happen to all of us sooner or later."

"Very true; but it was so sudden!" said Blifkins.

"Yes; but he has been going rather fast lately."

"Ah, he has, I know. And therefore I wonder at the nature of the remarks that were made."

"He was always ready."

Blifkins nodded; yet he couldn't reconcile the word "ready" with any thing but a team and a pair of runners. He settled at last upon the argument with which he met the address, — kindness for the departed, — but remained silent for some time.

"Have you known him long?" the lady asked.

"He was the friend of my early days — one of the best

of fellows — possessed very few foibles, though some were severe upon him — called him a little fast, you know."

"Fast?" and her eyes blazed as though she was very much astonished. There was a little fun in the tone, too, he thought.

"Well, yes," he replied; "some would call it so; but those who knew him well enough to allow for the exuberance of his generous spirit would give it a softer name."

"Did you say 'exuberance of spirit'?" she almost screamed, causing the other persons in the coach to look round.

"I did," said he. "I have been with him myself when he might be open to the suspicion that has been breathed. Have seen him, indeed, at times, when he was not in condition to lead in class-meeting; yet a more honest and better-hearted fellow it was never my lot to meet."

The lady covered her face with her handkerchief, and Blifkins saw, as he supposed, the ill he had done in harrowing up her feelings by a recital of his good qualities. Her agitation was very marked, and she remained silent for some time. At last she looked up, without the trace of a tear in her eye, and said, —

"How well you must have known him! The character you have given him is very correct, though I must say that I never saw" —

Here the carriage stopped, and the driver, letting the steps down, interrupted the sentence she had begun. Blifkins handed the lady out with proper ceremony, and, offering his arm, they joined the procession, moving solemnly and peacefully through the shades of Mount Hope, that charming resting-place for the dead. An opportunity was to be afforded here to see the deceased; and Blifkins, as he went along, plucked a leaf from an overbending tree, which he was going to place in the casket, and recalled those sweet lines of Halleck's repeated so often, —

"Green be the turf above thee," &c.

Gathering in a solemn circle, amid the most impressive stillness, each stepped forward to take the last look. It was Blifkins's turn, and with demure countenance, he prepared to take his final leave of his friend, when, as he looked into the stony face before him, he saw, not Whiffletree, but Deacon Hardhead, a man whose reputation for closeness had won him a name by no means desirable, and who once had become possessed of a note of Blifkins's, which he pressed with most persistent energy till he paid it, putting him to some considerable inconvenience to raise the funds at a time when money was scarce. Blifkins had hated him cordially ever since; and to find himself now one of a retinue to do him honor, and his friend Whiffletree denied his tribute, caused a feeling that he could not overcome. Even his fair companion could not reconcile him to the false position he was in, — at the *wrong funeral*, — and stopping the carriage at the first railway track, he rode to town in the horse-car, feeling that he had been outrageously swindled.

It all came from that mischievous man's direction, for everybody knows that Puddle Lane isn't in that part of the city.

IX.

MR. BLIFKINS SEES KEAN.

"I should like to see Kean," said Mrs. Blifkins, at the breakfast table, reading a very eulogistic criticism of the Keans. "I suppose, however, that I must do without it, though Mrs. Brown has been, and says he is divine."

"Like to see Kean?" replied Benjamin, poising his cup on the way to his mouth. "I never saw one that could see keener. Those eyes, whose rays outshine the morn, have the penetration of gimlets."

"Now, do make yourself ridiculous!" said she, though a little moved by the flattery; and Blifkins, before he left the house, assured Mrs. B. that she should see Kean that evening.

This was on Thursday. Mr. Blifkins went to the store. There was an unusual rush of business during the day, and at five o'clock he set out, perspiringly, for home. He reached a horse-car that was passing, full to its utmost capacity, and catching the rail, he swung himself on to the platform, where he hung by one foot, like a fly, one gentleman puffing a broadside of tobacco smoke into his face, and another diffusing the same through his back hair, which came out around the rim of his hat, like steam from around a wash-boiler cover. There was some obstruction on the track, and Mr. Blifkins, in thinking of the home comfort that awaited him, was disturbed.

"These cars are nuisances," said he, spitefully.

"So are you," said an obese man, who was hanging to the same rail with himself.

"Why?" Blifkins asked, with some surprise.

"Because you have been kicking my corns ever since you got on here," said the obese man; "and if I hadn't seen jest how you was sitoowated, I'd ha' pitched ye off."

Blifkins's first thought was resentment; but his second thought, as he looked at the obese man, was pacific. It was nearly six o'clock when he arrived home, where he found Mrs. B. arrayed in all the magnificence of toilet of which her wardrobe was susceptible; and to his inquiry if she was going out, she opened her eyes wide with astonishment, and said, —

"Certainly! I'm going to see Kean. Where are the tickets?"

Blifkins was a truthful man generally; but he dared not encounter that eye whose rays outshone the morn, as he had said in the morning, and he replied, while pretending to look out of the window, —

"Couldn't get 'em. All sold before I got down town."

Mrs. Blifkins was exceedingly provoked; but as it was so evidently a case of ill luck, rather than stupidity, on Mr. Blifkins's part, she merely said that it was always the way, — she never lotted on going anywhere in her life that there was not some disappointment attending it, — and subsided into silence over her tea.

"You know I can't go to-morrow night, Benjamin," said Mrs. B., "because the sewing circle meets here."

"True," said Blifkins; "but as I go down, I will step in, and buy some tickets for Saturday night, ahead of any of them, and then we can have a choice of seats."

This being the understanding, a pleasant atmosphere pervaded the mansion of Blifkins, with the single exception of a disturbance in the kitchen, where Sailor Boy, the dog, indulged in the attempt to draw the cat by the tail through the back of a chair, and, pulling the chair over on to him, provoked certain yelps that brought the entire household to the spot. Blifkins reclined upon the sofa with Quentin Durward in his hand, trying to find out something about Louis XI., and dropped off into a sound sleep, mangre Mrs. Blifkins's conversation, which meandered among his dreams like the babbling of a brook.

The sewing circle was a success, and Mrs. Blifkins felicitated herself that the one held at Mrs. Jones's wasn't a circumstance to it. Blifkins dined at the club. He had purchased his tickets to see Kean, and his mind was as unperturbed as a morning in May.

He thought he would go home early on Saturday, and get ready for the play; but just as he was ready to start, as in the case of John Gilpin when about embarking on his wedding anniversary excursion, " he saw a customer come in," and, like the Gilpin aforesaid, he was disposed to " cultivate " him. The customer proved shy; stopped a good while to talk about trifles; introduced a good many outside subjects, including the settlement of the Alabama claims; and Blifkins, looking at his watch, found himself a full hour beyond his usual time of leaving.

" Bless my soul ! " said he; " I'd no idea it was so late. I am going to the theatre to-night, and should have been home two hours ago; " and calling to his partner, he turned the customer over to him, thinking all the while of the reception at home when he should make his late appearance there. He well knew that an excuse would be of no avail, because the normal condition of Mrs. B.'s mind was doubt; she was prone ever to see wrong motives, and to measure Blifkins by his weak side. She reserved her doubt as an exclusive right, and had one presumed to touch upon it by insinuating in the least degree that Blifkins was not immaculate for veracity, there would be a row.

" Well, you've come," said she as he entered the door.

Adopting the Duke's Motto, in a gay tone he replied, —
"I am here."

"'Tis a pretty time to come home!" continued she,
"when you know it takes one so long to get ready. I am
almost minded not to go."

"My dear," said Blifkins, holding up his tickets, "I was
delayed at the store by a customer" —

"Oh, bother!" she replied, interrupting him. "I've
heard that too many times. Had any one else wanted
your presence or service, I dare say the customer would
not have prevented you."

Blifkins whistled *Di Provenza*, and sat down to a hasty
supper. Mrs. Blifkins, with every thing laid out preparatory, had no very extensive exertions to make to be ready,
and they were soon on their way to the horse-cars, which
would take them within a few steps of the theatre. Before leaving the house, Mrs. Blifkins advised him to take
out his fare, as she thought it wrong for a man to expose
his wallet in the cars; and he came very near falling
under the wheels of a passing wagon, before they got in,
from the extra exertion she made to keep him from danger. There never yet was a woman of one hundred and
twenty-five avoirdupois that did not think her protection
necessary to save her husband from harm, though he were
as big as Goliath of Gath.

They arrived late at the theatre, as some genteel people
like to do, and, as the seats reserved for him were in the
middle of the longest row in the house, there was much
crowding of crinoline, and much ruffling of temper, as they
forced their way to the position assigned them by the polite usher. Once seated, they turned their attention to the
play, when Blifkins found that he had no bill. He blamed
the usher very much for neglecting him as he came in,
in not giving him a bill, and thought about getting a friend

of his, who is a reporter, to put something in the paper about it.

The play was strange to him. It was a story of robbery, and violence, and throat-cutting, and other unpleasant things, with lots of gunpowder; but Blifkins did not stop to criticise the piece, his mind being absorbed by the principal figure, a robber of a very superior class and fine manners, dressed in elegant clothes, that he knew must be Kean; every motion and word of whom he devoured. He had seen Kean when he was in Boston seventeen years before, and remarked to Mrs. Blifkins that he didn't seem a day older than when he saw him last; to which she, not understanding him, replied, "Yes."

Blifkins was rapturous in his applause. At every sentence his kids came together with the vehemence of two goats in a mêlée, and he made such demonstrations as he thought would show to outsiders that he knew a thing or two about plays, and that Kean couldn't get around his appreciation of any point he might make. He applauded some points so loudly, that people around him cried, "Hush! sh-sh!" to his utter disgust, and some laughed.

Mrs. Blifkins was not at all enthusiastic. She was a woman who always reserved her warmest praise, and never wasted any of the article at all. Blifkins was sometimes accustomed to say that if she had been present at the seventh day of the creation, she would have withheld her praise till next day. She made no sign of like or dislike, but sat with the close attention that the great actor merited, and when the play was over she expressed the wish to go home.

Blifkins thought that the highest compliment to be paid a play or an actor was to be content with it or him, nor allow any other to compete with them, and he assented without a murmur, not waiting for the farce.

"Ah, Blifkins, you here?" said his friend Jolliboy, coming forward and shaking him by the hand; "and Mrs. Blifkins! I declare this is an unexpected pleasure."

"Yes," said Mrs. Blifkins; "Benjamin wished to see Kean, and I thought it would be a relief from household cares to come with him."

Blifkins didn't think this was putting it quite right, but said nothing in reply, merely remarking to Jolliboy, —

"He plays very well for an old man."

"Not so old, either," said Jolliboy, who at fifty was still laying claim to juvenility.

"Why, he must be near sixty — over fifty, at least, said Blifkins, mentally calculating the difference of time betwixt then and now.

"Why, no," replied Jolliboy; "it can't be more than twenty years since he went to school in South Boston.

"Who?" said Blifkins; "Charles Kean?"

"No, Frank Mayo," replied Jolliboy; "what has Charles Kean to do with it?"

"Oh, nothing!" said Blifkins, squeezing Mrs. Blifkins's arm in order to keep her from saying any thing, seeing that he had made a mistake; "nothing, only I was thinking of Kean at the moment — that's all."

"I never saw the character of Charles de Moor played better," said Jolliboy, enthusiastically.

"Nor I," responded Blifkins.

Mrs. Blifkins said nothing.

6

X.

BLIFKINS'S MOONLIGHT TRIP.

"I never told you about my moonlight excursion, last summer," said Blifkins, smiling, as he sat and gazed "upon the bust of Pallas just above our study door."

There was something provokingly funny in his look, and he drummed the "Hallelujah" upon the chair, looking up at the bust aforesaid, as though he were exchanging private signals with the insensate plaster.

"What excursion was that?" we asked, looking up from the work whereon we were engaged.

He burst into a laugh long and loud, and his sides shook again with the accretive humor that had evidently been gathering strength for the present explosion, when it could break out in an unembarrassed atmosphere. Such boisterousness was unusual to him, and indeed it was offensive, because the sacredness of the editorial precinct, given to grave meditation, should not be profaned by exuberance that finds voice above the breath, and we checked him by telling him not to make a donkey of himself by braying so unseemly. He kept on laughing, though moderating his tone, and then said, —

"In the Nelly Baker."

"Why, the Nelly Baker has stopped running for a month," we said; "what do you mean?"

"I mean," he replied, "the most curious thing that ever happened to me, and one which I have wanted to tell you for a long time. I thought of it just as I came in here, and looked at that bust. Whose is it?"

"Pallas."

"Pallas, is it?" he continued; "but it looks amazingly like the widow Thompson."

"And pray who may be the widow Thompson?" we asked, looking Blifkins in the eye, and through that avenue away down into his soul; "who is she?"

He smiled mysteriously in reply, still beating the "Hallelujah" on the arm of the chair, and turned his eyes again towards the bust of Pallas.

"Well, the matter was here," he said: "Spear, of the Nelly Baker, invited me to go down in the harbor on one of the moonlight excursions that they had last summer, and I went home with the invitation fresh in my mind to induce my wife to go with me. The normal condition of Mrs. Blifkins's mind being opposition, of course as soon as I mentioned it, with all the eloquent force of my enthusiastic temper, she met it with a rebuff that almost drove me out of the house. I was, I confess, a little discomposed at this, having expected a different reception for a proposition that sought her happiness, and seated myself moodily by the table, with my head upon my hand, thinking, I am constrained to say, upon other scenes than those that surrounded me, and another form than that which made the central figure of my domestic picture, murmuring to myself, inside, 'It might have been.' Excuse the digression; but Whittier has by those few words let many people into the secret of their unhappiness who never otherwise would have dreamt of it. Had he been a married man he never would have written them for politic reasons. I was giving way to these fancies, when —

"'Mr. Blifkins,' said my wife, 'you know I'm tired to death, delving and slaving all day, and that's the reason why you ask me to go, I suppose, thinking I will refuse. I'll go.'

"'Why will you impute such mean motives to me?' I

asked; 'must I be your devoted slave for another twenty-five years before you are convinced of my devotedness?'

"She made no reply.

"The night was a charming one. The full moon made every thing bright and beautiful, and a refreshing breeze swept over the water, cooling the fever that the day had caused. There was a large party on board — a curious mixture of materials, thrown together at random, and as incongruous as well could be. All were ripe for a good time, which was the harmonizing element — the oil that neutralized antagonisms, and fused the mass into saponaceous completeness."

" Soap ! " we said.

" Don't interrupt me, please; the simile is a good one. We steamed down the river in fine style, the waves bright with moonbeams and sparkling like silver. The sound of dashing water is pleasant to the ear, and to me is suggestive of many dreams. I love to look over the rail and see the foamy wake that follows the stroke of the paddle-wheels, and list to the hissing murmur that rises from the water, indulging in fantasies that realize the magic tales of Undine and the Naiads. And it is not bad either, to take a cigar and sit by the prow, and watch the bone that ripples up from the sharp cutwater in a gentle and trickling song, as soothing as a lullaby. On coming aboard, I had introduced Mrs. Blifkins to my friend Hodges, and leaving her very busy in conversation with him, I was strolling to the forward part of the boat to enjoy a cigar, when a light hand was placed upon my arm as I emerged from the shadow of the awning, and a soft voice said, —

" ' Good evening, Mr. Blifkins.' "

" Mrs. Thompson ? " we queried; but without moving his eyes from the bust of Pallas, Blifkins went on : —

"I started at the well-recognized tones, and there, un-attended, was the widow Thompson.

" 'My dear Mrs. Thompson,' I said, 'this is an unex-pected pleasure; to what fortunate star am I indebted for this sweet surprise?'

" 'That,' she replied, pointing to the moon.

" 'Thanks, most propitious planet,' said I, with enthu-siasm: 'Luna shall hereafter be my lodestar, and that "the devil's in the moon for mischief" shall be placed among the forgotten slanders hatched in the poet's teeming brain.' I took her hand as I spoke, and then we stood by the wheel-house together, and talked moonshine, and the nonsense born of romance, for many a mile. She informed me that she was on board in company with a young couple who had as much as they could do to think of themselves, without looking after her, but thought it prudent to join them, which she did, and I returned to Mrs. Blifkins.

" 'You are very gallant, I declare,' said that excellent woman, 'leaving me in charge of others. It was a fortu-nate thing that Mr. Hodges was on board, or I don't know what I should have done.'

" 'My love, it shows what confidence I put in you,' I said, trembling, as conscience gave me a castigating thump; 'I am not jealous, you know.'

"Hodges pretended that he saw somebody he wished to speak to, and hurried away, leaving me to Mrs. Blifkins.

" 'Been enjoying yourself, I dare say,' said she.

" 'Entirely,' replied I; 'I thought I would go forward and smoke a cigar; had an excellent time.'

" 'There must be a great deal of fascination in a cigar,' she said, tartly, 'to attract a man away from his wife at such a time.'

" 'I thought you were very comfortable with Hodges,' I replied: 'a good fellow is Hodges.'

6*

" 'He will do,' she replied, 'if one cannot have one's husband to speak to.'

"I endeavored to make myself agreeable. I pointed out the beauties of shore and sea; talked poetry, improvised speeches, essayed apostrophes; but it all fell on unheeding ears, and I was not glad when the boat stopped at Nahant.

" 'Hodges,' said I, 'look after my wife again, will you? Your eloquence has so eclipsed mine that all I can say fails to move her. You are a fascinating fellow ' — chucking him under the ribs as I spoke.

" I was glad to see him as carefully handing her up the steep steps at the landing as though she were made of glass. She looked round at me with eyes of wonderful indifference, I thought, and as she disappeared above the bank I gazed upon the other climbers, and close by my side was — Mrs. Thompson.

" 'Bless me,' said I, holding out my hand; ' how fortunate ! — allow me,' and I assisted her up.

" Taking my arm, we walked along together, communing most delightedly. Her delicate hand burned and palpitated on my coat sleeve, and its electric influence coursed through the veins of my arm, and thence to my heart.

" ' Blessings on the hour that brought you here,' I said ; 'and blessed be the moon, whose power moved you to come ! '

"I hurried away with Mrs. Thompson upon my arm, and we seated ourselves by the sea, in the crevice of a rock that the cliffs overhung; and there, with the waves dashing at our feet, we enjoyed the full beauty of the scene. Said I, —

> ' In such a night as this,
> When the sweet wind did gently kiss the trees,
> And they did make no noise ; in such a night,

> Troilus, methinks, mounted the Trojan walls,
> And sighed his soul towards the Grecian tents,
> Where Cressid lay that night.' "

" 'Mr. Blifkins,' said my wife, looking round a projecting angle of the rock; 'are you smoking again?'

"She disappeared as she spoke, and we sauntered along the sands, throwing pebbles into the water that almost laved our feet, as happy as children, and innocent as the babes in the wood. We stood in the shadows and looked out upon the sea, heaving, like our own hearts, with emotion, and looked into each other's eyes, tender with mellow light, and we sighed, 'It might have been.' Her thoughts, perhaps, were with the deceased Thompson — where were mine?

" 'Mr. Blifkins!' said my wife. Mrs. Thompson's hand slipped from my arm, the sea rolled away, bearing her off on its breast, the rocks settled to a grave, the moonlight grew opaque, and a passing sea-fowl gave me a smart rap on the ear.

" 'Mr. Blifkins!' said my wife, 'wake up.'

" 'Has the boat gone?' said I, starting from my seat at the table where I had dozed: 'where's Hodges and the widow Thompson?'

" '*Who?*' said my wife, in a tone that made the rims of my hat curl up as I put it on my head. 'Who?'

" 'Nothing, my dear, nothing,' replied I; 'it was a dream, that's all; and half of life is but little better.'

"We didn't go on the excursion. 'Tis wonderful how much that bust of Pallas looks like Mrs. Thompson."

Said we, "Blifkins, you are in a bad way. Drink cooling fluids, eat no meat, abstain from stimulants. The dream of Mrs. Thompson is but the residuum of bad fancies, and the sooner you are rid of them the better."

XI.

BLIFKINS'S SILVER WEDDING.

"Blifkins," said my wife, "we have been married twenty-one years to-day, and you have never manifested by any demonstration, on the returning anniversary, that you were sensible of the blessing you enjoy. Now I propose that we celebrate our silver wedding."

"Very well, my dear," replied I, "have it your own way; only it strikes me that the twenty-fifth anniversary is the one that is usually remembered as the silver wedding."

"That is just the way with you," said my wife, bursting into tears, and showing evident signs of temper, which, I am sorry to say. have increased somewhat of late; "that's just the way with you."

I told my wife that I was not sensible of any particular "way" in the premises, and begged that estimable woman to explain what she meant; indeed, I am not certain that I did not use the words, "what in thunder" she meant, as I frequently hear them used to strengthen our idiom, somewhat deficient in emphatic terms. She condescended to inform me that I had, by leaving it to her in the first place, manifested my indifference, and in the second had destroyed her anticipations by mentioning the fact of the twenty-five years' custom; as though only four years made any difference; as though twenty-one years of our wedded life had not been fully equal to twenty-five of that of anybody else.

"Equal to forty, my love," I interposed, "of some." My wife looked at me inquiringly. "Reckoning the time by happiness," I quickly added, to save the domestic bark

from going over on its beam-ends. I explained to my
wife that leaving the matter to her was another proof of
my confidence in her wisdom that twenty-one years had
not shaken.

"Then," said she, "Blifkins, we will celebrate our silver
wedding to-day; because life is very uncertain, and we
don't know what may happen."

"Very well," said I; "go ahead."

I went home at night a little later than usual, and was
agreeably surprised to find my wife's mother, and my wife's
three sisters, and my wife's two maiden aunts, assembled,
all dressed in their best "bib and tucker." I essayed to
look cheerful; but as I entered I felt that I was regarded
as an offender. My wife was dressed in her black silk, a
sure augury of trouble, for that black silk ever has been as
significant to me of disaster as the black cap of a chief
justice, assumed while pronouncing sentence of death.

"How d' do? Glad to see you!" I shouted, and attempted to kiss the sisters, who appeared to be as rigid as
those damsels mentioned in Tennyson's "Princess," offering no resistance, but caring nothing about it.

"*Mr*. Blifkins," said my wife, "if you had been as ener-
getic in your motions while walking as you are in your
rudeness now, you would have been at home sooner. We
can judge of a man's interest by the manner in which he
moves. Anybody else would have been home an hour
sooner than usual on such a happy occasion."

"My dear old wife," said I, attempting a mollifying expedient that had at other times proved successful, "be
reasonable" —

"Yes," she broke in, "that is just your way. *I* am the
unreasonable one of course; *I* cause all the trouble; *I* am
to blame for every thing; and as for being your *old* wife,
were I younger perhaps you would treat me differently."

I attempted a *coup de grace* by kissing her, as she was taking a loaf of cake from the oven. She held it towards me to prevent my approach, and I gave it a warm embrace, which it as warmly returned. I uttered my feelings with a degree of vehemence that might have answered to express the concentrated spite restrained for twenty-one years. My wife screamed, and the whole party rose to their feet, and held up their hands in horror at the atrocity. In vain I strove to laugh it off — the mother-in-law and the maiden aunts came over my spirits like a cold pack in January. The sisters simmered a little, but their laugh sounded to my perturbed spirit like the rustle of a chicken's feathers trembling at the appearance of a hen-hawk. I subsided into silence, and read the evening paper.

"Mr. Blifkins," said my mother-in-law, abruptly, in a tone that made me start to my feet as though I had been shot, "you ought to feel happy at the return of this joyful day."

"Happy?" I repeated, my mind dwelling on the doings of the broker's board; "discount ninety-five per cent, sales moderate."

"How?" she repeated, sharply.

"*Very* happy," I said, correcting myself, and putting a jolly emphasis on the very, relapsing into the broker's board again.

"And I dare say you properly value the treasure you have in your wife!" said one of the maiden aunts, solemnly.

"Value declining; four and a half, dividend off," I said, thinking of Erie, and my two shares that I had bought on speculation.

"How?" she queried in her turn.

"Most assuredly," replied I, in a tone that testified my proper valuation of the treasure.

"And you would probably take the same step if you could live your life over?" queried one of the sisters.

"Buyers positively decline purchasing," said I, reading a line relating to a class of fancy stocks.

"How?" asked the sister, not hearing distinctly.

"Certainly I would; of course," I said, redeeming my imperilled reputation by my earnestness.

The children came rushing in, and in a few moments I forgot my momentary annoyance. The whole thirteen have a natural taste for music; and while Juliana, my eldest, who is nineteen, and is courted by a long-limbed young gentleman in the city, played the piano, the others engaged in a pleasant little dance, till the tea bell sounded, when we repaired to the dining-room, where Mrs. Blifkins had prepared our little repast. Every thing was commemorative of the event. There were twenty-one plates upon the table, twenty-one cups and saucers, twenty-one spoons, twenty-one knives and forks, twenty-one slices of bread, and twenty-one pieces of pie.

"Sit down and eat," said I, "in welcome at our table."

"Mr. Blifkins," said my wife, "check your exuberance, please, and act more like the head of a family of twenty-one years' standing. Pay a little attention to your guests, do. You don't seem to have any more idea of waiting upon a table than nothing at all."

It was an old comparison of hers, though perhaps it might be objected to on the ground of grammatical impropriety. I immediately did the honors in my most approved manner.

"What were your emotions twenty-one years ago this minute?" said my mother-in-law, stirring her tea.

"To the nearest of my recollection," said I, "I had just smoked a bad cigar, and my emotions were any thing but agreeable."

"How unfeeling!" was echoed around the circle.

My wife didn't look altogether so amiable, I thought, as she had twenty-one years before. The supper came to an end, and all adjourned to the parlor. I went slyly down stairs, and brought up a couple of silver-necked bottles, and held them behind me. "I can," said I, "call spirits from the vasty deep."

"Can you?" said one of the aunts; "then you must be a mejum."

"Certainly I am," replied I; "come up here, my spirits, and let us keep our spirits up by putting spirits down."

I produced the bottles, and one of the circle said, "He is sich a man!"

"Mr. Blifkins," said my wife, "think of the example you are setting your children."

"I'll think of it, my dear," said I, cutting the wire. Pop! went the cork, followed by a discharge that flew all over mother-in-law's silk dress.

"Pray be careful, Mr. Blifkins," said my wife.

"Ladies," said I, "allow me to fill your glasses for a toast: The State of Matrimony — of which we to-day have become citizens through a twenty-one years' residence — may it always be the brightest star in the union."

The toast was drank, and Juliana played, at my mother-in-law's request, "Meddelsome's Wedding March."

Said I, "Ladies, I am not a poet, but I have been endeavoring to write something to-day expressive of my feelings for this great occasion — I may say the anniversary of the greatest occasion of my life. It is the excuse that I have to offer for my tardiness." My wife looked amiable then. "If you will listen I will read what I have written." I then proceeded, with my usual excellence of tone and gesture, that always win applause at the club, to read the following : —

MY TWENTY-FIRST WEDDING DAY.

Twenty-one years! — and it weren't at all strange
If in that time had happened many a change;
The jolly young boy, in waist but a span,
Is now a married and corpulent man;
And my wife, then a damsel so tender and shy,
Is as fat as a seal, and equally spry.

I've sown my wild oats; I've cut all the crew
With whom in my youth I put matters through;
I gave up cigars as a tribute to love,
And punch, that I prized all comforts above;
I have put all pleasures of old under ban,
Determined to live like a true married man.

With my children around me, my wife by my side,
Who's as dear to me now as when first my bride,
I envy not those who are soaking their clay,
Or are burning their lives in tobacco away,
Content to remain here just as I am,
As happy as is at high water a clam. .

Let fate do its best, or its worst, as it may;
All luck is·but accident, just, of a day;
The good and the bad, the sorrows and joys, .
Are nothing at all but trifles and toys;
I'll sit at my ingle, and say, as they fly,
I'm watching the harvest to come by and by.

"Mr. Blifkins," said my wife, in a severe spirit of criticism, clouding up again, "hadn't you better specify that it
is the *anniversary* of the Twenty-First Wedding Day, be-

cause unborn generations, who may read it, may suppose you was married twenty-one times, which is not to be supposed of any man."

I accepted the amendment, when she submitted that likening her to a seal was not very complimentary, and as for her being fat, she weighed but one hundred and eighty!

The evening passed very pleasantly. The champagne did the business. Before we parted, my mother-in-law embraced me, and avowed for the thousandth time that no one could have a better son-in-law; the maiden aunts were tractable, and the sisters stood still, like sensible girls, to be kissed; and thus ended my Silver Wedding.

XII.

BLIFKINS THE BACCHANAL.

"Do I look like a debauchee?" said Blifkins, as he came in the morning after the Re-union of the Jolliboys at Parker's. We told him that we didn't think he did. We turned him round to the light, so that we could look into his eyes. They were as clear as a bell, and as full of laugh as an egg is full of meat.

"Why do you ask?" we said, as he sat down on the damask lounge in our back room, in front of the great mirror that had in the early days of the republic reflected the features of the Father of his Country. He looked up, with a very roguish expression, as he said, "Mrs. Blifkins," and broke out with a laugh that shook things. We took another look at him, to ascertain if our first impression were not wrong, for it seemed to us that a sober man would not have acted thus. He cooled down, and then again attempted to explain the reason for his mirth. After several commencements he managed to tell his story.

"Mrs. Blifkins will have it that I was tight" said he, "though there isn't a Jolliboy that will not say I was right as a trivet. It was about three when I got home, and when I unlocked the door there stood Mrs. Blifkins in a spirit of patience, and a long flannel bed-gown, waiting for me.

"'So you've come,' said she, as I entered.

"I assured her that such was the fact, and asked her if she wasn't afraid that getting up so early would be injurious to her health. Whereupon she informed me that her health was the last thing I cared for — that no man who cared for his wife's health would expose her to the danger of sitting up till three o'clock in the morning, and he away indulging in dissipation.

"'But,' said I, ' my dear, there was no need of your sitting up. I was fully competent to take care of myself. I have that prudent regard for myself that never leads me over the bounds of sobriety, and to-night, in particular, I am wonderfully correct.'

"I attempted to salute her, but she drew back with a contemptuous and deprecating 'Faugh!' as though she detected odors of bacchanalian haunts in my breath. But I saw that a change was coming over her face, and she immediately assumed the patronizing and sympathetic.

"'Come, Mr. Blifkins,' said she; 'you had better go to bed, and sleep it off. Your head will ache fearfully in the morning, and serve you right, because a man with a family ought to know better than to make such a brute of himself.'

"' But, my dear,' said I, interrupting her, 'I assure you your fears are groundless. See me walk that seam in the carpet.'

"I attempted it; but I stepped on a confounded marble that one of the children had dropped on the floor, and came nigh falling down.

"'I knew so,' she sighed; 'what a pity! But I am used to it. I am glad the children are not up to witness their father's disgrace — little dears.'

"'But I'm not,' cried I, trying to save my credit.

"'Don't say another word,' said she: 'go to bed, and sleep it off.'

"I made no further parley, but walked up stairs, and in five minutes was enjoying the sleep that only the innocent know. When I awoke in the morning, Mrs. Blifkins was standing over me with the most severely virtuous face I ever knew her to wear.

"'Well,' said she, 'I dare say your head aches finely this morning — good enough for you, and all such as indulge in such practices.'

"'Nary a headache,' said I, sitting up in bed; 'never felt better in my life. Give us a cup of chocolate, and I will soon join you.'

"'Chocolate!' said she; 'chocolate after a debauch! You mean a cup of strong tea.'

"I thought of Mrs. Joe Gargery's tar water, and said no more. She was determined, I saw, that I was 'an example,' although I assure you, on my word as a member of the Association for the Promotion of Universal Good, that I was as straight as a die. Isn't it strange?"

We assured Blifkins that the saying, "Once a rogue, always suspected," applied to him, and that he ought to be grateful for the never-tiring interest thus disposed to watch over his unguardedness; but he didn't see it.

XIII.

BLIFKINS THE HORTICULTURIST.

It may not be very generally known that Mr. Blifkins has bought him a new house lately, on a new street; and since he came in possession of it he has devoted himself to deep thought, and taken counsel of others, regarding the improvement of his "grounds," as he terms the enclosure that forms his lot. He had a high respect for horticulture from early associations, — had, indeed, while a mere boy in the country, raised considerable fruit, much to the surprise of his friends as to how he came by it, — and he determined to devote this spot to horticultural purposes, looking forward to the time when he should be able to sit under his own vine and eat his own fig tree.

Friends advised this, that, and the other, each one eloquently advocating his particular plan as the best to beautify and benefit. One advocated flowers, another favored arboriculture, another dwelt on the beauty of a lawn, another gave conclusive arguments in favor of a greenhouse.

"Why, any one can see, with half an eye," said Mrs. Blifkins, "that it is beautiful for pears; but I don't suppose my advice is worth any thing, as it is never asked."

"Your advice is excellent, my dear," said Blifkins, raptuously; "never was man blessed with so wise and sweet a counsellor: a perfect Solomon in petticoats."

This last was uttered as an "aside," it being regarded a precarious venture.

Full of his idea of stocking his place with pears, he immediately visited all the nurseries in the vicinity, to consult catalogues in order to get the best varieties. It was a severe tax upon his time, but he resolved to get the best. He saw many scores of names that he didn't understand, for which he felt a profound respect; and of those he selected a half dozen with the most formidable and unintelligible titles, assured that he had got just the thing. The trees looked thrifty, the green just coming out — his own case he thought — and engaging an Irish gardener — " born wid a shpade in his fist," as he averred — he soon saw the trees transferred to his grounds, sods beautifully plastered over the bare patches, and the place really assumed the look of cultivation. But, alas! the chill winds did not agree with the tender trees; the cool air and the heat of the sun, acting in opposition, killed the shoots between them, as Mr. Pickwick came nigh being overwhelmed between the two belligerent editors.

"You've got a glorious place there for a grape vine," said Mr. Planit, his neighbor, looking over the dividing line between the two lots; "'twill fit over that balustrade splendidly."

"'Twill shut out the sun," said Mrs. Blifkins, overhearing the remark.

"Not a bit of it, my dear madam," replied he, "more than is agreeable; a grape vine is just like a child — train it up, and away it goes."

Mrs. Blifkins did not take very strong ground in opposition, though she afterwards mentioned to Blifkins privately that she thought Mr. Planit had a great deal of presumption in recommending it; that some folks' impudence led them a great ways in meddling with other folks' business.

"Why," said the neighbor, taking up the thread of his remark regarding the vine, "the first year you'll have at least a bushel; next year, two; and in five years you'll have grapes enough to supply the town."

Even Mrs. Blifkins melted before this delicious argument, and the vine was decided upon.

Blifkins immediately visited Sweetwater, the gardener, who had vines to sell.

"There," said Sweetwater, holding up a piece of stick about as big as a lead pencil; "there's a grape, now, that I can recommend; a choice kind; a hybrid betwixt a 'Jerusalem Pucker' and a 'Huckleberry Twist;' berries as big as grape shot, sweet as sirup, and three weeks earlier than any other variety."

"But that's dead — isn't it?" said Blifkins, touching the twig suspiciously.

"Dead! bless your soul, no!" he replied; "do you see that?" pointing to a rough spot on the bark; "that's a fruit bud, and that, and that," pointing to other rough places: "'tis one of the most healthy vines I've got. Plant it, and it will grow like Jonah's gourd."

Blifkins bought it, took it home, and prepared to plant it.

"You're not going to plant it yourself?" said Planit, putting his head up on the top of the fence.

Blifkins thought he should.

"You'd better get a gardener to do it, — begin right, and always right; a good grape will pay for all care."

So Blifkins went to the original "Shpade," and, engaging him to plant the vine, proceeded quietly to his business. About an hour after, while employed in some particular matter, an Irish head, hatless, protruded through his door, and the body of his friend "Shpade" appeared soon after.

"Plase, sir," said he, "if yez haven't got any bones, — and bones is allers best, — it ud want about two loads of manure, yer honor."

"What does!" cried Blifkins, in amazement.

"The grape vine, sir," said Spade.

"The deuse!" replied Blifkins; "well, go to Drury and get what you want, and send the bill to me."

Off went Spade, and Blifkins resumed his business till dinner time, going home then to witness the progress of his horticultural experiment. He could see nothing of Spade. An immense heap of dirt lay before him, while on one side was a black and offensive pile as high as his head.

"A pretty piece of work you've made of it!" said Mrs. Blifkins, thrusting her head out of a window over the balcony, and drawing it in again, as if offended with the odor.

"I think so," said Blifkins. "Where's Spade? — Spade!"

"Here, yer honor," responded a voice the other side of the heap, as though it came out of a grave; and at that instant a shovelful of earth fell at his feet. He climbed up on the pile, and beheld the original digger delving like a gopher at the bottom of a huge hole, as earnestly as though he were working a new mine, and was anxious to get enough specimens together to secure it a place on the list at the brokers' board.

"What in the name of Moses are you doing?" said Blifkins, in some heat.

"Making the bed for the vine, sir," said Spade, wiping his forehead.

Blifkins took the vine in his fingers — it hadn't grown an inch — looked at the hole, and the heap of manure, and the Irishman, and then went into the house to look at Mrs. Blifkins.

To say that that estimable woman was disturbed would not be exaggerating the fact. She was. She had in her mind's eye imagined an umbrageous growth of green, that at the very outset would flourish — she was too impatient to wait for ordinary results. But she had the good sense to see that Blifkins was troubled, and simply remarking that he might have known it would be so, and if he had taken her advice, — which she never expected him to do, — it would have been different, he ate his dinner in silence, going down town thereafter as quietly as possible. On going home at night he found the planting completed. The sward was blackened by the fouling dirt; but there was the lead pencil planted, come what might of it, and done, too, as Mr. Planit had advised, thoroughly.

The next day the Irish head appeared again, the body immediately after, and Mr. Spade presented the following little bill: —

"Misther Bliffkens to Mich. Spade dether,

To too lodes manoor, witch it is pade fur meeslf out ov my one pokit, not wishen to trubble a gintleman . .		$6.00
To doin bed for graipe vyne		5.50
Tottle,		$11.50

Reccept pay,   Mich. Spade."

Blifkins paid the bill, thinking all the while he had been more thoroughly "done" than the vine.

XIV.

BLIFKINS THE LINGUIST.

We had not met Blifkins for some time, and were much pleased to see his round, good-humored face thrust through an opening in the door, and to hear his voice salute us with its old-time sincerity of tone, for there is the genuine ring of honesty in his "How are ye?" which, though not meaning any thing in particular, always gives us a pleasure to hear it. He came in and seated himself, hung his hat on the antlered tree that graces our sanctorum, and knocking the ashes from his cigar, he began to speak of the news. We asked him where he had kept himself, and he said he had been engaged in a little speculation that had taken him from the city. He had been travelling, he said; had explored oil-wells and coal-mines, had made a thousand acquaintances, and had had a big time generally.

"A queer thing happened to me last night," said he. He looked funnily, as though he were internally chuckling with a thought that must have expression.

"Out with it," we said, "and don't keep it, like a hen looking about to steal a nest."

"Well," replied he, "I will not. You see my new friend Spratt, of Titusville, was on here, and was engaged in a little business transaction that also concerned me; so I thought I would take him round some, maugre the admonition of my wife that I had better know whom I associated with, and that married men had better stay at home. I accordingly took him to see Booth, and after enjoying a portion of the cheerful play of Macbeth, we went out to refresh ourselves with a mouthful of fresh air, or its equivalent. We sauntered into a restaurant that looked neat and cheerful, and getting seated comfortably, I proposed that we should have a steak and a cup of coffee, which were ordered, and we enjoyed a half hour of pleasant converse — plunged into caves of coal, swam in rivers of oil, and talked ourselves into immense fortunes. We saw ourselves millionnaires, with coaches and horses; with costly houses in town, and summer villas in the country" —

"The effect of the coffee?" we queried; but he took no note of it.

"And so on, till the time of leaving arrived, when I

arose and stepped to the counter to settle the bill, throwing down a two dollar greenback. The gentleman behind the counter took the bill in his fingers, turned it over and looked at its back, then turned it over again, as if to satisfy himself of its genuineness, while I waited to receive my change. He was, I saw, a French gentleman that was waiting upon me, or, rather, upon whom I was waiting, and I said to him in as good French as I could muster, —

"'Pardonnez moi; I wantez mon chango.'

"I saw that he looked at me somewhat surprised, as if he hadn't expected me to speak in his 'native vermicular,' but made no sign of paying me.

"'Monsieur,' said I, 'etes-vous Francais and avez-vous de postage currency?'

"'N'importe,' replied he, shrugging his shoulders, 'beaucoup de postage-stamps!'

"I felt my indignation rising.

"'I demandez de 'echange,' said I.

"'Four dolliar and a quartier,' said he, tapping the bill of fare.

"'What!' said I, in a surprised roar.

"'Morbleu!' said he, in a manner considerably excited, running his finger down the bill of fare; 'four dolliar and a quartier; biftek, pommes de terre, pain, moutard, potpourri, beurre, etc. Four dolliar and a quartier, messieu.'

"I remembered that there had been certain patches upon the table of minute proportions, and not wishing to appear small before my guest, I handed him three dollars more.

"'Ah,' said he, 'where was I thought? bigar, I forgot ze cafe noir. It is four feefty, messieu.'

"'Well, well,' I replied, now speaking in my mother tongue, for indignation rather overcame my French manners, 'give me back my change, and be hanged to you;

for if you read that bill of fare again, you will take every cent I've got in the world.'

" He grinned as he gave it me, and said, in very excellent English, ' That's so.'

" I've found out since that he was born in Vermont, and wasn't any Frenchman at all.

" When I got home I had to take a severe lecture from Mrs. Blifkins on the loose habits of the times, who repeated, what I had become rather accustomed to, that all men who were heads of families should be at home evenings, and not be gallivanting round with this or that person, or going to places, where, perhaps, their wives might not follow them. I dropped to sleep right in the middle of her lecture ; but it kept on buzzing in my ear till, in my sleeping fancy, I conceived myself tormented by a swarm of blue-bottled flies, that flew round and round me with a fearful din, from which I could not escape ; that after being subjected to it for a year, I was relieved by a tornado that swept them all into the sea. I waked up as the clock struck twelve, having been to sleep but fifteen minutes, while Mrs. B. was snoring vehemently by my side."

This was Blifkins's story. Not much of a story, either, to those who see more of the world ; but Benjamin Blifkins, the domestic and patient, makes a mountain of such little episodes, and it delights us to listen to them.

XV.

BLIFKINS'S DOG SAILOR BOY.

ABOUT a month after he had bought the dog Sailor Boy, and the remembrance of the fifteen dollars he had paid for him had mellowed into an indistinct idea of a rather profitable investment, Blifkins went home one day in a very happy frame of mind. He had that morning made a successful speculation, and had, by a most delightful accident, found company in the car up town that had smoothed the wrinkles completely out of his temper, rendering his feelings as beatific as they were susceptible of being. He applied his latch-key, humming, "Ever be Happy," and entered his door with a bound. He was met by the chill that one at times feels when the wind comes round suddenly east on a warm day — a sort of home atmosphere that the over-ardent will at times encounter, providentially to save them from a too exuberant state of feeling.

"What's the matter, my love?" said he, as he saw Mrs. Blifkins coming towards him from the darkened side of the hall. "Any good news to tell me? You are looking remarkably pleasant."

He spoke at random, for he could not see distinctly how she looked; but he *felt* that trouble was brewing for him — conscience jogging his memory regarding his recent contraband mile of enjoyment in the omnibus with one whose name, in that precinct, would be a signal for an immediate storm. He felt timid lest some winged spirit of the air had anticipated his arrival, and had revealed his innocent delinquency, as Mrs. Blifkins came out into the brighter light, and he saw her face red and hot, looking as though she had been assisting the cook in frying doughnuts. It is bad when the happiness of one is the bane of another, and harmless indulgences are concealed from either through dread of a scene — a prudential measure rendered necessary, but which is to be deprecated, nevertheless; and Blifkins, from being one of the most ingenuous men in the world, had become so close, that he hesitated about telling Mrs. B. what o'clock it was, when asked, for fear it might involve the necessity of an explanation.

"If I look very pleasant, I don't feel so," said she, with a slight degree of tartar in her tone.

"Just as I feared," Blifkins thought to himself. but mustered courage enough to repeat his question, "What is the matter?"

"I have been afraid all along that that dog would cause us trouble; and now it has come — just through your persistence in keeping the brute."

His persistence! This, when he remembered one weary day's search for him, through her own wish to have the dog found after he had turned him out of doors. It was provoking, but Benjamin Blifkins had long ago taken a position on principle that he would not be disturbed in temper by man or woman; and should he now abandon a principle so well maintained on account of a woman and a fifteen-dollar dog? No; forbid it, consistency!

"Get out, you good-for-nothing dog!" cried Mrs. Blifkins, vehemently, much to his surprise, imagining the remark made to himself; but following the direction of her eye. he saw "Sailor Boy" at the head of the stairs, wagging his tail violently, with a very curious expression of countenance, — as if of half fun and half fear. — but not daring to come down. As Blifkins caught his eye, he rubbed his nose with his paw, very intelligently, looked significantly at Mrs. Blifkins, and disappeared,

"What's the matter?" said Blifkins, for the third time.

"Frederick Augustus!" she cried, naming the youngest boy, "come down here and show your papa what the naughty dog has done!"

The boy came when called, with his forehead bound round with a handkerchief.

"Show papa where the dog hurt you; but I suppose he wouldn't care if we were all killed by the worthless brute. Dear, dear, what cares a mother has! I don't know what would become of the children if it wasn't for mothers!"

This was uttered with a half sob, as Frederick Augustus unbound his head, and revealed, beneath the customary brown paper and rum, a dark bruise upon the forehead as big as a dime.

"There, that's what your beautiful dog did," said Mrs. Blifkins, in a tone of triumph, as though she were delighted with the prospect; "and it is a mercy, I am sure, that his skull was not crushed and his brains spread all about the floor."

Blifkins looked at the contusion, and heard the agony culminate with wonderful equanimity, almost justifying Mrs. Blifkins's charge of indifference. He saw that no great harm had been done, because the boy's appetite had not failed him, as he was then engaged upon an extensive undertaking of bread and butter, a sharpener of his appetite for dinner.

"How did he hurt you, Bub?" said Blifkins, stooping down and parting his hair.

"Frowed me down stairs," replied Frederick Augustus, blowing a cloud of crumbs upon his paternal's shirt bosom.

This charge looked serious, and casting his eyes up he saw that Sailor Boy had returned, and was lying at the head of the stairs, with his head stretched out upon his paws, the picture of innocence, as if listening to the testimony against his character that was being heard in the "court below."

"Tell papa how it was," said Blifkins, coaxingly.

"Ride on Sailor Boy's back — fall down," was the reply, making an angry gesture towards the dog with his fist, as big as a cent apple.

"'Tis wonderful how that child resembles its mother," thought Blifkins, as he saw the expression on the boy's face. He learned from this that in an insane attempt to ride Sailor Boy down stairs, he had been thrown, and saying he was glad it was no worse, proposed they should go to dinner.

"I don't see how you can think of dinner at such a time; but that is just so inconsiderate as men are. Dinner, indeed, and that dear blessed boy escaping eternity by a quarter of an inch. Such unfeelingness!"

But an odor of good things filled the air, as if, while denying him the privilege of thinking about dinner, her thought had been busy in that direction, and the promise made to the olfactories was not broken to the taste. Mrs. Blifkins as a cook is not surpassed. Sailor Boy feeling some doubts as to his status, from the remembrance of an application of Blifkins's Malacca cane in punishment for his offence, prudently kept out of the way.

Mrs. Blifkins has told us twenty times what a wonderfully sagacious dog Sailor Boy was; and well she might admit it. Among the evidences of his sagacity was a thorough understanding of her various moods. He knew when the domestic breeze was east, and no barometer could more plainly demonstrate the atmospheric changes of home than his demeanor. It is true he had literally had this "beat into him;" but it required only a few applications of the foot, or of such weapon as chanced

to be handy, to convince him of the necessity of watchful-
ness.

Having a very social disposition, Sailor Boy attracted
quite a coterie of dogs to the Blifkins neighborhood; and,
being desirous of showing them hospitalities, they were
always welcomed by him in the back yard, to the great
delight of the children, who rummaged all the closets for
cold victuals, and nearly ruined Blifkins by their attacks
on his larder, rendering quite impossible that hope of an
economical household, a " picked-up dinner." The unfortunate beggar woman, who for a long time had come twice
a week to get the odds and ends, withdrew her patronage
in disgust because of the insufficient supply, much to the
delight of Sailor Boy and his friends, who escorted her
to the gate and barked their adieus, one of them retaining
a shred of her ragged shawl as a memento. The coterie
at last was broken up by the cook, who poured a skillet of
hot water upon one of the dogs, who had ventured into
the kitchen, and was helping himself to a veal cutlet.
They found they were getting into hot water, and left.

Professor Agassiz couldn't have a better illustration of
reason in dogs than that displayed by Sailor Boy. He
reasons from principles; cause and effect are duly considered by him. This latter was proved in the case of his
treatment of Blifkins's butcher's boy. Seeing the boy in
the butcher's shop was *prima facie* evidence to Sailor Boy
that he was good to eat; therefore, whenever he comes to
the house, S. B. is sure to have a nip at him. The boy, by
a judicious application of his brogans, endeavors to dispel
this illusion, but as yet unsuccessfully. He is, besides, an
amateur in music, as is manifest whenever a hand organ
performs near the Blifkins mansion. Sailor Boy, at such
times, will sing so furious an accompaniment to the strain,
that the teeth of the whole neighborhood will be set on

8*

edge thereby — superstitious people, and those with no ear for music, regarding it as howling. Mrs. Blifkins averred that the harmony with the organ was perfect, and that the one who turned the crank was so jealous of the dog that he swore a fearful oath at him in Italian, and tried to kick him.

His hospitality was exemplified one day in a remarkable manner. He had made the acquaintance of a respectable dog in the neighborhood who was accustomed to run in on an occasional visit. One day he came in as Sailor Boy was discussing a savory bone, who with a growl seized the bone and ran with it to the dog-house Blifkins had built in his shed. A moment after he seemed to say to himself, "Well, this is rather small business for a fifteen-dollar dog;" and, coming out, he laid the bone at the feet of his visitor, wagged his tail as if inviting him to fall to, which he did, to Sailor Boy's great delight.

He is a constant companion of all the boys in the neighborhood, taking part in their games, and is as big a boy as any of them. Indeed, all idea of race seems to be overlooked by all parties, and whether they are all dogs or all boys, when pursuing their play, it would be hard for either of them to say. It was a marvel to see him one day gravely sitting contemplating a game of marbles, and appearing very angry when he saw one of the boys trying to cheat.

"Well," said Blifkins, pushing his chair back from the table, "then Sailor Boy must go; such a trick as this to-day never can be excused — endangering the peace of my dear wife, and the lives of my precious children."

There was a blank expression on the faces of the children as he said this, and Mrs. Blifkins looked troubled. At this moment Sailor Boy came into the dining-room, as though he had been listening outside. There was a melancholy droop in his tail, and a general air of penitence in his whole demeanor.

"Yes, you bad man's dog," continued Blifkins, addressing him; "a stop must be put to this, sure, and to-day ends your continuance with us as a boarder. My dear," said he, turning to Mrs. B., "I will send some one up for him this afternoon. Poor Sailor Boy!"

"You are in a great hurry about it, I think," said Mrs. Blifkins, "but that is as reasonable as you men are. Of course I didn't expect you to ask my advice about it — that would be out of the question."

"But my dear," replied Blifkins, tossing Sailor Boy, who was having a jolly time with Frederick Augustus, whom he had thrown down stairs, a cube of meat, "I certainly understood you to express the wish to be rid of him, and was willing to gratify you. He has been a cause of trouble" — rubbing his roguish eye — "and perhaps it would be as well to get rid of him. I can give him away."

"Give him away! Yes, you can give him away, I dare say. But what will the children do when they go in swimming next summer, and get into deep water, if the dog isn't there to pull 'em out? They'll certainly drown; and then who will answer for it? Not I, to be sure."

"Well, I won't give him away, then," said Blifkins, "though I know somebody that will be very glad to have him."

"Who?" asked Mrs. Blifkins, with some animation.

"Mrs. Simkins," replied he, carelessly.

"Then she shall not have him," said she with warmth; "and you should be ashamed of yourself for naming her to me. But I have done expecting any thing else but ill-treatment and insult.

Blifkins put on his hat and went out, satisfied that he had secured a permanent home for Sailor Boy as long as he chose to live. He felt, as he went down town, that his forte did not lie in merchandise, but that Nature had developed him largely for a diplomat.

XVI.

BLIFKINS TAKES A STAND.

"How far does woman's sphere extend?" said Blifkins, as he paid us his customary Monday morning visit. We informed him that, though it was not very definitely assigned, it was generally understood to be all round. "I should think so," said he, reaching over and taking a match, with which he proceeded to light a cigar, and puffed some time in silence, gazing upon the serene and pleasant countenance of Horace Greeley that hangs upon our wall.

"I can't smoke at home," he said, after a while, gently knocking off the ashes.

"Why not?" we asked, half diverted from an amusing paragraph in the Daily Advertiser.

"Mrs. Blifkins doesn't smoke herself, and rather insists upon it that I shall not," was the reply.

There was a tenderness in his tone that betokened an aggrieved spirit.

"Won't she let you smoke?" we asked.

"Why, 'won't' isn't exactly the word," he replied; "there is a qualification put in that redeems it from positive prohibition; but, after all, it amounts to the same thing. The smoke, she says injures the curtains, discolors the ceiling, impregnates the clothing; she wonders how I can smoke, and when I would show her, she runs away, declaring I want to choke her."

We saw there was something more on the poor fellow's mind, and so let it go off with the smoke without saying a word to him.

"It is pretty much the same with every thing else," he broke out at last. "I can't do right. My wife will be boss over every thing. I was fixing the coal-pen a day or two ago, and had done, as I supposed, wonders in a mechanical way, when my wife said, —

"'Mr. Blifkins, you should have put the boards on the other way.'

"I raised my foot to kick — don't start — to kick the pen to pieces again, but my guardian angel whispered a suggestion of the folly and expense of the thing, and I refrained. Why, I can't have a pair of pants or a vest made without her interfering. She presumes to answer for my religious faith, my social relations, and my political creed — to do every thing but pay my bills. Worse than all this, I was shaving this morning, in a state of mind as tranquil as a man can be under the sorrow of a dull razor, when my wife came in.

"'Mr. Blifkins,' said she, 'your lather isn't good.'

"I scraped away without speaking, though I felt the irritation crawling through my veins to my very finger-tips.

"'Mr. Blifkins,' said she, 'you don't hold your razor right. You'll cut off your nose some time by your carelessness.'

"I could contain myself no longer.

"'Mrs. Blifkins,' I cried, with some heat, as the razor scored a half-inch incision into my cuticle, 'any thing but this. You may be boss in every department of the household, from the mending of coal-pens and sawing of wood to the blacking of boots and the hanging of clothes-lines; but here is a job that I choose to boss myself. I feel positive that it is an operation quite outside of your sphere. Nature, Mrs. Blifkins, has fixed bounds here — settled them to a hair — by depriving you of the beard that is such a delightful ornament to the masculine sex; and it is full bad enough to have to take care of it without female interference.'

"I was clear, decisive, firm. There was a shower of tears, a volcano of reproaches, a vocabulary of expletives, of which 'brute,' often repeated, was the principal, and the scene closed with — *Exit Blifkins.*"

We soothed the poor fellow by telling him that there must be some drawback to felicity; that all mundane bliss had its temporary offset; and that he really was the happiest fellow in existence; for what could he do if the interest thus expended on his behalf were withdrawn, and indifference substituted? He thought of this a moment, said he supposed it was all right, and, as his cigar was out, he went out also.

Excellent Blifkins!

XVII.

BLIFKINS THE PATRIOT.

"WE must show our colors," said Mrs. Blifkins, one morning at breakfast. "We are surrounded by 'copperheads,' and shall not be distinguished from them if we do not hang out our banner." She was fiercely loyal.

Blifkins was as delighted with the prudence of Mrs. B. as was Cowper's John Gilpin at the wholesome suggestions of his wife on their wedding day; and with a promise, on leaving, that a flag should be hoisted, and that right speedily, he went out to secure the services of Mr. Plane, the joiner, in putting up a sufficient pole for the desired bunting. Mr. Blifkins thought it would not be necessary to put up a pole as tall as some, though his patriotism stood at the loftiest altitude; and telling Plane to procure him one of twenty-five feet, he went down town to buy a flag. This was procured, — a beauty, blazing with the glory of thirty-six stars, — and forwarded to Blifkins's residence, to await the elevation of the flag-staff, soon expected.

Day by day passed, and Plane did not make his appearance with the desired staff; day by day did Mrs. Blifkins urge upon her husband the necessity for his " seeing about it; " for she had mentioned their intention to neighbors, who were expecting it, and she had overheard some boys looking over their gate, speculating as to where it was to be put, one mischievous little wretch saying to another, " Don't you wish you may see it!"

Upon several consultations with Plane, Blifkins was told that it was " got," " finished," " gone to be painted," " at the blacksmith's; " and in the mean time Mrs. Blifkins, with patriotic ingenuity, hung the banner in her window, glorifying the end of the domicile that looked towards the street, leaving no doubt in the minds of passers-by that all was right in that house.

" The flag-staff is up," said Mrs. Blifkins, with a voice of triumph, as Blifkins came home one evening, " and you must get up early in the morning to see about putting out the flag."

It was too dark for Blifkins to observe how the work was done, but he could see the slender pole traced against the sky, that seemed pointing among the galaxies which his own bright banner was to symbolize. He hummed to himself a line or two of Drake's ode, —

" When Freedom from her mountain height," —

and then went in to make preparations for a good time at the consecration of the flag. He would have a band of music, a free lunch, and fireworks in the evening. Probably it would get into the papers, and he would be famous. Blifkins went to bed to dream of skies of red, white, and blue, and Goddesses of Liberty in short skirts dancing all around him, to the air of the Star-spangled Banner, played by invisible bands.

Just as Blifkins fancied he had got soundly to sleep, he awoke, and found it was morning. He arose, and his first thought was to look out of the window at the pole which proudly occupied the position in his premises, the flag on which was to delight the residents of three streets. He sent down to Crotchet for a dozen pieces of music, got his sandwiches all ready, and at the time appointed quite a crowd was present. Mrs. Blifkins, who had told her female friends that it was the proudest day of her life, sat in full view of the scene, with a coterie of admiring and envious neighbors around her, as Blifkins came out bearing the bunting, which he was prepared to hoist with his own hands.

Blifkins looked at the pole, looked at the flag, looked at the people. He was reduced to a dilemma. He was no philosopher, and he was perplexed to know how he was to get the flag up to its position. He had seen flags floating from mast-heads and flag-staffs, and wondered if they were nailed there.

"You must hoist it!" screamed Mrs. Blifkins from the window.

"Run it up, Blif!" shouted a friendly voice from below.

"Up with it!" yelled a fiendish boy on top of the wood-shed.

The musicians were all already with the Star-spangled Banner, and the people all ready to cheer; but Blifkins looked very red, and beckoned to a friend among the crowd to come up and help him. They were seen to confer a minute, then the friend burst out into a roar of laughter, and Blifkins looked the picture of disappointment. They had discovered, what nobody had observed before, that Plane had neglected to reeve any halliards. There was no remedy but patience, and Blifkins had had his tried too severely in a twenty years' married life to allow it to be overcome now. His was a temper to lift man over his accidents; and dismissing the band, much to the disgust of the boys, he invited in his friends, and, with the flag hung upon the gas chandelier over the table, as good a time was enjoyed as though the thing had " come off."

Plane was summoned, who received a lesson from Mrs. Blifkins that made him see more stars than there are in the American constellation, and "sent down" the pole to receive the proper halliards. This being done, Blifkins was instructed how to hoist the flag; and soon the proud banner was seen moving heavenward with ostentatious show. Nobody but a small boy was near, who shouted, " Hi, hi!" as it ran up. There was now another dilemma. Plane had made the staff shorter by some five feet than that agreed upon; and there were eddies of air playing about between the buildings, antagonistic to patriotic demonstrations not more than twenty feet high. They were true national airs, and flouted all trivial demonstrations. The flag had a prevailing tendency to wind itself around the top of the staff, like a night-cap; and at last Blifkins, finding it impracticable, went down to Plane again, with an order to add twenty feet more to the pole at once.

The neighbors, with that kind sympathy which commiserates failure and misfortune by laughing at it, shouted to Blifkins, as they went by, " When are you going to hoist your flag?" which he answered mildly, and was content to wait until, with twenty feet added to his flag-staff, he could confound them, especially his "copperhead" neighbors, who had been outrageous in their abuse of him. He longed for his hour of triumph, which he was sure would soon come, as Plane had promised to have it done in a fortnight. The fortnight, however, passed, and the staff was not done; another fortnight was consumed in lying and promises, and it did not come; but one day, as he came home, resolved that he would next day seek some other carpenter, Mrs. Blifkins met him at the door, her face radiant with smiles.

"Did you see any thing as you came in?" she asked.

"Yes," replied he; "I saw your own bright face, which is always my delight."

"Nonsense!" said she; "you are so provoking! Didn't you see our flag?"

"No," he replied.

"Well, it is up," said she; "I put it up myself, and it has attracted lots of attention. More than twenty people have stopped to look at it. It blows out splendidly!"

He stepped to the window, and looked out. There, sure enough, hung the flag, blowing out, as she had said, with great freedom; but, alas for his peace and her taste, it was Union down, and at half staff! There were six people watching it from the street — all "copperheads." With almost a howl, Blifkins rushed out, and in less than one minute the flag was in his hands; in a moment more it was reversed, and floating from the top of the staff.

It is with malicious satisfaction that Blifkins, on any occasion where Mrs. Blifkins asserts her superiority, asks her which way she will have the Union hoisted; but, though she is subdued, she is not conquered.

XVIII.

BLIFKINS THE CONSUMER.

"Grocers are terrible fellows," said Blifkins to us one morning, as he took us by the arm. We had just got past the store of Firkin & Tubb, and observed that he looked in there very timidly as we went by.

We asked him what he meant by the remark he had just made. He hesitated a little, and then proceeded to confess that he was a victim to fear of grocers and provision dealers.

"When I first began housekeeping," said he, "I got along very well. I could go into the grocer's, and order an article with considerable confidence, and with a half-belief that I was conferring a favor in buying of him. But I soon found my mistake. That was a mere delusion. I found that I was the obliged party, and that the sale of goods to me was a matter of condescension. That grocer was a terrible man. He sold me bad butter, bad sugar, bad molasses, bad every thing; but there was such a sternness about him that I didn't dare to say a word.

"'Mr. Blifkins,' says my wife, 'this tea is wretched.'

"'So it is, my love,' I would reply; 'but what can we do?'

"This was a settler of a question, and, like a sensible woman, she held her tongue.

"'Mr. Blifkins,' says my wife, 'the last barrel of flour didn't hold out very well; it was not full when it was bought.'

"'My dear,' said I, 'we will have another barrel.'

"'Mr. Blifkins,' says my wife, 'that butter you sent

home is awfully rancorous; we never shall eat it; hadn't you better speak to Mr. Firkin about it?'

"I did so, and the shock I received settled me.

"'Do you pretend to say,' said he, looking into my eye, 'that the butter was bad?'

"'Really, Mr. Firkin,' said I, mustering courage, 'I have seen better.'

"'Better, sir!' said he, in a voice of thunder and lightning, 'I never had better butter in my store in my life; and if you don't like it, I won't sell you any more.'

"I apologized, and we went on again.

"'Mr. Blifkins,' says my wife, 'this is wretched oil.'

"'Well, my dear,' said I, 'what can we do?'

"'Buy somewhere else,' says she, promptly as the catch of a steel trap.

"I looked at her to see if she wasn't a little out; but her cerulean eye never wore a clearer expression.

"'My dear,' said I, 'sha'n't we give offence by doing so?'

"'That for the offence!' said my wife, snapping her fingers contemptuously.

"Down town, a few days afterwards, I went into a grocery, and sent home groceries enough to last for a month. I met Tubb in the street soon after, and says he, —

"'Blifkins, I half suspect you are buying goods somewhere else. Now, I'll give you fair warning: if you do, I'll sue you for defamation of character, implied by your leaving us, and for damages in the profits we shall lose.'

"I went down and saw a lawyer, and he told me, for ten dollars, that they couldn't do any such thing. I buy where I please now; but I haven't got so that I can look him in the face yet, and go round the other street to get to my house, because I dare not meet him.

"The provision dealers are just as bad," continued he; "for when I bought a quarter of lamb, the other day, down town, my provision dealer found it out, and raised a particular storm about it; and as for buying vegetables out of a cart, though I can get them a good deal cheaper, that is out of the question."

We felt for Blifkins, and believe he is one of a great many who are victims to grocers and provision dealers in one way or another.

XIX.

BLIFKINS THE RURALIST.

BLIFKINS had leased a house at a convenient distance from Boston, and every morning he might have been seen with the "innumerable caravan" that streamed down town from one of our railroads, and, as the evening shades prevailed, with his basket of purchases, entering the railroad depot as regular as a cow accustomed to come into a byre for milking.

When he first moved to his country residence, Mrs. Blifkins and her mother — Blifkins was blessed in his mother-in-law, she was so good to advise — thought the place was charming. It was delightfully situated on the outskirts of the village, with a hill rising from the back door to a respectable altitude, and a brook but a short distance from the house, in which the children and the ducks could paddle with perfect freedom, and where the frogs came at night to serenade the neighborhood, and soothe it into peaceful rest by their dulcet notes.

His nearest neighbor, Mr. Sparin, dwelt in the house opposite, who, as Blifkins found a short time after he had located, was in the habit of indulging in occasional "times," — "benders" the initiated call them, — when he would be away for several days in the enjoyment of sublime indifference to home and every thing else; but he was harmless to everybody except himself; and, after the fit was over, he would return, and settle down to work again as quietly as though nothing had happened, looking his neighbors in the face as composedly as though he had returned from a political convention, or a missionary meeting in some other place. If any one inquired as to where he had gone, he had an answer always ready, that, to those unfamiliar with his habits, was of the most satisfactory character. He informed Blifkins, who was at first curious regarding his disappearance, that he had been up in the country to see about some property that had been left to his wife; and Blifkins had nothing more to say.

Sparin had been away three days at the time the grand incident of this veracious story transpired; and, as Blifkins alighted from the cars on his return from the city on that day, he was informed that Sparin had been seen by one of the neighbors going towards home across the pasture. On arriving home, he was surprised to find his wife, and his mother-in-law, and all the children arranged along the front of the house in a sort of evening dress-parade, gazing intently up towards Sparin's house. The night was calm and pleasant, and he thought at first, before he joined them, that they were enjoying the beauties of the evening. He was past the dressing-gown and slippers period, and therefore knew the parade was not complimentary to himself; but he said, by way of a joke, —

"This, now, is really kind of you. There is nothing that cheers a man up so, on returning fatigued from business, like a kind reception from 'wife and weans.' This is really pleasant."

"Blifkins, don't be a fool," said his wife; "but look up there."

She pointed to a front upper window in Sparin's house, and a queer sight met his startled gaze. A bright light that sat on a table near the window shone full upon a *human face*, that with staring eyes seemed to glare wildly upon vacancy, with a meaningless expression, motionless, while, at intervals of a few moments, alternate hands stole up to the top of the head, and then, with a seeming effort to grasp something, dropped again from sight.

"A pretty place you've brought us to!" said Mrs. Blifkins, with the acid slightly preponderating over the sweet.

"I'm glad to hear you say so, my dear," said he; "I knew you would like it. The quiet of the place and the convenience of access — 'five minutes' walk from the depot,' as the advertisement said, though I must confess that the five minutes seem rather long between the railroad and my treasures."

Gallant Blifkins!

"Don't be a fool always," said Mrs. Blifkins; "what is that?"

She pointed up at the window opposite, where the face yet remained — the eyes staring out into vacancy, and the hands alternately clutching the air, as it appeared. Poor Blifkins was as puzzled at the sight as was Belshazzar, when he saw the writing on the wall. He scarcely dared to breathe his suspicions to himself; but it at once ran through his mind that the face opposite belonged to Sparin, who he deemed had come home, and was then in a fit of delirium tremens, fancying the air full of snakes and other venomous reptiles, and he was engaged in the interesting game of catching them. The idea was a horrid one, and he imparted his suspicions to Mrs. Blifkins with some timidity. Her mind immediately took alarm.

"What if he should kill his family," said she, "with a carving-knife, and then go round murdering his neighbors, and setting fire to their houses, and then finish with himself! Gracious goodness, it makes my blood run cold."

"I guess he won't do any hurt," said Blifkins, with affected cheerfulness. At that moment the figure gave what seemed a desperate grab, as though a particularly big snake were aimed at, and Mrs. Blifkins, in a tone of great earnestness, said, —

"Why don't you do something, stupid?"

"What can I do?" responded the unfortunate Blifkins.

"Why, go over and tie him," said the excellent woman, with a quick mind that never lacked for expedients. Blifkins, however, looked timidly at the stony face and the staring eyes and the hands grasping at the snakes, and did not jump at her proposition with the alacrity that a tender husband ought to have done, she thought.

He had a half-formed plan of raising an alarm of fire, and bringing out the engine company, but was stayed by the imperative question from his wife, —

"Why don't you go?"

Mustering courage, he ran across the street, when it occurred to him that Uncle Bean, as he was called, a soldier of the "last war," lived in the house with Sparin, and would undoubtedly go in and see how it was with his unfortunate neighbor. Uncle Bean, however, was in bed, and in response to Blifkins's knocks a window opened over the door, and a voice harshly demanded, what the deuse was the row. Blifkins explaind the matter as well as he could, which was poorly enough, as the veteran was a little hard of hearing. As soon as he could make the story out, he told Blifkins that he must be excused from doing any thing, as he had just retired on four fingers of whiskey and a bad cold, and didn't want to be disturbed. He advised Blifkins to go down the street to Constable Grabem's, and get him to come up and attend to the affair, as it was his especial business.

The office of constable had been filled, from time immemorial, by some unfortunate who was unable, from bodily infirmity or otherwise, to get a living, but who was deemed sufficient to preserve the peace and dignity of the town, though a home guard of seventy men are now enrolled for that purpose.

Blifkins assured himself, as he came out again into the street, that the unfortunate was still there, though Mrs. Blifkins and the domestic forces had retreated to the citadel.

"Mr. Blifkins!" said his wife from an upper story window, "have you tied him?"

Without deigning a reply, because it might involve too long an explanation, and provoke unpleasant remark, Blifkins started at double quick for Grabem's, who lived some twenty rods down the street. The old fellow was cooling off in the porch of his house, tilted back in a chair made of a flour barrel, which just admitted his spacious person, and smoking a clay pipe. He heard the story patiently, but vouchsafed no reply to Blifkins's prognostications regarding the inebriate's performance of mischief, except "Let him."

"He'll cut his own throat, and then murder his family," said Blifkins.

"Let him," replied Grabem, puffing away.

"He'll set fire to the house, and burn the neighborhood!" screamed Blifkins.

"Let him!" shouted the constable.

"He'll kill everybody, and play the deuce generally!" yelled Blifkins.

"Let him!" roared the official, breaking the clay pipe as he tipped energetically forward.

Blifkins went back, and bethought himself that Sparin had a son, — a sort of second edition of himself, — who was disposed of an evening to make merry, with boys of his age, by the grocery at the other side of his residence, about as far as he had come to find the constable. He would go and see him, and have him go home and look after his eccentric paternal. He accordingly rushed, as fast as his weary limbs would carry him, to where he expected to find the lad. He looked up at the house as he passed by, and there was the face still there, with the set eyes and the busy hands.

Fortunately for Blifkins, the boy was found; and on being informed of the suspicions concerning his parent, and expressing his own convictions thereon in a very precocious manner, involving sundry unfilial remarks, implying a wish that he might be permitted to punch his head, they started down the street together. The outposts of the Blifkins stockade saw them coming down the street by the uncertain light of the stars, and the whole garrison turned out to meet them, with the remark of Mrs. Blifkins, that he had been gone two hours, and that all of them might be killed and scalped if they depended upon such as he for protection. It was an exaggeration with regard to the time, because not more than half an hour had elapsed since he had arrived from the city; but something must be allowed for excitement, when a maniac, threatening violence, and perhaps death, was in she case.

Blifkins thought it would be best for the boy to go in, while he would wait outside of the door, armed with a bludgeon, to rush in at the first alarm. He accordingly provided himself with a cat-stick, and stood with a beating heart to await the result. He heard no sound from within. The stillness of death prevailed. Could it be possible that the maniac had rushed upon the lad suddenly and strangled him! He glanced up at the window, and saw that the stony face had disappeared. He couldn't leave his youthful ally to perish. The respect of the neighborhood, his self-respect, and, more than all, the respect of Mrs. Blifkins, whom he still saw watching him from the opposite side of the way, forbade so cowardly a thing. He seized his cudgel with a firmer grasp, and was lifting his foot to take a step nearer the door, when he heard a step upon the stairs inside, and the door opened. He was relieved by seeing that it was the boy, who said, —

"It's all right."

"What's all right?" cried Blifkins, taking him by the collar, and dragging him across the street to where the impatient group were awaiting the denouement of the scene.

"It's only mother," said he, as soon as he could speak; "you see she wears a wig, and was sitting there where you saw her, pulling out the short hairs that were growing on her head — she's as bald as a plate."

"Just as I thought," said Mrs. Blifkins, "and anybody but a fool would have seen it at once. I declare I believe Blifkins is growing stupider and stupider every day. I'm thankful none of the children take after him."

"True, dear," chimed in his mother-in-law; "but it couldn't be expected any different, because men are never so considerable as women. Though he hadn't ought to try your feelings so at such a time."

"Oh! my feelings are not of any consequence," said Mrs. Blifkins; "I never expect any consideration for them."

Blifkins with a tried spirit went into the house, the light had disappeared from the pane opposite, he heard his children say their prayers as he put them to bed, and sat down in velvet slippers and tranquil meditation, thanking his lucky stars that he had been saved from participating in what might have been a tragedy, had the fates so willed it.

XX.

BLIFKINS'S MIDNIGHT CALL.

Mr. Blifkins in his domestic economy for many years has retained the allopathic system of medicine, and, by his liberal encouragement of apothecaries, has established quite a reputation with that class. As, in the event of sickness, each application required new bottles and new pill-boxes, it may be supposed that during the twenty years of his experience, there was about his house a formidable aggregate of half-used prescriptions, reminders of several moderate fortunes that had been thrown to the dogs in the form of physic, about the use and effect of which the memory of Blifkins ceased to be cognizant. Mrs. Blifkins, however, insisted upon keeping them, from an economical desire that nothing should be wasted; for she is a great economist, and there is not one in the neighborhood that excels her. Her house is a curiosity shop of relics of past economies, that have survived all earthly uses, and lie mouldering in a hundred nooks around the house, and bottles and boxes in a closet handy are numerous enough to set up a druggist of not inordinate desires. She pretended, and actually thought, probably, that she knew the difference between a cough mixture and a wash for weak eyes, could discriminate betwixt rheumatic and dyspepsia pills, and knew cantharides from Dover's powders readily. Blifkins had long been doubtful about this, though, which doubt recently produced an entire revolution in his household pharmacy. But Mr. Blifkins tells his own story best, and we leave its recital to him.

"'Mr. Blifkins,' says my wife, suddenly starting up in the bed, and looking wildly into the face of little Tommy, 'I believe this child is going to have the croup, or the scarlet fever, or something. Mr. Blifkins!'

"I had got to the stage of sleep when one is conscious of sleeping and waking at the same time — the senses steeping with somnolent poppies, but not quite narcotized into forgetfulness.

"'Mr. Blifkins!' repeated my wife, giving me this time an unmistakable pinch.

"'What in the name of tribulation is the matter?' I cried in something like a pet; 'is the house on fire?'

"'No; but something is the matter with Tommy,' she replied; 'perhaps he's going to have the croup — maybe he'll have a fit — he's very restless.'

"I started up and looked in the face of that little innocent. They always said he looked just like me, and certainly that midnight inspection gave very little encouragement to self-vanity, for a more disagreeable-looking little cub I thought I had never seen. He was evidently in trouble, for his features worked, his tiny fists were clinched hard, his eyes were partly unclosed, and his skin seemed quite dry and hot. I immediately took my wife's alarm.

"'What's to be done?' I asked.

"'Mr. Blifkins,' said she, 'we must give him something.'

"'Exactly,' I responded; 'but what shall it be? You, who are such an excellent nurse, shall decide.'

"I arose, and, 'accoutred as I was,' stood ready to execute her command. I signified this to her by saying, —

"'Now, my dear, say the word.'

"'Let me see,' said she; 'if it is the croup, the medicine in the bottle on the left hand side of the closet is the one. It was bought for Mary, two winters ago.'

"I immediately proceeded to the closet adjacent to our

room, the interior of which was revealed by the dim light
of the gas. There were long rows of phials on the shelves,
backed by bottles of hair dye, and boxes of undefinable
articles in the domestic dispensary. I saw what I supposed was the needed bottle; but, in extricating it from
its position, I threw down some half a dozen of the inter-
vening phials, that rattled and clattered upon the floor in a
manner that sounded fearfully, some of them breaking, and
the glass scattering around, to the dismay of my bare
feet.

" ' *Do* break every thing to pieces !' said my wife, in a
tone not very sweet, considering her amiability of temper;
but I imputed it to her anxiety. I brought the bottle, and
placed it in her hands.

" 'Good Heavens, Mr. Blifkins,' said my wife, 'would
you kill the child ? This is volatile liniment.'

" 'The d— it is,' cried I, with unwarrantable heat. My
wife sobbed out, —

" 'O Mr. Blifkins! suppose we had given him some of
this by mistake ! — *you* never would have forgiven yourself.'

" I thought the change of person in her remark a little
invidious, and somewhat unkind, in view of the fact that
she had command of the medicine chest.

" 'I took the bottle from the place you told me,' said I,
almost fiercely.

" 'You couldn't have done so, Mr. Blifkins,' replied my
wife; 'I saw it on the right hand, just inside the door, no
longer ago than Tuesday week, when Mrs. McGonagle
cleaned the paint.'

" '*Right* hand?' I repeated after her; 'you said the *left*
just now.'

" I heard her sigh out something about 'cruelty' and
'unfeelingness' as I went to make another plunge among
the army of bottles.

" 'This must be it, then,' said I, seizing a four ounccr, nearly full of a dark fluid, by the neck, and bringing it out to my wife.

" 'Gracious goodness!' exclaimed she; 'are you determined to kill the child? That's arnica, for the rheumatism. Mr. Blifkins, are you awake?'

"Without replying this time, I made a dive for the closet, taking down phial after phial, and reading the smeared inscriptions as well as I could. What an ocean of lotions, and mixtures, and vermifuges, and preparations, and washes! At length I got hold of one that I felt sure must be it, because I could not by any ingenuity decipher the label. I accordingly carried it to Mrs. Blifkins with the confident air of one who has achieved an immense exploit, holding it out to her with a '*There!*' expressive of my satisfaction.

" 'That!' said my wife; 'that's not it; that is the chalk mixture, bought for Bub two summers ago.'

"I broke down at this, and with a voice tremulous with cold, though my wife always wrongfully said it was with anger, I asked her why, in the name of some deity or other, she didn't get up and find it herself. She immediately arose to the occasion, like a speaker at a Fourth of July dinner, and sublimely strode towards the closet, returning, a moment thereafter, with two bottles that had escaped my notice, which she held up before me with the simple but comprehensive remark, —

" 'Stupid!'

"I felt that I was stupid, and was ready to admit the fact, when I was struck by the puzzled look that appeared upon my wife's face.

" 'Let me see,' said she.

"I made a motion to turn up the gas, so that she might see, but found that she required a clearer vision re-

garding some mental problem that she was solving; so I
let her see as she best might.

"'I declare,' said my wife, 'I don't know whether this
is the bedbug poison or the croup specific, they are so
much alike.'

"'Perhaps he hasn't got the croup,' said I, as I stooped
over the bed; and there lay the little fellow wide awake,
threshing the air with his two tiny fists, and making up all
sorts of faces at the shadows upon the wall. I saw in a
moment that we had deceived ourselves, as most parents
will; and, turning away, I wickedly said, —

"'Give me the medicine! I think he's going to have a
fit' —

"My wife shrieked.

"'Of laughter,' I immediately added, and received a box
on the ear for my reward. I addressed my wife solemnly,
for I felt serious : —

"'Here we have been collecting together this precious
amount of trash for years for an emergency, and now,
when the emergency comes, what is it good for? I tell
you what, wife — this is the end of such nonsense. Will
you be so kind as to open that window ?'

"She did so, and in three minutes every phial and its contents were in the street. People opened their windows to
ascertain the meaning of the crash of glass, and were much
astonished the next morning to learn the cause of it, but
more so to hear me say that I would have nothing more
to do with doctor's stuff, unless it was in the form of small
pellets, so harmless that nightshade could be taken as well
as catnip, for the same diseases, with impunity."

XXI.

BLIFKINS THE EXPERIMENTALIST.

"THERE," said Blifkins, as he laid a small paper package upon the table, while a strong smell of camphor pervaded the apartment, "I guess that will fix 'em."

"Fix who?" asked Mrs. B., wildly, as she thought of her children, or some other poisoned victims of Mr. B.'s sudden insanity.

"Have you seen Amos?" he continued, without answering her question.

"Amos? What Amos?" she queried, half rising from her chair, as if to cry for help in the event of his being violent.

"Amos-quito!" he almost shouted.

"Now, don't make a jack of yourself, Benjamin, if you can help it," said she. "The little brains you have got should be devoted to better uses than making fun of the wife of your bosom; but I have learned to bear it, and am now ready to 'suffer and be strong.' What have you got in that parcel?"

"That? Dead Shot for mosquitoes — Amos, you know. I read it in the paper that gum camphor, burnt in a room, is a certain antidote against 'em, and I'm bound to try it. But now, little wife, let us have supper, for I am as hungry as a meeting-house."

"Do be a little more choice in your comparisons, Benjamin. The children all copy you in spite of all I can say. Only yesterday little Jimmy said he didn't care 'three shakes of a sheep's tail' for his uncle Joshua, who is always giving him moral lessons."

10*

"Well, let's have supper, wife, and then, —

> ' When the evening shades prevail,
> We'll take an old tin pan or pail,
> And straightway with the burnt camphire
> We'll give the skeeters Jeremiah.'

See Watts for the authority — quoted from memory."

"That's right; go on making fun of the most serious things. No wonder the children get all sorts of queer notions into their heads; but they shall never blame me for it when they grow up."

Blifkins chatted with his children, said a cheerful word to his wife, praised the cooking, and as the table girl, who was quite good looking, passed his chair, he gave her a smile that Mrs. Blifkins detected.

"That's pretty," said she, "for a married man to do right in the presence of his wife and children! But I have no right to expect any thing else. Hadn't you better install that minx in my place, and done with it?"

"No, my dear," said Blifkins; "I am very well contented with the one I chose, among fifty, to preside over my mahogany, and am not disposed to change at present."

After supper Blifkins romped with the children, joked with Mrs. B., and forced that estimable lady into a degree of pleasant humor that was quite startling. Before they well knew it, the hour of bed-time had arrived, when the children were kissed good night previous to being put in their little beds, and Mr. and Mrs. B. retired to their chamber, which had been terribly invaded by hordes of mosquitoes, making sleep impossible for several nights.

"I declare, my dear," said Blifkins, when just ready for bed, "I've forgotten, in the pleasures of the evening, my camphor. It is on the dining-room table. I'll run down and get it."

"What!" almost screamed Mrs. Blifkins, "and meet, perhaps, the servant girls on the stairs! I'll go myself."

And go she did.

"And now," said he, "little wife, for some implement in which to burn the camphor. Let me see : your little dust-shovel will do. Where is it?"

"What a plague you are, Benjamin!" replied Mrs. B.; "and I don't believe it will amount to any thing, after it is all done. There's the shovel."

Blifkins crumbled up about a great spoonful of the camphor, and, placing it in the shovel, held it over the gas-burner, waiting for it to burn. He was soon rewarded by seeing it smoke, and then, a moment after, there was a poof! and a blaze, and Blifkins, starting at the suddenness of the conflagration, dropped the shovel. and Mrs. B. turned off the gas. The camphor fell into the wash-basin, where it soon burnt out, the faces of Mr. and Mrs. Blifkins looking ghastly in the light while it lasted, and their night-dresses rendered the scene very spectral.

"Better luck next time," said Blifkins, smiling in the dark, and feeling round for the camphor.

"Nonsense!" replied Mrs. B., sententiously.

"I'll succeed or perish in the attempt," said Benjamin, brandishing the shovel, as he relighted the gas.

"You'll never do any thing with it," replied Mrs. B.; "and if I were a mosquito, I should laugh at you."

"By the way," said Blifkins, as he crumbled the camphor, "did you ever hear that it was the female mosquitoes that do all the stinging?"

"A story invented by a man," replied she, "to slander us poor women, as though we hadn't enough laid upon us already."

"Well, here we go again," said Blifkins, holding his shovel over the blaze.

This time the gum ignited finely, and a bright blaze and a dense smoke followed, the latter rising to the ceiling in a black cloud, and rolling along the wall in opaque convolutions. This experiment was followed by another; and as B., like the fabled Colossus of Rhodes, as depicted, stood with his hand raised aloft, holding the blazing shovel, he passed the open door where his children lay, the oldest of whom, waking, shouted, " Fire ! " and rushed for the entry, where the servant girls were huddling, having already smelt the smoke. They opened the door, and all rushed in pell-mell, as Blifkins was completing his last grand round before the flame sunk to its grave, and then rushed out again, as Mrs. B. threw herself into the breach, and forced them back. The cry of the child had attracted attention in the street, besides ; and Blifkins, hearing a murmur of voices below, looked out upon a crowd of people assembled, and a voice demanded. —

" What the deuse is the matter ? "

He assured them that nothing was the matter; that his child was frightened, that's all, with a nightmare; and told them there was no need of the hose-carriage they had brought from round the neighboring corner. After some altercation, the crowd dispersed, an opinion being expressed that Blifkins was " a humbuggin' cuss."

The house at last was still, and the pair retired to sleep in an atmosphere of camphor smoke that was almost suffocating.

" Now, my dear," said Blifkins, " I hope we shall enjoy a quiet night's sleep, free from the trumpet-notes of the mosquitoes."

B-z-z-z, b-z-z-z ! right in his very ear.

At that moment, Mrs. B. gave herself a severe slap in the face, as if she were inflicting personal chastisement ; and Blifkins, with both arms out of bed, thrashed the air like a windmill.

"I told you so," said Mrs. B.. giving herself a dig in the eye, and bringing her elbow plump on Blifkins's nose; "but you never will take my advice. I am done expecting that. Men nowadays had rather ask the advice of other people's wives than their own, and I suppose it is all right; but don't think it is just the thing (slap) to expect every thing of a woman, and withhold confidence (slap), and smile at servant maids, and visit other women (a vicious slap); and now this last farce that you have played (slap), with a shirt so ridiculously short; and Heaven knows where it will end (slap), which was disgraceful enough; and the girls rushing in as they did" —

She drew the sheet over her head, her voice died to a confused murmur, and Mrs. Blifkins slept.

Blifkins fought in silence with his fate. The enemy had been driven from the ceiling above, and had attacked, front and rear, in the field below, coming not as single spies, but in battalions, until he was fain to beat a retreat, and hide his head beneath a defence of cotton cloth, vowing to himself, as he passed into the land of dreams, that he would do on the morrow what he should have done long before — buy some mosquito netting.

Next morning it was found that the snow-white wall was grimy with the smoke, the paper smutched, and a villanous smell remained, an abiding evidence of the night attack. The whole affair was the subject of a severe lecture at the breakfast table, and a re-affirmation by Mrs. B. of the often-repeated statement that there was never a woman so cruelly treated as she.

When Blifkins arrived at the store, he took up the Post, and the first item that met his view was : —

"There was a slight fire at the house of Mr. Benjamin Blifkins, No. 16 Cliff Street, last evening; but it was extinguished by Officers Mudhead and Spinks without causing a general alarm."

THE MODERN SYNTAX.

DR. SPOONER IN SEARCH OF THE DELECTABLE.

119

INTRODUCING DR. SPOONER.

Those who have been privileged listeners of Dr. Dionysius Spooner, as he has described to them his adventures
while in search of "the Delectable," will not be offended
at this imperfect rendering of them; while others who
have not been thus privileged will see in them the struggles of a great mind towards the attainment of an object,
and may receive from their example an impetus in the
right direction, as though it were from the toe of an
intellectual boot, energetically applied. The writer became acquainted with the doctor through a train of very
singular, yet natural, circumstances — singular from the
manner of their occurrence, rather than from their character. Passing through the streets one day, he overheard two
gentlemen in earnest conversation, one of whom said,
"Well, Dr. Spooner said so." This sentence forced itself
upon his mind, and he pondered upon what Dr. Spooner
could have said, and who Dr. Spooner was, with no hope of
solving the mystery. He was afterwards at a picture sale,
where the fate of an original Rembrandt, the subject of
which none could make out, was hanging on the blow
of the auctioneer's mallet. "Why, gentlemen," said he,
will you let this go so low, when Dr. Spooner vouches

for its authenticity?" The bids then ran rapidly up to a dollar and a half, when it was knocked off. Dr. Spooner again! He was evidently a connoisseur, but there was no room for inquiry. When the steamboat Henry Morrison went down, in Boston Harbor, it was stated that Dr. Spooner was present, and lent able assistance in preparing the chowder. He thus proved himself an epicure, — an "epicac" Mrs. Partington called it, — and again provoked the inquiry, "Who is Dr. Spooner?" The answer to the question was further withheld, and on a day some months later, while the writer was in a store matching some calico for home consumption, there was quite a commotion near the door. He asked the meaning thereof, and was told that Dr. Spooner was passing by. "Tell me," said he, suddenly seizing his informant by the collar, "who is Dr. Spooner?" The person extricated himself, and, simply saying "I don't know," passed out. There was no one present who could answer the question. But Fate was kinder. One day, while purchasing his dinner at a stall in the market, a remarkable and very imposing person was cheapening a leg of mutton at the same, having purchased which, and given a very lucid direction as to how it should be trimmed, he threw down a card, to the address of which he wished the delicacy sent. Glancing at it, the writer read,—

"Dr. Dionysius Spooner,

CHIROPODIST,

111 Q Street."

Here was a discovery! "Hesitating then no longer," the writer hastily said, "Pardon me, sir! but I am very desirous of making your acquaintance. Your name has reached me so favorably, that you need not produce vouchers of character; for myself, try me." "I should, perhaps, leave the tribunals to do that," said he, blandly, "but I like your impudence, and will encourage your advances. Come and see me, and we will make an equal exchange — you try my mutton, and I will try you; sheep for sheep, you know." The victim was annoyed, but gulped down his chagrin. This was the commencement of an acquaintance most beneficial to the writer. While, paregorically speaking, sitting at the feet of this modern Gamaliel, the narration of his efforts to attain the Delectable has fallen in showers of soporific illusion about the ears of the listener, until, inspired, the Muse plumed herself for the flight that should portray the persistency which strove for so much and gained so little.

The walks through which the modern Syntax wandered in search of the Delectable are not so varied as those pursued by his ancient prototype, in quest of the Picturesque, because the space devoted to the subject is not so extended; reminding the reader, doubtless, of that classical incident where the three wise men of Gotham went to sea in a bowl, and it was said, in excuse for the brevity of the narrative, —

"If the bowl had been stronger,
The song had been longer."

The incidents, however, have herein been compressed agreeably to a wise editorial admonition, but recently promulgated, to "boil it down," meaning just this kind of matter; and therefore the latter production bears the same relation to the former that Leibig's extract of flesh does to the "stalled ox."

The author trusts that the recital of the several incidents described may afford pleasure and profit to the reader, and win for the distinguished subject thereof new renown.

THE MODERN SYNTAX.

DR. SPOONER IN SEARCH OF THE DELECTABLE.

I.

On Monday morning, with the sun uprist,
   Good Dr. Spooner ate his steak in haste,
And hurried down his coffee and his twist,
   As though no moment he would idly waste,
Then took his cane within his sturdy fist,
   With animation on his features traced,
And started forth in attitude reflectable,*
To seek, 'mid airs mundane, the goal Delectable.

* The author at the outset — before he has led the good doctor
through any of the labyrinthine walks of life — with the independ-
ence of the poet, who will not be limited by the conventionalities
of dictionaries, grammars, or common sense, claims the right to coin
as many words as his opinion, or the needs of rhyme, may require.
Hence the word "reflectable;" and the claim is introduced to disarm
the critics of the Atlantic, North American, or Foreign Quarterly,
who might snap at this seeming and only fault, as a pickerel might
at a frog's leg.

II.

Before him lay the undeveloped scene
    That Fate, impatient, waited him to show;
He stood a moment with a thoughtful mien,
    As if uncertain which path he should go,
Then held his cane his finger tips between,
    That, by its falling. he his course might know.
North-east!   'Tis well.   Now all my doubts at rest,
Since chance so wills it, I'll go sou'-sou'-west

III.

Not he, alone, to go adverse to Fate;
    Some do, with all prognostics pointing clear,
And full success attending at the gate ;
    They do not stop propitious hints to hear,
But clutch at phantom shapes that tempting wait,
    Till, to their disappointment and their fear,
They see their error and neglected track,
With little hope of ever getting back.

IV.

All have desire to win the happy goal,
    And all strike out o'er some illusive gravel,
Investing hope and earnestness of soul
    The mystery of the future to unravel,
Finding, too oft, to their dismay and dole,
    Their road, like Jordan, very hard to travel —
Their delectation, like the Paddy's flea,
Within their grasp, and yet not quite to be.

V.

Diversity of tastes prompts divers aims,
    And, as the whim controls, men blindly go it,
Pursuing here and there their little games,
    Through which, for bliss set out, they think they'll
        show it;
Each plays his part, with equal hopes and claims,
    Trusting that Fate propitious will bestow it;
But very few attain the culmination
That gives the sought-for boon of delectation.

VI.

Though, for that matter, comes the question up,
    What is the boon for which they thus are striving?
Fill to the brim Joy's most enchanting cup,
    Some would reject it, other draughts contriving,
Being more happy far to take a sup
    From sombre springs, or in their depths be diving;
A strange anomaly we too often see,
Where happiness is sought in misery.

VII.

No sympathy have I with such as these;
    But what they do is what they deem the best;
The genial soul, the heart in fullest ease,
    Comes up the nearest my ideal of blest;
We will not quarrel — each his pathway sees,
    And travels it for happiness in quest:
Each to his taste, as the old lady said
What time she kissed the tenant of the shed.

VIII.

So Dr. Spooner, with his heart aglow,
    Stood ready to attain the boon I speak of;
The Fates had fixed the path that he must go
    By his cane's falling — you recall the freak of —
He rested as he felt the breezes blow
    From a fair hill of which he saw the peak of,
And thus addressed them, like a necromancer
Demanding of unsentient things an answer:

IX.

"Tell me, ye wingèd winds, as on ye fly,
    Hast come from scenes where delectation waits?
Point me, O winds! that sport beneath the sky
    Where perfect joy the craving spirit sates;
Direct my steps, that I may quickly hie
    Where bliss unfolds its amaranthine gates!"
The winds deigned no reply, but swifter sped,
Tearing the doctor's hat from off his head.

X.

There is no more provoking thing I know
    Than this: to have one's hat torn from his pate.
No sympathy doth any one bestow,
    And grins the awkward accident await;
The curious crowd look on to see us go,
    As we pursue the fleeing thing of hate,
Until, perhaps, some chap, a little faster,
Plants his thick No. Twelves on our new castor

XI.

He stood a moment when regained his tile,
  And on the incident reflecting dwelt;
He paid the fact the tribute of a smile, —
  A feeling tribute, for the hat was felt.
"I've chased this hat the fraction of a mile,"
  He said, "and this sage thought comes through my pelt:
That, as I've won it, racing with the wind,
'In the long run' I happiness shall find."

XII.

And, thus assured, he sped with eager feet,
  Caroming here and there as on he flew,
Pushing some off the sidewalk to the street,
  And by collision bringing others to,
Exciting talk we will not now repeat,
  And angry thoughts awaking not a few,
When to a full stop was he quickly brought,
Like a blue-bottle in a fly-trap caught.

XIII.

There moved along, exactly in his way,
  One of those well-made-up, artistic women,
Who are, as one might very justly say,
  One quarter flesh and blood, and three fourths trimmin':
He tried to pass her, giving ample play
  To all the furbelows about her streamin',
When, spite of all his wary care and pain,
He found his boots entangled in her train.

XIV.

He turned about and gazed on what he'd done,
  Confounded at the seeming mischief dire;
But when he saw the spitefulness that shone
  Forth from her eyes, like that same baleful fire
We read about, excuse he proffered none,
  But said, " If I am sorry I'm a liar;
What right had she, at just that time, to spread
Above the spot whereon I chose to tread ? "

XV.

But in a moment more he felt contrite,
  And held his head down with emotion humble;
He o'er the pave had no exclusive right,
  And, 'mongst her things-come-afterwards to stumble,
He had endangered an annoying plight,
  At which she well might frown on him or grumble;
And then he turned, repentant, but, a goner,
He saw the lady turn a distant corner.

XVI.

And this impressed itself upon his mind;
  No one is happy disregarding others,
As men are so untwistingly combined
  That rending one the great remainder bothers;
And but as one is just, polite, and kind,
  And all his selfish aspirations smothers,
Can he expect that happiness below
Which the exalted soul alone can know.

XVII.

He moved along 'mid scenes of active life,
    And stoutly strove his object to attain ;
There was excitement in the pressing strife,
    But with it all there mixed a sense of pain ;
With selfishness society was rife,
    And finding all his expectation vain,
Heart-sick and weary, with unlevel head,
He turned himself towards home, and went to bed.

XVIII.

And then the dreams born of his urgent wish !
    Led through fair scenes that waking ne'er reveals,
Feasting on spreads of flesh, and fowl, and fish,
    Quaffing rare drinks of most attractive seals,
All right side up his favor-beckoning dish,
    Holding such cards as kindest fortune deals,
Waking at morn with resolution stout,
His quest for happiness to carry out.

  .   .   .   .

XIX.

One day is like another in the race
    For some pet object, every else forgot ;
So the good doctor daily held his chase
    To find 'mong mundane scenes the blissful lot,
The one strong hope to rest his weary pace
    When he should reach the delectating spot.
Of all the spots that I know worth the trying
A fifty spot is the most satisfying.

XX.

Thus, as with zeal elate he wandered out,
　　His mind intent on seeking delectation,
And with an eager eye he looked about,
　　Giving all things a wise examination,
Unheeding an admonitory shout,
　　That of some danger made ejaculation,
There came a snow-slide from some upper height,
And Dr. Spooner disappeared from sight!

xxi.

A mingled feel waits accidents like these :
　　A grateful thrill like an unuttered prayer,
As one from peril saved his status sees,
　　And then a pressing tendency to swear,
Which from oppressive wrath the temper frees,
　　— So some folks think, in which I take no share, —
But the good doctor, as he moved once more,
Took stock in neither mood, nor prayed nor swore.

XXII.

In fact, just then in search for happiness,
　　And doubtful if 'twere pious or profane,
He would not compromise his chance for bliss,
　　But non-committal would a while remain.
Many another does the same as this,
　　Desirous some pet object to attain;
For policy and selfishness prevail,
While interest steers, and caution trims the sail.

XXIII.

The greatest pleasure that the world can give
  Is that we draw from intellectual sources;
Freed from the sensuous dross in which we live,
  We 'mid the purer ethers vent our forces,
And misspent hours we happily retrieve
  In following those crystal water-courses
That flow from founts in mental mountains springing,
And to our feet the choicest gifts are bringing.

XXIV.

So Dr. Spooner thought he'd take to books,
  And bought them lavishly, — all subjects choosing —
Having them placed in their adapted nooks,
  With catalogues their resting-place disclosing;
Bound handsomely in calf, that graceful looks
  Might add attraction, and enhance the using, —
All books that might a reader's thoughts awaken,
From Blood-and-Thunder Nibs to Friar Bacon.

XXV.

His heart ached at the woe of thrilling stories,
  Fraught with depictions of unreal life;
He read in histories the crowning glories
  That flowed from fields of sanguinary strife;
Philosophy and physics passed before his
  Eyes, with the light of ripe reflection rife,
Yet betwixt Reade and Bacon he confessed
He'd neither read, but thought Reade was the best.

XXVI.

Then borrowers came, and fastened on his hoard,
   Splitting his sets remorselessly to pieces;
And in those cases where they were restored,
   They came back dog-eared and defiled with creases;
Until, at last, beyond endurance bored,
   Said he, "From now henceforward all this ceases!"
Then locked his door upon his precious shelves,
And left his authors pondering on themselves.

XXVII.

The tempter whispered, "Go it while you're young!
   Taste the delirious tumult of the hour;
The siren sings as sweet as e'er she sung,
   The senses plead with unabated power;
Bring your dull soul joy's halcyon scenes among,
   And pluck, while yet it blooms. life's brightest flower;
Don't mure yourself till felt years' chilling blasts,
And quaff the cup of pleasure while it lasts."

XXVIII.

In dissipation did the doctor dip,
   And strove to find what fun there might be in it.
He pressed the sparkling goblet to his lip,
   Till his old head hummed like an ancient spinet;
He joined in pleasure's jolly partnership,
   In wild adventure mixing every minute;
But when he found his nose all raw and red,
"There's very little fun in sport like this," he said,

XXIX.

A wholesome lesson this, that all may learn
    Who try such roads to find the bliss they crave.
They're lit by lamps that oil Plutonic burn,
    And lead through scenes that weaken and enslave;
Brigands of Passion lurk at every turn
    To trip the feet of those their prowess brave,
And the "good times" that lured the soul away,
Are drafts on time, with no funds left to pay.

XXX.

Many of those these sprightly lines who read
    Know how it is themselves — no slang intended.
Though fair the promise all too pronely heed,
    With honeyed hope and expectation blended,
The hope soon prematurely goes to seed,
    And winter comes before the summer's ended;
The roses turn to ashes 'neath the tread,
And dirges wail the season that has fled.

XXXI.

Were I disposed a moral to indite,
    Here most unquestionably is its place:
Don't wait repentance until appetite
    No more has power its progress to retrace;
Complete worn-outness surely's not the plight
    To give repentance much, if any, grace.
'Twas no great merit in old Uncle Ned
Corn-cakes to eschew with his teeth all shed.

XXXII.

He walked and pondered, with his brow erect,
    Devising in his mind which way to turn
To gain the point his fancy did affect,
    Convinced, indeed, that he had much to learn
Before he saw the beacon-lights reflect,
    That on the coast of pure enjoyment burn,
When, lost in reverie, his reason fled,
He found himself down cellar — on his head.

XXXIII.

A cellar doorway, though a fearful trap,
    Affords a cautionary moral, clear,
To every visionary, dreamy chap,
    Impelled by contemplation high or beer,
To heed his steps, lest they should chance, mayhap,
    To lead him, witless, into trouble drear.
Although 'tis well uplifted gaze to show,
We should have half an eye for things below.

XXXIV.

And the good doctor lay a moment thus,
    Not knowing how or why he should be there,
The world all muddled in a precious muss,
    Concerning which he didn't know nor care;
And then he rose, and said, " Ridiculous!"
    Running his fingers through his matted hair,
In which confused and much-mixed-up condition,
He felt just fit to be a politician.

XXXV.

In politics the doctor took a stand,
   And blurted with an unremitting zeal,
Retailing dogmas up and down the land,
   Professing earnestly the public weal;
Condemning all who, on the other hand,
   Chanced differently regarding them to feel,
And was a cog-wheel active as could be
In the great whirl of party enginery.

XXXVI.

As legislator, in the town and state,
   Across the stage with giant steps he strode;
His was the dictum on which hung the fate
   Of mighty hobbies that the lobby rode;
He took no bribes his act to compensate,
   And voted as the "greatest good" was showed;
Rich only in the sense of duty done,
And — certain *gifts* his self-denial won.

XXXVII.

Strange fancy his who seeks in politics
   For happiness; as well might he essay
To honey find in husks, or oil in bricks,
   Or new potatoes in New England May;
His chiefest recompense the meed of kicks
   Constituents ungrateful always pay,
And find he's purchased, when it is too late,
A tiny whistle at a monstrous rate.

XXXVIII.

Sure delectation must be found in Fame,
  As Solomon had said 'twas more than riches;
And so his sail he spread to catch a name,
  Courting each breeze to draw and test its stitches;
His name appeared, with eulogy aflame,
  And all the slabber that the vain bewitches;
Besides, his face graced each pictorial journal,
With praise or blame allied — alike infernal.

XXXIX.

He talked his mouth for fame in every place,
  Was always found, wherever wished or not;
From a street-corner speech to saying grace
  He rose to the occasion piping hot;
Sometimes a slap he'd welcome in the face,
  And a nose-pulling now and then he got;
But all such favors helped his little game
To win the " glittering height " on which was fame.

XL.

His head grew dizzy on his lofty perch,
  — His reputation mere factitious show, —
And, like a weather-vane upon a church,
  He turned just as the fickle wind might blow,
Till counter breezes gave a sudden lurch,
  And down he came 'mong common folks below,
The ridicule of every humble eye —
The golden cynosure but gilt, brought nigh.

XLI.

For fame he'd sacrificed all thoughts of peace;
  Had found antagonism everywhere;
Had lied and swore his chances to increase;
  Had tried philanthropy, and wore long hair;
For every wheel he had the needed grease;
  In every public movement had a share;
Denied himself all comfort for a name;
"And this," said he, "is all there is of fame!"

XLII.

In wit's display he next great effort made,
  And searched the dictionary through for puns,
While such extreme abandon he displayed,
  His jokes popped off as though they had been guns;
Grave people all around him were afraid,
  And 'gainst his influence bewared their sons,
Bidding them think their sires ne'er acted thus,
And calling him "disreputable *cus-*

XLIII.

Tomer," which softens some the verbal force —
  Like the old clergyman of whom they tell,
Who, vainly trying to secure his horse,
  By his momentum in the brambles fell;
And, angered thereat, made the mattter worse
  By shouting out vehemently, "O hell!"
But seeing in an instant his offence,
"*Lelujah*" added, which quite changed the sense.

XLIV.

The doctor made a laugh where'er he went —
  He had no scruple thus to serve them so;
Even a funeral scene could not prevent,
  And where an undertaker had to go,
His mates such unction to the season lent,
  He said, " What '*sprit de corpse* these folks do show!'
' Twas villanous, but those the rue that quaffed
Looked through their sables and at Spooner laughed.

XLV.

The Lecture Bureaus then must have him out,
  And curious people came from far and near,
With buttons sewed on more than extra stout,
  Fearing to burst them with the fun they'd hear;
He heard, one side, the injudicious shout,
  But something like a groan filled t'other ear;
Snowed in and criticised, self-reproved and weary,
He felt, as did admiring friends, 'twas dreary.

XLVI.

And next in Fashion's walks the doctor pressed,
  And clothed himself in most approved attire,
With brainless glorying at being dressed
  Up to the standard that the modes require;
From hat to boots resplendent as the best,
  With but to shine the limit of desire;
And every one inferred, who chose to scan,
That Dr. Spooner was a " killing man "!

XLVII.

But then the thought upon his senses stole,
   " What am I but an ape ? — though not so mean
Is mine as Darwin says was man's first role
   Before the footlights of this earthly scene, —
The copy but of others, with a soul
   That grasps infinitude — too grand, I ween,
To spend its faculties in such base use
As hatching goslings from a tailor's goose."

XLVIII.

" This, then, is evident," he further mused,
   " That delectation does not come to those
Who spend their strength in attributes abused,
   Or ripen into gorgeousness of clo'es ;
Neither to those with qualities unused,
   Who dawdle, to day's dying, in a doze ;
But unto those who try, by work or wit,
The world's great family to benefit."

XLIX.

In gentle recreation did he strive,
   Attending all the small fêtes that were going ;
Was great at fairs, where ladies so contrive
   To keep the cream of human kindness flowing ;
Tried summer picnics with their glee alive,
   That such a wealth of promises were showing ;
Joined social clubs and literary coteries,
And took a stand high up 'mong Pleasure's votaries.

L.

Thin dissipations, such as these, at best,
  Gave little recompense to his ambition;
He seaward turned, and on the ocean's breast
  He thought he saw his ardent hope's fruition;
He sang sea-songs, and "Heave ho'd" with the rest,
  But found the sea unsteady in position;
He didn't relish his first evening's supper,
And closed his "Heave ho's" in the leeward scupper.

LI.

He murmured faintly, "Please set me on shore;
  I love the grand and ever-restless ocean,
But I believe that I can love it more
  On *terra firma*, where, unfelt its motion,
I can delight to hear its mighty roar,
  And throw myself with rapturous devotion;
But here, alas! the power that rules the sea
Rules it too crookedly by far for me.

LII.

Then Dr. Spooner ventured into trade,
  And learned to buy and sell with ready art;
He many paying operations made,
  And got the trick of traffic all by heart;
So shrewd was he in action he displayed,
  He won the fame of being "devilish smart,"
Which means — well, any thing respectable —
But found that trade was far from the delectable.

LIII.

It would have done you good to hear him lie —
    Or froze your blood — just as you felt inclined;
He'd swear that black was white a trade to tie,
    And all so plausible, that caution, blind,
Took stock at once, without a how? or why?
    Such marvellous integrity to find;
And then he slapped his pockets, well content
That he had made a mighty big per cent.

LIV.

"Mercantile shrewdness," though it fleece and skin,
    Is ne'er dishonest by the rules of trade,
And those who deepest plunge and largest win
    Sleep lightest on the bargains they have made;
Conscience to such makes no unpleasant din,
    And, at the future not one whit dismayed,
They "will" their wealth with most complacent air,
And lay them down the just's reward to share.

LV.

To Education then the doctor flew,
    The very field for happiness, he thought;
The total that he guessed, and what he knew,
    Were into active requisition brought;
He went to all Conventions with a *gout*
    That was a substitute for what he sought,
And, being quite a favorite in the city,
They made him member of the School Committee.

LVI.

Then pleasure turned to business — early, late,
  His door-bell rang with clamorous appeal,
Permits to grant, parental doubts to bate,
  Teachers to hear, vexatious feuds to heal,
New books to choose, the salaries to rate,
  The pangs of interrupted peace to feel,
The public growling in its discontent,
And watching, lynx-eyed, each invested cent.

LVII.

With not a chance to steal, and snubbed and bored,
  His privacy invaded as a right;
His motives doubted and his claim ignored,
  His life a constant, ignominious fight;
The slave of school-book agencies, that poured
  Their arguments so thick, that, vanquished quite,
He vowed no more his soul with such to vex,
Then "handed in" his thin official "checks."

LVIII.

The doctor next dipped fiercely into morals,
  Went regularly every morn to prayer;
Mixed earnestly in theologic quarrels,
  Where men for truth's sake pulled each other's hair;
Had for all ill the formulaic abhorrals, —
  Two words, I think, you'll not find anywhere, —
Struck for hair-splitting dogmas left and right,
And deemed that he was "fighting the good fight."

LIX.

He drew his skirts aside when others passed
    Of different belief from that he held;
He fanned dissension with persistent blast,
    And with a Pharisaic rapture swelled;
He'd gained perfection in belief at last,
    And, from his lofty perch, all else beheld
In darkness lost — salvation's chances slim —
But *he* was safe, and what were they to him?

LX.

Small delectation could he find herein,
    And worry of contention grayed his hair;
He'd searched in every other one for sin,
    And looked within to find it rampant there:
He'd thought through self-perfection bliss to win,
    But saw its fallacy in half-despair,
And then backed out, not finding what he'd fain,
Placing his baggage on some other train.

LXI.

He'd be a Mason: surely he could find
    Within those ancient halls the thing he sought;
It seemed delightful to his ardent mind
    That happiness, like onions, could be bought;
And so he acted as he felt inclined,
    And soon was to the ancient gridiron brought,
Seeking for blissfulness one seldom sees,
As lawyers get to heaven, by degrees.

LXII.

He spread himself on mystic pins and seals,
  And knew more signs than doth the Zodiac;
Was letter-perfect in the springs and wheels
  Of night-trains running the mysterious track;
Took every step the Order's scope reveals,
  Until, from the "ineffable" looking back,
He wept, like what's his name, who lived of yore,
Because he couldn't master something more.

LXIII.

Then Dr. Spooner took to rural shades,
  And dressed himself in most unique attire,
A costume something like the knave of spades',
  As odd as piscator could e'er desire;
And then he followed brooks through grassy glades
  To catch the trouts that epicures admire ;
But ne'er could he by any subtle crook
Induce the fry to bite his baitless hook.

LXIV.

He sought dim nooks by water's babbling streams,
  He breathed the sweet "balm of a thousand flowers,"
He laid him on the emerald sward for dreams,
  He hid himself within the woods' deep bowers,
He revelled in the morning's opening beams,
  He sweltered through the sultry evening hours—
Poisoned by dogwood, bit by bugs and flies,
He fled from happiness 'neath rural skies.

LXV.

And then despairingly he made complaint:
  "Oh! who can tell me where is happiness?
With much endeavor I am worn and faint,
    And each step seems to show the progress less
In striving for that boon which hope did paint,
    Which seems more distant as my steps I press.
Tell me, ye wise ones, in earth's mighty bound,
Where, tell me where, may happiness be found?"

LXVI.

"Here stay your steps, my boy," a veteran spoke;
    "I'm just the chap 'll point you to the spot;
I've sought for happiness through fire and smoke —
    My brierwood pipe — and here is where I've got:
The search for happiness is but a joke,
    For which you needn't go all round the lot;
I'll ease your caput of its great quandary —
For delectation — see the dictionary."

LXVII.

Then laughed aloud that execrable hind,
    While Dr. Spooner turned in strong disgust.
But as he thought of it, he felt inclined
    To think the rough man's ribaldry was just;
For to himself he said, "I nowhere find
    The delectation of my hope and trust
But in the book; and therefore I will wait,
And let things happen — as it pleases fate.

LXVIII.

And then he took things as they came about,
   Nor strove from fate his happiness to wring;
At unpropitious luck he made no rout,
   But was serene as when joy's birds did sing,
And in contentedness of purpose stout,
   He found himself as "happy as a king," —
Feeling true delectation did not rest
On any thing outside the seeker's breast.

Note. — The author read the foregoing to a young and charming critic, who had just completed the ecstatic story of " The Bloody Hand, or the Avenger of Darrville ; " and she immediately suggested that if Dr. Spooner had found some amiable being worthy of his choice, — as in the instance of which she had just read, — he would undoubtedly have found the happiness he sought. It seemed to her that he had thrown away a great deal of valuable time.

ORACULAR PEARLS.

BY MRS. P.

STRIPPINGS.

I.

AFTER the great thunder-storm that shook things up so a neighbor came in with her face clothed in wonder. She sank into a seat, fanning herself; and after recovering her breath, which threatened to leave her, she said, —

"Well, Mrs. Partington, did you ever?"

Mrs. P. looked at her as if wondering whether she ever did or not, but waited further development.

"Don't you think," the visitor continued, "that our neighbor Goggles was struck down by the lightning, and was carried into his house in an incomprehensible condition!"

"Indeed! was he?" said Mrs. P.

"Yes; he was standing in a doorway, when the lightning came down, throwing him to the ground; and he swallowed a pint of the fluid, they think."

"You don't say so!" ejaculated the dame, notwithstanding the neighbor had just said so, and made a sort of mental calculation while tapping her snuff-box reflectively. "A pint!" she said, at length; "well, it must have been stronger than any fluid they have round here, for a pint of no other kind could ever have served him so. It shows what a difference there is betwixt Jersey lightning and the real article, and should be a warning to him as long as he lives."

They talked it over between them, with an accompaniment by Ike on a sheet of zinc, in attempted imitation of the thunder.

II.

"POLITICAL canvass!" said Mrs. Partington, as she read the accounts, in the papers, of party engineering in numbering the clans. "What can they be going to do with it, I wonder?"

"I know," cried Ike, looking up from the floor where he was framing a kite with two of her best curtain sticks.

"What?" she asked.

"They are going to canvass the State with it," he replied.

"That may do very well for hams," said she; "but for the State 'twould be ridiculous. I wonder now if these breaches of political faith that we see advertised in print, are not made out of it; and it must be poor stuff, that gives way so easy. If it is cheaper than satanet, it may do for the straightened Democrats, poor creaturs, who have so little to bless themselves with."

"Political canvass," said the schoolmaster, who had come in and heard, unperceived, the most of her soliloquy, "is simply the count of political noses, in trying to find out how many are going to vote for certain parties."

"Ah! thank you," said she, as she sniffed up a few titillating grains of fragrant rappee; "is that it? Well, people use such strange terms that it is hard to understand, sometimes. But it is just as well, perhaps; at any rate, a mistake is no haystack, as Paul used to say, which is unfortunate with hay at forty dollars a ton."

III.

"If any one understands the anathema of a turkey, they can desecrate it better," said Mrs. Partington, as she stood, carving-knife in hand, endeavoring to make her way through the bones and muscles of a veteran of the gobbler species. The connections would not sever, and in vain the guests waited.

"I think anathema would do some good," responded Dr. Spooner, smilingly; "at any rate, I think I should try it."

"Dear me!" she continued, still persevering in her efforts; "did anybody ever see such a provoking thing? The butcher said it would be a good, serviceable bird, and I declare it is as tough as a blacksmith's apron. I wish everybody had it."

"And yet," said Old Roger, "although it is so tough, there is, I should judge, considerable tendonness about it," winking at the company.

"It may be," replied she, "in further than I have got; but the elementary apparatuses that can digest this must be like that of the oyster of the desert, that they say can eat nails and such things with the greatest felicity."

The afternoon was devoted to riving the turkey, but Ike made it up in the small matters.

IV.

IKE rushed in one day, with his eyes opened to their widest, and threw his cap into a pan of custard pudding that Mrs. Partington had just prepared for baking.

"Do be careful, dear!" said Mrs. P., extricating the cap, and shaking off the accruing matter. "There's your new cap, now, completely satiated with custard!"

"I wish I could be," muttered the boy. Then he broke out with, "Oh, I've seen such a sight! I just saw a woman go by here with more'n fifty pounds of hair on her head!"

"Don't say that," replied Mrs. P., severely; "that is a falsehood, which isn't any better than lying; and though some say such things with impurity, I cannot allow it. I know the chinyons and the waterfowls are large enough, but fifty pounds is impossible. You should not say so, because you remember how Hannah Nyas and Sophia were struck dead for lying; and, though very few have suffered so sence, it isn't because they don't deserve it, mercy knows, but because there's so many of 'em that there wouldn't be any left."

"It isn't a lie, neither," said Ike. "She did have fifty pounds of hair on her head."

Mrs. Partington turned on him the burning disk of her large round spectacles. There was a concentration of rebuke in the look she gave. Her finger was raised like the note of wonder.

"This is original sin, total depravity, and close communion all together," said she with a tone of horror.

"I did see it," he repeated. "'Twas a woman who had been picking hair, and was carrying it home in a bag on her head."

She smiled forgiveness, and the custards were a success.

V.

"What a label it is upon the character of Boston!" said Mrs. Partington, as she read a speech on the liquor bill that reflected on Boston. "There is no place where benevolence is so aperient as here. For my part I don't know where so much is done for the suffering, — and anybody can see it that can read, — for how often we see 'free lunch,' in the windows of our humane institutions! You never see sich things in the country, as much better as they think themselves."

Mrs. Partington paused, looking over the top of the paper at the country member, as though she were resting her gaze there preparatory to making another shot, while Ike sat on the floor, lathering the cat with raw custard.

VI.

"I have never liked Prussia," said Mrs. Partington, "since a peddler swingled me in selling me some blue clay for Prussian blue; and as for the war, I have no doubt that General Benzine will take spots out of 'em, to say nothing of General Troches, who will undoubtedly realize all the expectorations of the French people."

The old lady carried the matter no further, except to deprecate the war that was so destructive to life and patience in trying to make out the reports, while Ike was taking French and Prussian towns, made of the household effects, alternately, upon the floor.

VII.

"Are you in favor of the prohibitive law, or the license law?" asked her opposite neighbor of the relict of P. P., corporal of the "Bloody 'Leventh."

She carefully weighed the question, as though she were selling snuff, and answered, —

"Sometimes I think I am, and then again I think I am not."

Her neighbor was perplexed, and repeated the question, varying it a little.

"Have you seen the 'Mrs. Partington Twilight Soap'?" she asked.

"Yes," was the reply; "everybody has seen that; but why?"

"Because," said the dame, "it has two sides to it, and it is hard to choose between 'em. Now here are my two neighbors, contagious to me on both sides — one goes for probation, t'other for licentiousness; and I think the best thing for me is to keep nuisance."

She meant neutral, of course. The neighbor admired, and smiled, while Ike lay on the floor, with his legs in the air, trying to balance Mrs. Partington's fancy waiter on his toe.

VIII.

"The mortification of the nincom tax," said Mrs. Partington, as she heard Ike read that it was to be modified, her countenance revealing in its expression the depths that lay below, "is just what people are complaining about, and gracious knows it is bad enough without making it more mortifying; for a good many nincoms can't stand it, and so get exemptied, and don't have any thing at all when the tax impostures come round, which is very mortifying, undoubtedly, to them, where they would like to swell the government coiffures, as good loyal citizens. But I declare, though I don't hold any mosity against the ones who tax, — because, like punishment, it is for our good, — it does seem hard to tax a widow's might to raise enough to pay a nincom on three dollars, which is about as much mortification as an assessor can cause, and I should like to tell 'em so."

"But," said Ike, thrusting in his oar, which, like a crow-bar among cog-wheels, caused the machine to come to a sudden stand-still, "this isn't a mortification at all; 'tis a modification — m, o, d, mod."

"No matter, dear, however it may be spelt," said she, pausing a moment to balance her answer, like a javelin, before hurling it, "nor what it may mean; it is the same old imposition, any way, and all are nincoms if they don't complain about it."

She ran down here, like a jolly old clock, while Ike employed himself by filling the sails of an improvised boat in the milk-pan with the bellows.

IX.

CHRISTMAS Ike was made the happy possessor of a fiddle, which he found in the morning near his stocking.

"Has he got a musical bent?" Banfield asked, of whom Mrs. Partington was buying the instrument.

"Bent, indeed!" said she; "no, he's as straight as an error."

He explained by repeating the question regarding his musical inclination.

14

"Yes," she replied; he's dreadfully inclined to music since he had a drum, and I want the fiddle to see if I can't make another Pickaninny or an Old Bull of him. Jewsharps is simple, though I can't see how King David played on one of 'em, and sung his psalms at the same time; but the fiddle is best, because genius can show itself plainer on it without much noise. Some prefers a violeen; but I don't know."

The fiddle was well improved, till the horsehair all pulled out of the bow, and it was then twisted up into a fish-line.

X.

"Your neighbor Kloots has grown quite obese," said the schoolmaster to Mrs. Partington, as they sat by the window.

Mrs. Partington greatly deprecated any ill remark about any one. and she heard the observation in silence, until the schoolmaster continued, —

" Don't you think so ? "

" Why, as to his being a beast," replied she, "I am not willing to say, though some say he is very glutinous in his habits, and sometimes is indicted to steamiousness; but there is nothing harmonious about him that I know of; so I should be loath to call him so. The least we say is soonest mended. and none of us are any better than we ought to be, with corruption without and temptation within, and the Lord knows what. to disturb our equal Abraham, and bring us down all of a sudden, as Mr. Buss cut his leg "—

" I meant fat — obese — fat, madam," said the schoolmaster.

" Well," she replied, "perhaps he is, which you might have said so at first; but that has no weight against his character, that I know of if he came honestly by it, which is none of my business."

The rebuke was well received, and Ike, who had listened attentively, drew with charcoal the picture of a fat man on the white closet door.

XI.

"Our Indian Relations!" said Mrs. Partington, as she read such telegraphic head in her paper; "well, I wonder what they will trump up next! Our Indian relations, indeed! for my part I never shall allow that they are relations of mine, the red-skinned vagabones. I know they are apt to call the president their Great Father, which is a scandal and a shame, I dare say; but that is no reason why we should be called their relations, of which we have enough already that are white, though some are not so respectable that we can brag much about 'em. It is constitutional and proper to take the black man as a brother, and giving him the right of suffering with the rest of us; he isn't so bad in any thing but color, and useful in a window-washing point of view; but these red skins as relations! It makes my blood boil to think of it." She fanned herself vigorously with a long-handled dipper, as Ike took up the paper, which had fallen on the floor. "It don't mean relations," said he "that come to see you and stay till you get tired of 'em. 'Tis only the way things stand betwixt Indians and the government." "Is that all?" she said, smilingly; "well, I wish the papers would be a little more obscure in stating a thing." Ike went out impressed with the importance of knowing a great deal, and lost all his marbles at "in the ring" before he came in.

XII.

It was suggested in the Boston Medical Journal that May-day be observed on the fifteenth instead of the first of the month, on account of the coldness of the latter in our latitude, and the danger to the children, who will parade, weather or no. "Bless their little hearts!" said Mrs. Partington, meaning the children to whom the paragraph referred; "it is a spettacle to see their arms blue as gold fishes, with chaplains of paper roses round their heads, and their noses as red — the little dears — as lobster sallet. I do hope they will differ it, I'm shore, for I always said May had got turned hind part afore. or that there was something wrong about it, I couldn't tell which, and I am glad folks are becoming conscientious of the fact. Putting it in the middle of the month, 'twon't make no difference which end comes first, and it will be such a relief to the poor children who go out to pick violence and roses on the first of May, and get brown critters in their throats and newrology in their limbs. To say nothing of the young people who ride on horseback, like turtle doves, out of town to breakfast, and take cold and die early and often, and " —

"Where's my marbles?" said Ike, pulling out a drawer, and throwing the contents in a chair.

"Don't be so hasty," said she, interrupted in her May-day reflections as a stream may be by an invidious fall of earth, and she hastened to preserve order, and find the alleys, but there were none; and he went to bed to dream of a five-cent investment in twozers next morning. The thread of May-day was broken, and Mrs. Partington subsided into her knitting.

XIII.

"What is the matter?" said Mrs. Partington, as she passed by the corner of Hamilton Place on the morning the tickets were sold to Mr. Dickens's readings; "what is the possession forming for?"

There was a human lining to the whole of Hamilton Place, and she had taken it for a procession.

"Dickens," was the reply.

"The Dickens it is!" she replied, contemplatively; "and right opposite the Park Street Church, too, where the truth is dispensed with every Sunday; and goodness knows there's no use to run after the Dickens, when he is always so ready to come at any one's beck and call. But things have changed, to be sure, and a good coat covers up the original sin of tail, and the cloven foot is not visible in No. 8 boots."

"This isn't the *old* fellow," said a struggler; "this is a horse of quite another color, mem."

"I don't care what sort of a color he is," replied she, "though the original black was respectable; and they do say he keeps it up in some societies where it is necessary to preserve appearance, and touches the young ladies' white shoulders with a hand as soft as velvet; but I don't know. At least he's bad enough in whatever dress he comes, or no dress, for that matter; and Heaven knows we must watch him who goes about seeking whom he may devour somebody."

"He means Charles Dickens," said Dr. Spooner, who was by her side, "the writer who" — He proceeded with a long panegyric, which it is needless to repeat. to which she responded with a long "Oh!" like a distended hoop, as if it were a relief at being extricated from her

14*

dilemma, while the crowd moved on to get their tickets. Ike was making motions to all of the cars to stop, and more than twenty drivers shook their whips at him.

XIV.

"Dear me!" said Mrs. Partington, as she swept three tea-cups from the table in an herculean effort to annihilate a fly that was buzzing round her head. "Dear me! I don't see what they were made for. Sich an annoyance to one, to say nothing of the pieces! and goodness knows if my life isn't tormented out of me by 'em, getting into the molasses jug, and covering every thing with perfect impurity, for we can't help ourselves, and taking sich freedom with us that they go into our mouths and noses, which is not pleasant, though when mixed with huckleberries it doesn't make much difference in cake. It does seem to me a great waste of time and material to make 'em."

"But," said Dr. Spooner, "flies were not made in vain. They are undoubtedly a species of humble scavenger, taking up the offal, as it were, in the atmosphere, that but for them might induce disease."

"That may be so," replied she, calmly. "I don't want to find no fault with Providence; but they are awful troubles, if that's what you mean; and as for the disease, I'll risk it without 'em."

There was determination in her eye, and a wet towel in her hand as she said this, and every observing fly would have made himself scarce at once; but many that night failed to answer at roll call. Ike puzzled Dr. Spooner by asking him if *tempus fugit* didn't mean fly time.

XV.

"Have you got any consecrated lye ?" asked Mrs. Partington of the druggist, during anniversary season. "No," replied he, winking at his chief clerk, "but you can get it anywheres round here all this week." "Indeed!" she continued; "is it so common as that? I thought only the pothecaries had it. But no matter. I dare say it isn't any better than the old kind, for a lye is a lye, any way, whether 'tis consecrated or not; for the purification is what is wanted, and a lye well stuck to will be jest as well, if the clothes is clean; that's what's looked at, and the lye isn't thought of. I dare say you haven't got any desecrated cod-fish, either? You haven't? I thought so, though some ain't so particular. They'll desecrate any thing for money; and what else can you expect when everybody seems to be coveting his neighbor's goods? and Heaven knows where it will end, with beefsteak forty cents a pound, which John Rogers himself couldn't have stood. Why, Isaac!" The remark was caused by Ike, who stood practising hydrostatics by douching the flies on the wall with a new syringe.

XVI.

"How limpid you walk!" said a voice behind us, as we were making a hundred and fifty horse-power effort to reach a table whereon reposed a volume of Bacon. "What is the cause of your lameness?" It was Mrs. Partington's voice that spoke, and Mrs. Partington's eyes that met the glance we returned over our left shoulder. "Gout," said we, briefly, almost surlily. "Dear me," said she; "you are highly flavored! It was only rich people and epicacs in living that had the gout in olden times." "Ah!" we growled, partly in response, and partly with an infernal twinge. "Poor soul!" she continued, with commiseration, like an anodyne, in the tones of her voice; "the best remedy I know for it is an embarkation of Roman wormwood and lobelia for the part infected, though some say a cranberry poultice is best; but I believe the cranberries is for crisipilis, and whether either of 'em is a rostrum for the gout or not, I really don't know. If it was a fraction of the arm, I could jest know what to subscribe." We looked into her eye with a determination to say something severely bitter, because we felt allopathic just then; but the kind and sympathizing look that met our own disarmed severity, and sinking into a seat with our coveted Bacon, we thanked her. It was very evident, all the while that she, or they, staid, that Ike was seeing how near he could come to our lame member, and not touch it. He did touch it sometimes, but those didn't count.

<h2 style="text-align:center">XVII.</h2>

"For pity's sakes, what are you doin'?" said Mrs. Partington, as Ike came in, and threw himself forward on his hands, elevating his heels in the air, and falling against the clean buffet in the corner, his gravelly shoes endangering the ancient china; "what is the meaning of this? Are your brains so decomposed that you have forgot the end you should keep uppermost?"

Ike recovered, and simply said he was trying a little gymnastic exercise.

"I should think it was nasty exercise," said she, wiping the dirt from the buffet with her apron; "but you should be keerful. Only think of conjecture of the brain, and see how many men kill themselves during operation of mind, and let it be a warning to you. Besides, it isn't pretty nor proper. What should you think of my turning heels over head, now, and cutting up antiques like a circuit rider ? "

" Bully ! " shouted Ike, clapping his hands; "jest try it; you can't do it, I bet."

" I sha'n't, you disgraceless boy ! " said she, blushing to the roots of her cap; "and if I see you trying any more of your nasty tricks, my shoe shall teach you which end belongs up."

She looked at him severely, as if she meant it, and the boy went out, appearing as if he were regretting she didn't try the experiment, kicking over the dust barrel on the sidewalk in his effort to jump over it.

XVI.

" It is roominous enough in here," said Mrs. Partington, as she hung her bandbox and umbrella upon the side of the car on the Eastern Railroad, and took her seat. " I declare, I am very lucky to get so good a seat, when the cars are so crowded by execrationists going to the mountains or the sea-shore. It is quite ill-convenient to travel at such times; but with an agreeable company, and a nice car like this, it is very pleasant."

" This is not an ice car, madam," replied the gentleman to whom she addressed her remark.

" Well, I must say that tobacco smoke is not so nice as it might be, and I don't think people behave themselves altogether so well as they might who smoke where there is ladies; but we must take folks as we find 'em."

" Have a cigar, madam ? " said her acquaintance.

" No, thank you," she replied, astonished at his audacity, as she saw him rub a match, and light his weed.

"Go it alone!" said a voice behind her.

"Yes," said she, "I'm alone," thinking herself addressed.

She looked round to see a game of euchre progressing. As Batchelder, the conductor, entered, he saw the black bonnet and the kind eyes, and whispered in her ear, "You are in the smoking-car;" whereupon she went out, and found her sphere in the next car.

XVII.

Mrs. Partington, speaking of the over-activity of Ike in mischief, says it proceeds "from the axis of fidelity in his system." Heaven bless the boy, then, Mrs. P., and if he has excess of "fidelity" in his system, do not try to reduce it; for there are so few who are troubled with fidelity in any form that one so gifted is a *rara avis*. She meant "excess of vitality." Her rhetoric is far ahead of her grammar.

XVIII.

"Arranged for selling liquor!" said Mrs. Partington, the morning after the arraignment in court of the dealers for sentence. "That's the place for doing things right, and I have always noticed that everybody there is arranged for what he does. How many there are arranged for drunkenness, with large swallows, I suppose, every Monday in the court; and goodness knows where they get their liquor, unless they are arranged for that, too, or somebody arranges it for 'em, which is impossible, because nobody has any to sell, I know, for I wanted some gin to put into camphire for a vortex in my head, and the stationary agent wanted my name, and where I was born,

and the color of my grandmother's eyes, and I couldn't
tell him, and so he wouldn't let me have it; and there is
sich doings! I suppose I am arranged to go without, and
I guess I can."

She looked rigidly at the profile of the corporal of the
Bloody 'Leventh that hung upon the wall, and thought of
the sacrifices he had made to secure liberty, — rum in-
cluded, — and she rammed a pinch of snuff home like a
cartridge, while Ike, taking a broomstick, charged upon
the stove-pipe with a spite that brought it down, and restored Mrs. Partington to her consciousness, who pursued
the boy with her shoe as he darted out of the door.

XIX.

"What a large family of daughters he must have!"
said Mrs. Partington, as she read in the papers an account
of a marriage at the residence of the bride's father. "I
never read a paper that I don't see one of his daughters is
married at the old gentleman's house. I'm shore I hope
they may turn out well, for, though it is very desirous that
so many girls should be married off, and become the heads
of families, if Heaven should so order it, though it doesn't
seem to nowadays, yet it is very essensual that they should
be well to do, too, and have something to begin life with.
There is a perfect manammonia among girls to get married; but they marry in haste to repent at leisure, and
Heaven knows what an end may be that begins so badly!
I hope the bride's father may have done his duty by pos-
terity, as well as he has for it, — and Solomon himself
couldn't have done more, — for half that marry nowadays
are no more fit for it than they are for preachers, and, instead of being helpmeets to their husbands, they are more

likely to help part, sometimes before the honeymoon is over. May Heaven bless us all, for we are none of us better than we ought to be, by a great deal."

Ike sat with a long string, and a piece of meat attached, angling for the cat.

XX.

"I've always noticed," said Mrs. Partington on New Year's Day, dropping her voice to the key that people adopt when they are disposed to be philosophical or moral; "I've always noticed that every year added to a man's life is apt to make him older, just as a man who goes a journey finds, as he jogs on, that every mile he goes brings him nearer where he is going, and farther from where he started. I am not so young as I was once, and I don't believe I shall ever be, if I live to the age of Samson, which, Heaven knows as well as I do, I don't want to, for I wouldn't be a centurian or an octagon, and survive my factories, and become idiomatic, by any means. But then there is no knowing how a thing will turn out till it takes place; and we shall come to an end some day, though we may never live to see it."

There was a smart tap on the looking-glass that hung upon the wall, followed instantly by another.

"Gracious!" said she; "what's that? I hope the glass isn't fractioned, for it is a sure sign of calamity, and mercy knows they come along full fast enough without helping 'em by breaking looking-glasses."

There was another tap, and she caught sight of a white bean that fell on the floor; and there, reflected in the glass, was the face of Ike, who was blowing·beans at the mirror through a crack in the door.

XXI.

"As for the Chinese question," said Mrs. Partington, reflectively, holding her spoon at "present," while the vapor of her cup of tea curled about her face, which shone through it like the moon through a mist, "it is a great pity that somebody don't answer it, though who under the canister of heaven can do it, with sich letters as they have on their tea-chists, is more than I can tell. It is really too bad, though, that some lingister doesn't try it, and not have this provoking question asked all the time, as if we were ignoramuses, and did not know Toolong from No Strong, and there never was sich a thing as the seventh commandment, which, Heaven knows, suits this case to a T, and I hope the breakers of it may escape, but I don't see how they can. The question must be answered, unless it is like a cannondrum, to be given up, which nobody of any spirit should do."

She brought the spoon down into the cup, and looked out through the windows of her soul into celestial fields, peopled with pig-tails, that were all in her eye, while Ike took a double charge of sugar for his tea, and gave an extra allowance of milk to the kitten.

XXII.

Tramp, tramp, tramp! Footsteps were heard along the passage-way leading from the gate to Mrs. Partington's back kitchen, ceasing at the word, "Halt! Dress! Shoulder arms! Support arms! Carry arms! Charge bayonets! March!" said a voice, in a rapid succession of orders.

Mrs. Partington opened the door at the word march, as Ike

15

charged through with a wooden gun, made of half a clothes-pole that he had taken for the purpose, and found herself "falling back" before the furious assault, not stopping till her main body lighted under the table, her right wing resting in a saucer of milk put there for the cat, and her left much demoralized by a flank blow from the leg of the table. She scrambled to her feet. Ike withdrew his force towards the door. There was a flush upon her cheek, and anger in her eye, as she brought her forefinger up to "present;" for what elderly lady of propriety and some fat would like to be knocked under a table by a mischievous boy, even to illustrate military science?

"What do you mean by doing this, you bad boy?" said she, as she found her tongue. "Do you think you are a squirmish, that you attack a body in that way? I'll let you know better, sir, when you go to bed. Dear me, how you have decomposed me! I come nigh knocking my brains out."

Seeing that she had not struck her head, it was wonderful how this could be; but it was to be pardoned to the excitement of the moment. Ike stood good-naturedly at "shoulder," and then remarked that he was only going through the manual.

"And what has a *boy* to do with the *man*-ual. I'd like to know?" asked the old lady, severely. "You'd better be a recrunet, and done with it, and go to Pamunky Creek, if you want to cut up sich monkey shines."

"Right about, face! March!" said Ike, wheeling towards the door.

"Stop!" said Mrs. Partington; but Ike kept on. "Stop!" she repeated; but he did not mind. Then her spirit was aroused, and charging after the withdrawing force, she seized him by the arm. "Why don't you stop?" she cried.

"The command wasn't right," said Ike; "it should have been 'halt.'"

"I'll make you halt!" said she, taking off her shoe in anticipation of the sentence of a drum-head court-martial. But, as she raised the shoe, she caught a glimpse of the profile of the Artillery Corporal on the wall in military rigidity, gazing out on nothing, the sword above it that had flashed over the Beanville muster-field in the Bloody 'Leventh, and her eye moistened with a new emotion. Gone was her anger, gone the excitement, and gone was Ike, who ran out the back door, and leaped the picket.

XXIII.

"WHEN one is exasperated with fatigue," said Mrs. Partington, with the ex cathedra touch emphasized by the suspended silver spoon, "there is nothing that has a more accelerating effect than a good strong cup of Oblong tea. Besides, there is nothing harmonious in it that will hurt any one, and none of the innovation that one feels who drinks Japan, and keeps jumping up and down all night, like a possessed critter, with no going to sleep till morning, and worn out next day so that he can't work, and has to take whiskey to steady his nerves, which is an abomination. There's a great difference in tea, and, though some fancies this and some that, I shall always think the Oblong is best."

She here ran down, like a Connecticut wooden clock, the spoon still pendent, the steam from her cup rising in a cloud of fragrant whiteness, through which her spectacles gleamed like stars; and Ike sat with his elbows on the table, and his chin resting on his hands, like a horse-car driver, waiting for her to turn out.

XXIV.

"Are those the Duchess Dangleworm's pears?" said Mrs. Partington, as she stopped at the street corner, and "hefted" one of a number marked "12 cents."

"No, ma'am," was the reply; "them's Easter Beurres."

"Well," replied she, "I hope Esther will find somebody to buy 'em at that price; but I think it is doubtful, they are so very high."

"Yes'm," replied the vender; "they was raised on very high trees."

"Ah, thank you," said she. "I declare, it is good as going to an intelligence orifice to meet with such a one as yourself. You ought not to dispense with your wisdom so liberally, because by and by it may give out."

She turned to go away, but felt that her reticule was heavier than it was, and found that some one had put a large pear in it, a gift, she deemed, from the fruit-vender; but Ike walked by her side demurely, and she could not see under his cap-visor the fun that was there. He could tell how it came there.

XXV.

"Mrs. Partington *et als!*" said Mrs. P., as Ike read an eulogistic notice of herself and retinue thus headed. "Is that so, Isaac?"

"'Tain't nothing else," replied he, thrusting the cat's head through the paper, which served as an elaborated choker.

"Et als!" mused she. "I never ate als in my life that I know of, though there is so many dishes with new names that one might forget 'em all, unless he is an epicac."

She turned every thing in her mind to remember what she had eaten, — her mind an oven full of turnovers, — but it refused to come to her; and she made a memorandum by tying a knot in her handkerchief, to call on the editor, and find out about it. Ike sat upon the leaf of the extension-table, swinging his feet beneath it, trying to make a tune out of the creak.

XXVI.

"A serious riot!" said Mrs. Partington, as her eye rested on such title to a paragraph in a paper. "I wonder if it was any thing like the riot in church, where the two ministers tried to read the lethargy in the same pulpit at the same time, and one of 'em got his surplus torn off by one of the deacons. It is too bad for serious people to do such things; but it shows how liable we are to get led into deficiency."

"The serious part of it," said Dr. Spooner, straightening himself up like a rake-handle, "I suspect, is in the magnitude of the act, rather than in the seriousness of the actors."

"Perhaps so," replied she; "but I have known the most serious people do as bad as others, going about with the cloak of hypocrisy in their mouths, and pretending they were saints. There are very few we can trust, and who we can put confidence into is a question."

Dr. Spooner was silent, and Isaac, who was mending a slate-strap with a fork, cried out, loudly, "Bother!" as the fork went into his finger. This was a diversion, though it was not very diverting to the boy, and the riot was forgotten.

15*

XXVII.

"HAVE you seena?" asked Mrs. Partington of the apothecary.

"Seen whom?" said he, smiling, as he recognized the dame.

"Why, seena, to be sure," emphasizing the word, "Seena!"

"I have not, my dear madam, the least idea of whom you are inquiring; but I have seen no one whose presence has given me greater pleasure than your own."

"Well, certainly," she said, "that's very kind of you; but I want to know if you have *seena?*"

"Madam, I assure you," replied he, despairingly, "that I do not know whom you mean. I have seen hundreds, thousands, multitudes, but have not seen *her*, among them all, that I know of."

"But you have manners?" said she; "and they go together."

"*What*, in Heaven's name?" he almost shrieked, starting the old lady into looking at him anxiously through her "parabolical" spectacles, and drawing Ike away from an attempt to carom three soap-balls on the counter, to the great amusement of the cat.

"Why, seena and manners," replied she, calmly, "for a gentle purgatory."

"Oh, senna and manna!" he repeated *sotto voce*, and procured it for her. She went out as gacefully as a seventy-four, and soon was hull down in the distance.

NEW AND OLD THINGS

FROM MY INKSTAND.

175

LES MISERABLES.

A LONG WAY AFTER VICTOR HUGO.

I.

JEAN VALJEAN.

Jean Valjean
A convict had been —
For nineteen years no freedom had known.
When from Toulon released,
He was feared as a beast,
And hooted and hounded from country to town.
The fourth day, near
To Pontarlier,
The place of his destination,
He was hungered and sore,
But men shut their door,
Nor pitied his desolation.
Even the dogs their kennels refused
To one so vile from bondage loosed,
Till, by men and dogs alike abused,
He grew savage with desperation.

Note. — The writer leaves the pronunciation of certain names to the reader's option ; " he pays his money and he takes his choice."

He swore to himself a bitter prayer,
As he passed on through Cathedral Square,
And shook his fist at the temple there,
As though he thought the church might care;
But it frowned in the dark with a frigid air,
    Nor heeded his demonstration.
        With failing strength
        He fell, at length,
    By a very strange fatality,
        At a printer's door,
        The whole world o'er
        The biding-place, on every shore,
    Of wisdom and morality.

Not a single crumb had he to eat —
He couldn't buy of bread or meat,
For the shops were shut along the street,
    And he fain would sleep,
    In its silence deep,
Forgetting his stinted rations;
        When a woman, — 'tis always thus I think,
        That, just as we're going to take a wink,
        And our eyelids peacefully 'gin to sink,
        The woman makes our tempers kink
With sharp interrogations, —
        A woman saw his sorry plight,
        Asleep in the street on a stone by night,
        A singular couch for one not tight;
        So she spoke to him as a Christian might,
And then he surlily told her
        That he was a soldier in distress —
        A claim that always its way must press;
        We every day its power confess,
        And do our best to aid and bless,
And never turn cold shoulder.

She heard and pitied the worthless scamp.
He swore he hadn't a postage stamp,
Had sought each door on a bootless tramp.
She said he mustn't lie in the damp,
    A victim of Fortune's malice,
But gave him twopence, and bade him go
To a house a block along or so,
    Next door to the Bishop's palace.

Now the Bishop was of men the best,
In whom the country round was blest;
A model man, whose every thought
With good of his fellow-men was fraught.
His soul reflected the beaming love
That streams direct from the throne above;
His constant wish to do for others,
And held the good and bad as brothers;
He acted without regard of self —
Gave up all thought of rank or pelf,
    And did his Master's duty;
The poor and needy ones he fed,
The languid and the erring led,
The strong upon their way were sped,
The hearts were soothed that joy had fled,
And his tears upon the sorrowing shed
    Sprang up in shapes of beauty.

With the insolent airs of a surly boar,
The loafer opened the Bishop's door;
I dare say left his mud on the floor,
To the great disgust of Madame Magloire,
Leaned on his stick the priest before,
    And told him all his story:
Jean Valjean was the name he gave,

For nineteen years a galley slave;
The while he'd managed a trifle to save,
Was able to pay for what he might crave,
 Wherein he seemed to glory.
The Bishop turned to Madame Magloire,
Who had placed for three at table before,
And bade her provide for one guest more;
 At which Jean was astonished.
He read to them his yellow pass,
A record of fearful crime, alas!
Of all he had done the world to harass —
A hopeless case for prayer or mass;
He asked for bread and a bed of grass,
Nor longer hoped with men to class;
 But vain was the Bishop admonished.
Without opening to Jean his head
He bade Magloire put sheets on the bed
In the alcove — then to the convict said,
 Sit down, *sir*, by the fire.
The man, surprised and wild to hear
A word of human love and cheer,
Felt, as might be supposed, quite queer,
And odd enough in his way did appear,
 But complied with the Bishop's desire.

 The table was set,
 And round it all met,
Jean Valjean on the Bishop's right.
The silver forks and spoons of state
Were put in honor beside each plate,
 When the Bishop complained of the light.
"The silver candlesticks!" he cried.
'Twas a matter with him of a little pride
To have them lit with a guest by his side;

And Madame Magloire,
    As she'd done before,
Obeyed him she'd never in thought denied.

'Twas a goodly feast you may be bound;
Magloire a bottle of wine had found,
And care in a little while was drowned,
    And the convict was in a bother.
Again he told the Bishop his name;
But the Bishop said it was all the same,
He felt his sorrow and his shame,
He knew his title ere he came,
    And that he told him was "BROTHER."

Then Jean Valjean went to bed;
But wicked thoughts spun through his head,
The good, and pure, and holy instead.
At midnight he arose from sleep,
And round the house like a cat did creep,
Doing such perfidious works —
Stealing the spoons and stealing the forks,
Then leaped the window and garden gate,
And left the Bishop minus his plate!
A wicked wretch, but such must be
From taking felons and like to tea!
        So thought Madame Magloire
        And many more,
But the Bishop smiled more glad than before.
They had taken his forks, but he said 'twas as good
To use spoons and forks that were made of wood.

Jean Valjean was speedily caught,
And into the Bishop's presence brought
By three gensdarmes — they had him, they thought;
    16

But the Bishop pretended he'd given the plate,
And told him he needn't have leaped the gate,
And wondered by what strange absence of mind
He'd left his candlesticks behind.
    Jean Valjean here opened his eyes
    In a wild and undisguised surprise.

Then the Bishop spoke. "My brother," said he,
"You're no more for evil, but good, you see.
I've bought your soul of you, and withdraw
It from the imp of perdition's claw,
To lift it from the ills of the sod,
And give it to the keeping of God."

A strange, strange trade,
As ever was made;
But, reader, if you'd find the key
To open up this mystery,
    I'd say, *do* go
To Lee and Shepard's, or where you please,
And hire or borrow, and read at your ease,
    The book by Victor Hugo.

II.

FANTINE.

Ne'er did monarch array his queen
Richer than Hugo did Fantine,
    With pearls of gold
    More manifold
Than she of Egypt wore of old—

More regal than those of the " Queen of the South,"
The gold on her head, the pearls in her mouth.
    Oh ! she was fair as nymph or fay,
    And she was sweet as flowers in May,
    And she was as lithe as a breeze at play,
    And she was as mild as a summer day.
      She was all alone —
      No parents had known,
A waif on the world for charity thrown;
      A sad, sad doom,
      For beauty and bloom —
Immortal seed on a soil of stone;
The fruit of love's unhallowed chrism,
Denied the right of blest baptism,
    Left to shame and human blame,
That follows the fallen like breath of flame,
      Called Fantine
    By *herself* — Fantine —
Simply because it was her name.
    She knew none else; 'twas at her cast,
    Like a bone to a dog, by a beggar who passed —
    'Twas Fantine only, first and last.

      .   .   .   .   .   .

    And Fantine loved ;
    Her heart was moved
    With a love more ardent than approved;
    But still it was a love as true
    As e'er in human bosom grew,
    Fed by Hymen's sacred dew,
    And blest in sacerdotal view ;
    For love is the same in poor and rich,
    Working them up to the self-same pitch,
And don't distinguish " t'other from which."
She loved, with all her little powers

— Hungry love that the heart devours —
A man of wit and ready tin,
But soiled by the world and touch of sin,
With carious teeth and a wrinkled skin,
And bad digestion — how *could* he win ?
His eyes were watery, too, and dim,
But she saw no blemish at all in him :
  . So true to him
   She flew to him,
    And stuck like Hilton's glue to him !
But he, the churl, I'm sorry to say,
Didn't love her in that same way.
His was a passion — a baleful flame,
That kindles in fervor and ends in shame ;
A blaze that burns with a lurid light,
Then leaves a darkness, as black as night,
Of broken heart and spirit blight ;
   And poor Fantine,
    With anguish keen,
  Felt cold desertion's direst harms :
   Her first love flown —
   Alone — alone —
  Bearing her woe in heart — and *arms.*

   . . . . . .

  In heaven above or earth below
  A purer love none e'er may know,
   Than in the mother's breast doth glow ;
Irrespective of sin or shame,
Glorying still in the mother's name,
Nature asserting its holy claim,
   In fortune's light,
   In poverty's blight,
   In sorrow's night,
It burns forever and burns the same ;

And sweet Fantine
Loved her poor wean
As 'twere a child of loftier fame.

On a dusty day
O'er a public way
Was Fantine and her child astray,
Weary and sad, and most forlorn,
Bound for the town where she was born,
Hoping an honest living to win,
Outside the vortex of deadly sin,
When she arrived at a wayside inn.
'Twas a queer, old nook,
With forbidding look ;
But there before it, in a swing,
Two children, bright as flowers in spring,
Rocked to and fro,
While, soft and low,
The mother a gentle air did sing ;
And Fantine felt
Her motherly heart within her melt,
As she looked upon the beautiful thing.
The mothers, with a motherly pride,
Put their children side by side,
And poor Fantine,
As she viewed the scene,
Thought of her fatherless babe, and cried.
"What will Mrs. Grundy say ?"
She said to herself, in a tearful way ;
For she dreaded the folk of M. sur M.,
And dreaded the lies she must tell to them.
So she gave up all of her little hoard,
And a promise of more than she could afford,
In payment for the baby's board ;

16*

Then with a heart of grief and pain,
And falling tears, like summer rain,
With empty pocket and giddy brain,
She wandered forth on her walk again,
Leaving her babe, without a fear,
With Mr. and Mrs. Thernardier,
By prudent folk considered queer,
    Because Fantine
    Must surely have seen
They didn't respectable appear.

   .   .   .   .   .   .

M. Madeleine
Had made great gain
By a patent he had chanced obtain ;
Godsend to those of M. sur M.,
An El Dorado 'twas to them.
    The little place
Grew up apace,
Under his grave and watchful care,
    And industry grew,
    And virtue, too,
And Fantine found employment there.
    Her toil beguiled
    By thought of her child,
That there in the distance lived and smiled.
But she kept her story within her breast,
And none her weighty secret guessed.
    But gossips were round, —
    They always abound,
Like canker worms, to curse the ground,
As clearly, in a moral way,
As the worms the farmer's hope to-day,
Filling his heart with dire dismay, —
Gossips who saw her proper life,

Who knew not were she maid or wife,
And whispered this and whispered that,
In hours of sly, malicious chat,
Until, alas for poor Fantine!
One came among them — *her child had seen!*
    And then the rout,
    The virtuous shout,
    To think that she had been found out!
Then were the arrows of hatred hurled,
And poor Fantine was thrown on the world.
    Alas for her,
    Sweet sufferer!
No friends to call on, far or near;
And how could she pay Thernardier?
He was pressing her for his pay,
Said the child was pining away,
Driving her crazed with fears each day;
Besides, her landlord wanted his rent,
But she had expended her last red cent;
    Had even sold
    The precious gold
That covered her head to raise the dimes,
    And the bright pearls, too,
    In her mouth that grew,
But not at premium of later times.

Dante mentions the rapid pace,
And the easy trip to a certain place,
When mortals fall from a state of grace;
'Twas certainly thus in Fantine's case.
It makes the heart of the virtuous bleed
The record of her shame to read —
Till she fell in the hands of the hard Javert,
And was brought before his honor the mayor,

Whose face she spat in then and there !
    But no angry glow
    Did his honor show,
    Who told Javert to let her go.
Then she, astounded, heard him tell
That he was one who wished her well;
Hadn't known she had left his mill ;
That 'twas others who had dealt her ill ;
    Then had her conveyed,
    For hospital aid,
Where the Sisters their heavenly mission fill,
Promising bliss in store for her yet
In union sweet with her little Cosette.

  .   .   .   .   .   .

Sad, ah, sad, was the closing scene
Of the little life of poor Fantine.
Crushed, and broken, and poor, and ill,
She saw her measure of sorrow fill ;
Her hope deferred, till her wasted breath
Became as one with the airs of death,
Then sunk to rest, and never met
The fond embrace of her dear Cosette.
Her last shocked gaze, with her closing gasp,
    Showing Jean Valjean,
    Her Madeleine,
Held like a vise in Javert's grasp.

MISSION OF A RARE-DONE STEAK.

" Do you take me for a cannibal ? " said the red-faced man, fiercely, addressing the waiter, who had put a steak before him that from its rareness might have awakened a doubt if it had ever felt the fire.

" No, sir, by no means; no, sir," replied the waiter, obsequiously.

" Then why do you bring me raw beef, sir ? " turning it over with an expression of intense disgust.

" Your order was ' rare done,' sir."

" Rare doesn't mean raw. This is raw. It roars, sir — it roars."

" Very well, sir, we will change it, and have one done better to your liking."

" See to it then, sir, and don't keep me all day waiting ; " and the red-faced man turned to a companion at the same table, with the remark, " Very annoying, sir."

" I suppose so," said the one addressed, who, having given his order, was balancing the bill of fare on his fork ; " but I consider eating-houses the next best thing to a calamity — the gout, for instance — for the trial of patience ; they are providential dispensations, so to speak, and those who will may profit by them."

" Nuisances, sir, half of 'em," said the red-faced man ; " pah ! raw beef."

" I smiled at what you said to the waiter about it," said the believer in the providential character of eating-houses, still balancing the bill of fare on his fork, and varying his performance with whirling the caster round, " because it called to mind something that occurred to some acquaintances of mine several years ago. 'Twas the strangest thing!"

He looked provokingly mysterious, and the red-faced man, with curiosity plainly visible, said, sharply, "What was it?"

"Two brothers, who had been apart and hostile for years, . identifying each other, and becoming reconciled through an under-done beefsteak! Strange, but true, 'pon my life."

He glanced up into the fierce man's face as he concluded, and saw the greatest incredulity depicted there. Indeed, his mouth was just puckering into a whistle ; but catching the earnest look of the informant, he commuted it by rapping on the table.

• "I have heard that it was good for a black eye," said he, at length, "caused, perhaps, by feelings like those named; but hang me if ever I heard any use so strange as that to put it to. How was it?"

"As it takes some time to cook what I have ordered," replied the philosopher, "perhaps I shall be able to tell you. Well, you see, old Farmer Wilbur, of Branch Creek, Vermont, had two sons — only sons — good, likely fellows, but they were always quarrelling. Cats and dogs weren't a priming to them. The old farmer was a widower, and they and their quarrels made him about as uncomfortable as one could well be. At last, when the oldest boy was about sixteen, after a terrible fight with his brother, he ran away; and soon after, the old man, having a chance to sell his farm to a railway company. improved it to good advantage, and moved West, where he became swallowed up, to all intents and purposes, for nobody knew where he had gone; 'out West,' in some unrememberable locality, being all that his old neighbors knew about it. 'Where's Farmer Wilbur?' strangers would sometimes inquire;

'Gone West,' was the reply. 'Whereabouts?' 'Don't
remember.' He was just as good as dead, you see — as
though he had been buried for a century. Nobody had
heard from him for twenty years, nor the runaway son.
But at the end of twenty years back came the runaway
son, with lots of money. He had been in California, and
was rich as a Jew. He tried every way to find out what
had become of his father and brother, but didn't succeed ;
and at last, as the next best thing to it, he bought back the
old homestead, and as much of the land as he could save,
married one of the pretty villagers, and settled down. In
buying back the old house, he restored the paint to its
original color, for Farmer Wilbur's taste had always been
peculiar. The house was red with white trimmings, the
blinds slate color, the doors yellow, and the roof blue — a
very peculiar looking house, and artists travelling in the
vicinity have been known to go five miles out of their way
to avoid seeing it. The returned wanderer, out of respect
to his father, had it painted exactly as he remembered it.
It was his custom to come to Boston once a year to col-
lect his dividends — arriving in the morning and going back
at night. I got quite well acquainted with him, and found
him to be an interesting and good fellow. We usually
took dinner together at his hotel; but on the occasion of
which I am about to tell, he didn't go to a hotel, and we
went into the French restaurant up here for a lunch.
While we were there, there came in a man of good appearance, but evidently a victim of misfortune. There was
care manifested in his coat, his pants looked shiny but
well preserved, his boots were patched, but they had lately
been blacked, his vest was a relic, and his hat of an uncertain period. He was seedy, but genteel — poor, but
respectable. His face was strongly marked by the small-
pox, and it was apparent from the way in which he half

closed his eyes, as he looked almost timidly around, that
his vision was impaired. 'A beefsteak,' said he, in a modest tone, 'middling well done.' The waiter gave him a
supercilious look, passed along his order, and turned to us
as mettle more attractive. Our order was 'steak rare
done.' The stranger took the unoccupied seat at our
table, and we in our conversation took no further notice
of him. By and by he had a plate set before him, and we
were again attracted towards him by the way in which he
regarded it; at the same time we saw that it was as raw as
the most desperate beef-eater could desire. He took an
antique looking eye-glass from his pocket, and scrutinized
his acquisition with much earnestness; then, leaning back,
he sighed deeply, and wiped his eyes on a faded blue cotton handkerchief. There was no anger on his face, but a
spirit of deep reflection was written there, and bitter sadness. After a while a smile played over his features, and
reaching over to us in a confidential way, he said, —

" 'You may be surprised, gentlemen, at my conduct;
but by some strange craze of the mind I am led to associate this raw beef with much of my early history. The
strangest fancy in the world, and I can't account for it.
While looking at that beef through my eye-glass, gentlemen, the first fifteen years of my life passed before me.
I saw wide-reaching meadows, and lowing cattle, and running
brooks, and gentle slopes, and a red house with a
yellow door, slate-colored blinds, and a blue roof, that I
used to call my home.'

" 'What!' cried my friend Wilbur, starting to his feet,
in great surprise; 'did such a picture as that present itself
to you? and was it a true picture? What may your name
be, sir, if I can inquire without being considered impertinent?'

" 'Not impertinent at all, sir, and I have no desire to conceal a name that has never had crime connected with it. My name is Nathan Wilbur—named for my father, a good old man, who owned the house I have described.'

" I saw through it all in a moment, and dreaded lest the old animosity should awake ; but it was buried beneath the years that had passed, and looking in my friend's face, I saw tears in his eyes.

" ' Is the old man yet alive ?' he said to the stranger.

" ' No,' replied he, much surprised ; ' it broke his heart to hear that my brother had become a Mussulman, and had forsworn his religion, my father being a strong Methodist.'

" ' Nathan Wilbur,' said my friend, in a voice of deep emotion, ' I am your brother Matthew.'

" I may as well cut the matter short," said the philosophical man to the red-faced one, " for here are our dinners coming. Matthew took his brother home with him, and they lived in delightful harmony. Strange story, isn't it, and all of an under-done steak ? Where would you be likely to hear another like it, but in an eating-house ? How is your steak cooked, sir ? Well, sir, we rail against 'em, and sometimes it is right we should ; but after all, sir, they're great schools for us, eating-houses are ; you may depend upon that, as trials of patience, encouragers of hope, and strengtheners of faith, — especially this last, — there's nothing like 'em."

The red-faced man ate his steak in silence.

17

A NEW RAPE OF THE LOCK.

PART I.

Sweet Madaline's hair was very fair,
Of ashen-gold hue, by which bards swear,
    Whose glorious curls
    Were the envy of girls,
Of kink divine and profusion rare ;
    And Madaline's power,
    Evinced each hour,
Rested, like Samson's, in her hair.

In such a glory it round her lay !
Crinkled in Style's adroitest way,
Burnt with irons to make it stay,
— With amount of effort best not to say —
Its every curl, in the light astray,
Seeming a streak from the source of day,
    Leading the rapt beholder,
Who saw it about her neck at play,
To deem it some amorous sunbeam's ray,
    Lit on her snow-white shoulder.

Not like the curls we sometimes meet
Out there upon the public street,
    To good taste oft offences,
That glisten and twist admiration to gain,
And excite the susceptible masculine train,
Till they find at last, to their shame and pain,
That _they're_ fraud, and the whole of their object, ·
    plain —
    Getting goods under false pretences.

At every feast, or dance, or fair,
In the burning blaze of the gas-light's glare,
Were seen those locks flash here and there,
Like fireflies in the summer air,
    Enchanting by their glitter;
Sought for by eligible beaux,
Subject for rivalry with those
Who ached to tweak each other's nose
    In the eager race to get her.

And her smile was bright as the curl she wore,
And equal kindness on all she'd pour,
    And each fond swain
    Perplexed his brain
    So far as that organ might obtain,
As he watched the smile her features o'er,
If for him it any promise bore;
    But all his watch was vain.

PART II.

'Twas in the glow of a festal night,
The social fires all burning bright,
The gas turned on to its utmost height,
Bathing the scene in its fullest light;
    Sweet Madaline,
    The pride of the scene,
The cynosure of enraptured sight
    To many a would-be lover,
Sat at the board with her golden hair
In affluent ringlets about her chair,
Catching the whole of the gas-light's glare
That streamed from the jet above her.

Toasted, and flattered, and praised, and pressed,
She caught each word with a fluttering breast;
And many a youthful, manly vest
Swelled at her beauty manifest,
And pulsing hearts, 'neath the glowing test,
The potency of her charms confessed,
With rapturous feeling overblessed
    If her eyes in kindness wandered,
And her golden hair a wealth possessed
That bosoms filled with as keen unrest
As any awaked by the golden west,
    In auriferous dreams long pondered.

Around her chair
Her votaries ther
Hung entranced her joy to share
    In each luxurious minute;
Already had passed the season of cream,
And trifles sweet as a maiden's dream,
And small talk ran like a babbling stream,
    When, a moment's hush,
    A push and a rush,
And then there came a mellifluous scream,
    Like the angry note of a linnet!
No one could tell the reason why,
But 'twas Madaline's cry, and Madaline's eye
That looked around on the standers-by
    With the fiercest temper in it!

PART III.

"On with the dance!" and with agile feet,
The music breathing its cadence sweet,
The dancers flitted with measure meet,

The gay hours moving on pinions fleet,
With saltatory joy replete,
    And Madaline,
    Again serene,
    Moved in the throng the regnant queen,
      The blissful scene enhancing;
There were polks and waltzes, galops and reels,
And those rare movements the dancer feels,
Thrilling all through from head to heels,
      That make the acme of dancing.

Again, "Choose partners!" every set
In just accordancy has met
For the gracefullest, grandest trial yet;
    There are twists and twirls,
    And swirls and whirls,
    And glowing bright are Madaline's curls
On the happy shoulder of George Manett!
(Perhaps that wasn't the very name,
But the truth of the tale is just the same.)
About they go in the mazy dance —
Chassez! Balancez! Back! Advance!
    When, just at the critical turning,
Fair Madaline seemed struck with a trance;
Her feet stood still, and with look askance,
Astonishment in her countenance,
    Her eyes in their sockets burning!

The dancers stopped in sore dismay;
The caller's call none would obey;
And there they stood in the light's full ray,
    Looking with vacant stare,
Till Madaline her finger put on
Her wondering partner's third vest-button,
  17*

Where, gleaming like gold,
On his waistcoat's fold
Was a lock of golden hair!

Like the fierce wild red man of the west,
Swinging a scalp as his valor's test,
So Manett wore on his sturdy breast
A *lock* of hers he loved the best,
And he vowed a vow that none of the rest
Should lift a hand to pick it;
Though how it came there he didn't know,
But Madaline the spot could show,
Where late the golden curl did grow,
That was torn by its roots from its soil of snow,
In the midst of the golden thicket.

And that was the secret of Madaline's scream,
Mingled with noise of spoons in the cream,
And waking the "spoons" from their little dream,
Coupled with glance of her eyes' fierce gleam,
That carried such a start with it;
And Manett clings to his beautiful scalp
As firm as the foot of an amorous Alp,
Determined never to part with it;
And Madaline she
Don't disagree,
Seeing he has his heart with it.

THE VERIFICATION.

I WAS in the old line brig Lively Sally, Captain Knaggs, the molasses lugger betwixt Cienfuegos and Boston, and was on my way home full of the joyful anticipations that a sailor indulges in, whose whole enjoyment is said to be in the fortnight preceding his arrival at any port, which he gives to pleasant anticipations. This is more the case now, perhaps, than then, because in the days of which I write, the sailor had a home and friends, now denied to the poor habitué of cheap boarding-houses in the purlieus of big cities, exposed to the temptations without and the corruptions within that tap his exchequer to the last farthing, leaving him to the tender mercies of a villanous landlord. The illusion is soon exhausted, and the poor fellow is glad to get to sea again, to recuperate during a long voyage, to again anticipate, and again be disappointed, till dissipation closes the drama, and "poor Jack" goes under.

We had a very good crew on the Lively Sally, and there was no prettier fellow ever walked a deck than Bob Small, who was a sailor from a love of the profession, and who had run away from his home in New Hampshire three years before, from which he had not heard a word since, and to which he had resolved to return after the present voyage. He was in my watch, and often, under the lee of the longboat, he would open his heart to me regarding his hopes and fears.

We were one night walking the deck in the moonlight, the sea just moved to a ripple beneath the tropical air, when he caught my arm suddenly, and cried, —

"Look there!"

" Where ? " I asked.

" There," said he, " in the wake of the moon.   Don't you see ? "

There, sure enough, swam an immense shark, just above the water, within a boat's length of us; and we felt that his evil eye rested upon us, as we stood there gazing at him.   I felt a sense of uneasiness as I saw the monster so near us, and was sensible of a violent tremor in Bob, as his hand rested upon my arm.

" Jack," said he, impressively, " that chap is after me.   I can read my fate in every wrinkle of the water as it plays around him, and I know very well that he will be my tomb."

" Nonsense," I said; " what is the use of·indulging in such feeling as that?   It is no unusual thing to see a shark; and what if every sailor should take it into his head that he was to be eaten; do you think he would be ? "

At that the monster gave a great swirl in the water, and the ripples flashed in the moonbeams.

" You see that, Jack," said he; " he knows what we are talking about, and it's a settled thing.   His mind is made up to have a pick at me, and he will do it."

" Why do you believe so ? " I asked.

" Oh ! " said he, " I have been too happy.   These joyful anticipations of seeing home again, and getting the forgiveness of the old folks, if they are alive, and seeing my little sister Myra, have filled me full.   Jack," he continued, turning me round, and looking me squarely in the face, " do you believe that a man who disrespects his father so much as to shut him down cellar and run away, has a right to anticipate happiness?   I served mine so.   See that shark; he seems to be laughing at what I say, the d—— beast, if I may be allowed the expression."

I comforted him by telling him that if he had served the

old man no worse than that, there was ample hope for him, and that I had known a young man who had pitched his father into a dry well, forty feet deep, and stolen all the old gentleman's tobacco that was in his coat pocket where he had laid it. I didn't tell him though, that that same young man had afterwards been eaten by the New Zealanders, which was doubtless a visitation for the offence. I further told him that he had no reason for his gloomy fears, and gently hinted that he was a consummate ass for borrowing trouble; but he mournfully shook his head. The calling of the "larboard watch" interrupted our conversation, and we turned in. I lay awake but a little while, and could hear Bob sigh deeply as he lay in his berth.

The next day the shark was not visible; but night found us again looking over the lee rail, and, as before, right in the wake of the moon, was the huge fish swimming along with his fin out of water, a boat's length from us.

"He's after me," said Bob, in a whisper.

"Nonsense!" I replied; "he's after me as much as you — or Bill Marline here," turning to an old salt of our watch, who had been to sea before either of us was born.

The old man didn't speak for a second or two, but chewed violently while he looked at the monster as he swam by, seemingly twenty feet long.

"Well," said he, at length, "I don't know how 'tis, but I don't like to see them fellows, nor to talk about 'em. They know too much, and it's a pretty sure thing when they are round that somebody's booked. Mabbe 'tis one, mabbe 'tis another; we don't know, but they do. They have a record of it all, and know their man just as well as we know one of our men."

Bob was deathly pale in the moonlight as he heard this. The slowly uttered words of the old sailor sounded to his ears like the burial service, "We commit the body of our dear shipmate to the deep," and I could see a tear in his eye. I then took him on one side and reasoned with him, but it was of no use. He was to die — how, he did not know — the shark was to have something to do with it — and he was to see his New Hampshire home no more. All this while the great sea-monster, with his dorsal fin out of water, swam lazily along in the moonlight.

I think that Bob could not have slept a wink all night. He turned and turned in his berth, and his sighs were piteous. He looked so haggard and worn the next morning, that Mr. Goodenough, the mate, noticed it.

"Ah, Bob," said he, "what's the matter? You look like a sick hen."

Bob simply replied that he did not feel very well, and turned his attention to his duties.

"Time's most up, Jack," said he, in a whisper; "and look there!"

Sure enough, there, scarcely a boat's length from the brig, was seen the ominous fin, the black flag of the buccaneer of the finny tribe; and I was for a moment shocked.

"This can't last another day," said he, seizing the rail; "and you believe it; I see you tremble. You must go up and see the old folks, Jack, and tell 'em how penitent I died, and that my life was not thrown away, though I was a runaway. Give them my chest, and give little Myra the sea-elephant's tooth with the carving upon it, to keep as a memento, and Heaven bless you, Jack."

The poor fellow wept like a child.

The whole crew were now attracted along the vessel's side to see the great fish that was so desirous of our company, and various were the comments made upon it, none of which were of the sombre character of poor Bob's, though they all looked upon it with a feeling of dread.

The cook — a Curaçoa darky of wonderful ivories, and as black as jet — stood looking on with the others, his face shining in the sun, his emotions evidently different from the rest, for his mouth was drawn out into a smile that almost divided his head, what was not mouth seeming but a sort of black ligament behind his ears.

"He wantee brekfus, guess," said Africanus to himself.

His mind at this seemed to arrive at a very decisive though comical conclusion. He darted into his camboose, from which he re-appeared again in a few moments with something rolled up in an old red shirt, that seemed to send out a steam.

"What have you got there?" asked the mate.

"Brekfus for shark, massa," was the reply, with an expansive grin.

He said no more, but threw his bundle far out into the water before the nose of the shark, who, waking from his supineness, darted forward, and immediately swallowed the object. For an instant the monster resumed his pace alongside the brig; but this was succeeded by an evident feeling of uneasiness, and a moment after he leaped his length from the water, falling upon the surface with a crash that sent the spray flying to our fore-yard. Then he swam furiously in a wild circle about the vessel, leaping occasionally from the water, and turned upon his back. Soon his motions ceased, and, rolling over, he lay a silent mass upon the water.

"Golly," said Curaçoa, "he got his brekfus, shu. Hot brick warmee tummak."

"Did you give him a hot brick?" said Mr. Goodenough.

"Yes, massa," said Blacky, with a grin; "and guess he don't 'gree wid 'em."

There was a loud laugh at the cook's experiment, and turning to speak to Bob, I found he had left my side.

"Where's Bob?" I asked.

"Don't know; saw him here a minute ago."

I went round to the other side of the boat. He was not there. We called him, and searched for him, but he was not to be found. Then it seemed sure enough that poor Bob's misgiving had been verified, and I mourned his loss, thinking of my own melancholy mission into New Hampshire to inform his weeping friends of his death. It in fact cast a gloom over all the vessel, and we could never understand how he disappeared so suddenly, supposing, however, that his mind, becoming morbid, had lost its balance, and he had leaped overboard while we were absorbed by the cook's adventure with the shark.

The vessel arrived in about eight days, and, after I had got clear of her, I set about the performance of the duty that had been charged upon me by Bob. I embarked for New Hampshire, having stowed Bob's chest in the baggage-car, and thought, all the way, what I should say to the mourning friends. It was something that I was not accustomed to, and I went on the voyage with much misgiving.

I stopped at the pretty little station of Spruceburg, among the hills, at which a coach was waiting to carry passengers to Rimmer, a town some four miles distant, that was the place of my destination. Upon this coach Bob's chest was hoisted; but, when I attempted to enter, I found it entirely full, and the driver's seat was also occupied by two besides himself. I therefore looked for some other means of conveyance. The depot master proved my friend, and, after a few moments, informed me that a young lady from Rimmer was in town with a wagon, who would return alone in a short time, and that she would be happy to accommodate me with a seat. So I gave directions that the chest should be left at the hotel, as I was informed there was one, in order that Bob's friends might not see it, and waited for my fair companion.

The wagon was pointed out to me, and the young lady soon came along, to whom I introduced myself, and, helping her in, I sat beside her. She insisted upon driving, of which I was very glad, as I was more familiar with a hawser than a horse. She was exceedingly pretty, about seventeen years old, and was in all respects interesting, being one of those bright and sparkling little fairies that are continual surprises to those who are predisposed to believe that all country productions of the kind are awkward and disagreeable; one of which, however, I was not. I found her chatty and pleasant, full of piquant remarks, in which she did not spare me, and I was perfectly delighted with her. The conversation at last turned on Rimmer.

" Do you reside there ? " I asked.

" Yes."

" Then, of course, you are acquainted with all the people there. Do you know a Small family ? "

" There are quite a number of small families," she said ; " in fact, none very large."

" I mean a family by the name of Small."

" Ah, yes, I understand. Well, I do."

" Is the name of one of its members Myra ? "

" Yes ; Myra Small and myself are very intimate. We sing in the same choir."

" She had a brother ? "

" Yes ; Bob Small. He was a wild fellow, and went away to sea years ago."

" Have they mourned him ? "

" No, not much. He locked his father in a cellar when he went away, and this rather set them against him."

" Well, I have sad news for them. I have just returned from a voyage with him, and he was lost at sea."

18

"Sad news, indeed, that will be. But he will never shut the old man down cellar again — will he?"

"No, I should think as much."

"Nor torment poor Myra?"

"No; but he thought of her at the last, poor fellow! and I have a parting gift for her from him."

I inquired about the old folks and about Myra, and the conversation lasted till we arrived at the hotel, where she was to put me down, which I chose rather than go to the home of Bob at once. I waited till the evening before I went on my melancholy errand. It was a fair night in September, the air just beginning to grow a little chilly, and I walked very slowly, almost reluctantly, to an encounter that I very much dreaded. My duty to Bob alone sustained me in the effort.

The homestead was a substantial old farm-house, with a lane leading up to it, and, turning into which, I proceeded on my errand, my heart beating a loud alarum on my ribs. The windows were all ablaze with light, and a strain of music floated to me from the house, auguring a scene of happiness and peace within, that I, fiend-like, was going to interrupt. Should I go on? Yes, duty to Bob impelled me.

I approached and rapped upon the door. All was still in a moment; but nobody came. I rapped again, and fancied I heard in response a titter on the inside. This time, however, there was the sound of turning a key or removing a bolt; the door swung open, and there, in the light of two blazing lamps, held in the hands of my fairy of the wagon, who "sang in the choir with Myra Small," stood my old shipmate Bob, in apparently excellent condition, and with an expression upon his face altogether unlike that which any ghost that I ever heard of wears.

"Bob Small, by all that's rascally!" said I, for a

moment regretting that he was not at the bottom of the sea. ·

"Yes, Jack," said he, after I had entered, "the very same. I hid away in the run on board the brig, ashamed of my wild prognostic when the nigger killed the shark, and I determined that even you should not see me till you saw me here, as I knew you would, because I knew you would comply with my dying request. So Myra has been down to the depot every day for a week to watch for the big chest, and the fellow along with it, thanking her stars to-day at the fortune which gave you her company. She knew you from my description and the chest."

"Well, Bob," I said, "I suppose I ought to rejoice that you are alive, though hang me if I would undergo so much inquietude on any account again. And Miss Myra must accept my apology for not recognizing her by instinct."

Then the old folks came in, and we had a good time all round, the old gentleman informing me of the trick put upon him in shutting him down cellar, which he seemed to relish as he recalled it; and the old lady looked as pleasant as an October evening, while Myra beamed ineffably on all.

Perhaps I ought to finish my story by falling in love with Myra and marrying her; but I found no chance for that, because she had a huge mechanic who was booked for her good graces, though she liked me as the friend of Bob; and I gave her the elephant's tooth, with his dying speech, which, years after, I saw her youngest babe cutting its teeth upon — I mean the tooth, of course, and not the · speech.

Bob is now one of the most successful shipmasters out of New York, and I am — the reader's very humble servant.

BUILDING THE BRIDGE.

A TRUTHFUL STORY OF OLD PEMIGEWASSET.

OUT spake the Plymouth landlord :
  " A bridge we'll straightway throw
Across Pemigewasset's tide
  To where the wild flowers blow."
Then out spake stout Seth Brownleaf,
  Conductor on the road :
" 'Twere worth a deal to all that here
  Mayhap shall find abode ;
And how can one do better
  Than herein show his skill,
For the credit of his genius
  And the power of his will ?

" So down the bridge goes, landlord,
  With all the speed it may ;
I, with two more to help me,
  Will build it in a day.
O'er that bright stream a pathway
  May well be built by three ;
Now who will stand on either hand
  And build the bridge with me ? "

Then out spake Jotham Hornbeam ;
  A rum'un rough was he :
" Lo, I will stand with axe in hand,
  And build the bridge with thee."

And out spake strong Jo Chesman —
  A granite boy was he:
"I will abide with boards supplied,
  And build the bridge with thee."

"Seth Brownleaf," said the landlord,
  "As thou sayest so let it be."
And straightway went on their intent
  Those sturdy builders three;
For such men in such spirit
  Were bound a bridge to throw,
That son and wife, in limb and life,
  Might safely over go.

The three stood calm and silent,
  And looked upon the tide,
Then planted first a joiner's bench
  That lay the stream beside;
And soon the boarders, looking on,
  Felt their hearts thrill to see
The joiner's bench and an old board fence
  A path for the dauntless three.

The axe and hammer sounded,
  As manfully they plied,
And the bridge stretched out behind them
  In its majesty and pride.
"Come back! come back! bold Brownleaf,"
  Cried the boarders with a burst;
"On, Hornbeam! on, Jo Chesman!
  And we will quench your thirst."

On labored Jotham Hornbeam,
  Jo Chesman pushed ahead;
  18*

The hammers rattled merrily,
  The work triumphant sped;
And when they turned their faces
  Towards the thither land,
They saw brave Brownleaf coming back
  With a stone jug in his hand.

Then, with a shout like thunder,
  They laid the last cross-beam,
And their voices echoed merrily
  O'er Pemigewasset's stream;
And a loud shout of triumph
  Rose from the other side,
As finished was the mighty bridge
  Across the rushing tide.

Alone stood brave Seth Brownleaf,
  For the others had gone in,
And the way they bagged those fluids
  Was what men term " a sin."
" He's done it ! " cried Si. Winkley,
  As he took another chaw;
" 'Twill squash ! " said old Lishe Porcina,
  Bringing down his dexter paw.

Round turned his broad face glowing;
  His mates were overcome;
Nor spoke a word did he to them,
  But looked towards his home;
He saw the hotel beaming fair —
  The boarders in a row —
And he spoke to the noble river
  That at his feet did flow : —

"Father Pemigewasset!
  Look at this bridge, I pray.
Its joiner's bench, its boards and nails,
  Take them in charge this day."
So he spoke, and gathered up the tools,
  His handsaw by his side,
And then upon the bridge he'd made
  He crossed the humbled tide.

And now the shore he reaches,
  Now on the bank he stands,
Now round him throng the boarders,
  Who shake his muddy hands;
But when, three weeks thereafter,
  The fresh came down apace,
Away went the bridge like a cobweb chain,
  And left not a single trace.

Yet Hornbeam and Jo Chesman
  Both swear, by main and might,
That they were sober as a judge,
  And only Seth was tight;
And say the bridge would e'er have stood
  Through all the tides and gales,
If the whiskey hadn't somehow got
  Spilt over 'mongst the nails.

NOTE. — The foregoing incident in Roman history will be remembered by some of the older sojourners at the Pemigewasset House, in Plymouth, New Hampshire. Seth's bridge was regarded a fine specimen of engineering, though he was not an engineer; simply a conductor. It is supposed that it was from this incident that Macaulay conceived his idea of the "Keeping of the Bridge" by Horatius and others, which he consequently put in feeble verse.

A MODEL MAN'S EXPERIENCES.

This story being about myself, my friends will readily understand that I am not parading myself as a paragon, a model of human excellence, and my friend Young, the artist, well knows that I am no model for his use; the term model has a significance peculiar to itself, which will be explained in the brief sketch here written. You will generally find model men, like a peach, only bright on one side — the other often being wormy and sour; the specious show outside, perhaps but skin deep, hides the defects, and the thing passes for much more than it is really worth. I know model husbands, who are pointed at as domestic copies for neighborhoods, because they never go ont nights, never mix in society, never have an idea beyond their own limits — a sort of " me and my wife " people, who are not remarkable for any thing except that they are models; but Heaven forbid that their selfish pattern should be followed by living men.

But this is not what I was going to say. When I came to Boston, some ten years since, I was in a severe corner. I had borrowed money enough to bring me here, but the last shilling was on the verge of being expended, and where to look for more I knew not. I had nothing to do, and to beg I was ashamed. Indeed I was a little particular as to what I might have to do, for I had graduated with some honor at the academy in my native town, and had chosen an entire suit of black for my outfit, at twenty-one, — my age when I left home, — implying that some genteel position was the one destined to be filled by me. Perhaps I should become a clergyman, or a lawyer, or a schoolmaster, — there was nothing in the way of a profes-

sion that was too high for my ambition, —and my let-down
on the last shilling and nothing to do was very depress-
ing. A fall in the mercury from ninety degrees to forty
could not be more so.

Like the man when treed by a bear, I felt that something was to be done, and I ran my thought along the
whole gamut of expedients, but couldn't elicit any thing
satisfactory. Some people have a special gift of luck, and
when out of employment run their noses by what seems
chance, but which is, in fact, providence, right into good
situations and good pay. I felt that I was not thus gifted,
but was called to work my way into place by the sweat
of brain and the power of tact. Then I thought it over
again, and resolved upon a plan. I would create a new
business, and use the press, that stupendous lever, to
hoist myself into notice. Full of this idea I took advantage of a slight acquaintance I had made with the editor
of the Herald to insert in his "valuable journal" the following advertisement : —

"A MODEL MAN. — A young man from the country, of good figure, manners, and education, desires to let himself as a model, for
the display of clothing, hats, boots, shirts, collars, or any articles of
dress, in a manner to exhibit all their beauty and excellence; or,
being in good condition, would serve as an exemplification of the
benefit of living at any specified eating-house. Terms moderate.
Apply at this office."

This was a bold stroke, and my friend the editor, as he
marked the advertisement before giving it to the printers,
with a latent idea that he was going to get his pay for it,
said that the conceit was a good one, decidedly original,
and, if it took well, was bound to be popular. The advertisement appeared, and I heard it discussed in various
places where I was not known, and coupled often with
very discouraging remarks, not complimentary at all to the
sagacity of the advertiser. But the next day after it

appeared, I was in the editorial room, when a gentleman came in and asked for the " model man," whom I immediately avowed myself to be, with a front as brassy as though I had been boarding a year in ———'s family, with the benefit of his distinguished example.

"I am that individual, sir," said I; "what can I do for you?" I couldn't have been more cool if I had been behind a counter, and he had come in to purchase a bill of goods.

He took a slip of paper from his vest pocket, read it, looked at me, and said, —

"This is all right, — is it? You're the model?"

"Yes, sir," replied I; "the first I think that ever operated here. In Paris they have long been established, also in London and Liverpool, but they have never before crossed the Atlantic."

" How is the business conducted? " he asked.

"Very simply," I said. "A merchant has clothing for sale. He fits me with a new suit, and sends me out to exhibit it, which I do everywhere, and send him lots of customers, he giving me the clothes and a moderate percentage on the sales. So of boots and hats; and these being essential to the better display of the clothes, I leave the tailor the office of finding customers for me in this line."

" And will they do it? " he inquired.

"Do it? Of course they will," I replied. " Why, I so alarmed a merchant in London, who was a little hard in terms, by threatening to be a model for another house, that he allowed me to hire a horse and buggy, and a boy to drive me round town. 'Pon honor."

" You don't say so! " said he. " Well, my business is wigs; do you ever do any thing in that line? "

" I can't say that I ever did," I replied : " that is regarded as the ornamental branch of the work, and commands higher pay, but I am disposed to attempt it if you wish."

He immediately engaged me at ten dollars per week to circulate as a demonstrator of wigs. It was in July when I commenced my perambulations, and I soon found that I had got my foot in it. There were varieties of wigs that I had to wear — thick wigs and thin wigs, long-tailed wigs and bob-wigs, curled wigs and shorn wigs, black wigs and white wigs — until I almost lost my identity. Passing through the street one day, a familiar voice accosted me with, —

" How are you, Roby ? "

This was the name I had borne in my state of native innocence, and I recognized one of my school companions. I turned towards him to express my delight at meeting with him, when he very confusedly said, —

" Excuse me, sir — mistaken in the person ; " and darting round a near corner he disappeared. I had that day paraded a brilliant red wig, and my natural hair was as black as the raven's wing.

This was but one of many similar accidents that happened. Once I was held as a witness about a street fight ; but when I came into court, my testimony was rejected, because the officer wasn't satisfied, from the color of my hair, that I was the person, which was made a point by the counsel opposed to us, and I escaped, thanks to a judicious change of wig. I continued in the wig business until my employer wanted me to wear female curls, which I objected to as unsexing the profession, and gave it up.

I had, in the mean time, made agreement with a fashionable tailor, and sported every variety of habiliment, — dress coats, frock coats, business coats, bobtail coats, — till, with those who only saw me in exterior, I was regarded as a brazen spendthrift ; and I heard, from one of those friends who love to tell us unpleasant things, that a story had been made up about me, wherein I figured as the

graceless heir to an immense estate, that I was spending
in a manner rivalling the reckless extravagance of the
prodigal son, was a libertine and gambler, had brought my
father's gray hairs in sorrow to the grave, broken my
mother's heart, and had rendered my sisters infamous
by association with my name! It was astonishing how
my acquaintance was sought, after this, by respectable people. I was an object of marked attention with the ladies,
and a formidable rival with rascals not half so lurid as I
was, who looked up to me with emulous ambition. In the
mean time I was a living and moving eulogy of my tailor,
and the firm who employed me increased in business so
rapidly that the original proprietors withdrew from the
concern. and retired to the *otium cum dig.*, as all sensible
people ought to do when they have got money enough. I
broke with them at last, and stood out on my own inde-
pendence, when they wanted me to introduce the kilt as a
summer costume. I remonstrated with them, with tears
in my eyes, but they were unbending, and, throwing my
trews in their faces, I departed. The firm failed, I was
happy to learn, in less than three months.

As a boot tree I was not so fortunate, my foot being
No. 10, and No. 8 the average wear; but by much crowding and taking the boot off round the first corner and
wearing the old ones, I got along pretty well. I was better with hats, and made the fortunes of several in exempli-
fying the beauties of some new patterns, by talking eloquently of allegiance to the crown, and advising people to
go and buy where I did.

My business was well established, and so adroitly managed that I enjoyed it in monopoly for a long time, no one
suspecting me ; but at last vague ideas of it began to prevail, and I was annoyed by all sorts of inquiries and the
queerest propositions. A man, a tobacconist, wished me
to stand at his door, in Indian costume, as a sign;

another, a watchmaker, asked me to dress as Father Time, and stand over his shop with scythe and hour-glass; and an undertaker asked my terms to lie in an open coffin, and dress for interment!

Business ran down after this, as rapidly as it had grown, and I was disgusted and disheartened with the annoyances. I was about giving it up in despair, when an aching tooth drove me to my friend Molar's, the dentist, to have it out. He looked in my mouth, thrust iron prongs into it, inserted a small looking-glass and turned it in all directions, and seemed at last ready to get in himself, when I stopped him to ask why he didn't go ahead.

"You've got a capital mouth for a set of teeth!" said he.

"I know it," said I; "I always keep a set on hand."

"Yes," he said again; "but these are giving out — they won't last a month — half of 'em are decayed now." Here he gave them a push this way and that, till the whole seemed in a painful dance round my mouth, and I yelled with misery.

"I don't see," said he, "why any one will suffer so, when he can have them out so easy, and new ones supplied. Let me take yours out, and I'll put you in a set that will be more beautiful than the real ones ever were. Besides, I will hire you to grin at all public places, to show their superiority."

"Insidious tempter," said I, quite cured; "you are rather worse in your proposition than the undertaker. I cannot think of it. Farewell."

And thus I left him. That same afternoon I received a visit at my lodgings — where I had located my office — from a tall, grave-looking gentleman, with spectacles on, who asked me in a slow, measured voice, if I was the model man. I told him such was my profession.

"Then," said he, "as I am a man of very few words, and

never say a great deal, deeming that talking, while it consumes the time, is really no great benefit to conversation, inasmuch as a short horse is soon curried, and a fool is known by his much babbling, according to holy writ, which it becomes us all to respect — being, therefore, as I said, a man of few words, and desiring to avoid all circumlocution in getting at my object — an object, I may say, that I have given some thought, and seen in it an advantage to another object that has long engrossed attention — being of a few words, allow me to ask you, sir, if you ever dwelt upon wooden legs ? "

He fixed his spectacles on me as he concluded, which burnt into my brain like two red hot interrogation points.

" Never," said I, " never; " not guessing his meaning.

" Then," continued he, " to come to the subject in the shortest possible way, with the least expenditure of breath, inasmuch as we have none of us any to spare where pure air is as scarce as lawyers in heaven — employing a saying derived from an ancient theological writer, though I trust not true — would you like to be a model, now, to show off around town a wooden leg we have achieved, that puts anatomy, physiology, and humbugs of that kind at defiance, sir ? "

I had risen to my feet when I got at his meaning, and when he had concluded, I yelled out " *No !* " in a tone that made the candelabra on the mantel chatter with affright.

" Very well," said he; " your manner, though abrupt and uncourteous, pleases me.   I always study brevity, and like it in others."   Saying this he left me.

I that afternoon went to New York with the little money I had saved, and soon became independent in the leather watchguard business in Nassau Street.   I was never a model man afterwards, though virtue and propriety have been, I may say, my grand characteristics.

WORK OF THE OLD MASTERS.

In the schools kept forty years ago, and perhaps later, the ferule was the emblem of authority, and a picture I once saw, illustrative of the "Work of the Old Masters," — not in Jarves's collection, — represented a boy undergoing flagellation with just such an instrument, in the hands of the conventional, lean, and lank individual designated the Schoolmaster. The picture was interesting to me as feelingly recalling scenes wherein I had taken unwilling part, no more pleasant than this — the contortions of the boy revealing a far from beatific state of mind under the progress of the work. Who of the older boys does not remember the day and dominion of ferules? Every master was supplied with one, either lying ready for use upon his desk or stuck in a socket by its side, in open sight of the scholars, held — as my friend the linguist says in Latin, which he speaks like his mother tongue — "*in te Deum* over them." There was often an exercise of fancy and taste in the form of the ferule, and the character of the master could be gathered from the implement employed to enforce his authority. The same peculiarities were apparent in the use. Some were but botches and bunglers, their simple aim being to get through with the flogging as soon as possible, striking heavily and in earnest: but the performance bore none of the masterly touches of genius. Others refined upon punishment, their motive apparently being to manifest to their subjects the superiority of their mode of "laying on" to that of any one else. I remember the first ferule at which I trembled. It was a formidable "ruler," of lignum-vitæ, broad, thick, and long, and woe to the delinquent unfortunate enough to be flogged with it!   An aching hand for a week secured a week's immunity from mischief; but oh, such hatred as it enkindled, and such bitterness of spirit, and such nursing of revenge, that even the good-nature of boyhood could not lull into forgetfulness!

.   .   .   .

The identical ferule, belonging to Master W——, the last that I suffered under, has become mine. after a lapse of thirty-five years.   The master has long since passed away, remembered kindly by thousands, who. though never spared for faults, were ever encouraged in well-doing by him, who had constantly their good at heart.   The writer hereof yields his tribute to his old master's worth, recalling the benevolence of his smile and the gentle words of admonition and loving counsel that marked their last interview. The ferule, as a relic, released a crowd of old-time memories, and reflections that took the form of rhyme, which he here appends.   They rather apply to the general ferule than the particular; and that its dominion has ceased is a matter for hearty gratulation, though the tyranny that prompted its use still exists in a degree; but that is dying out before the light of to-day's progress.

THE OLD FERULE.

Grim relic of a distant time,
More interesting than sublime!
Thou'rt fitting subject for my rhyme,
    And touch'st me queerly;
Unlike the touch that youthful crime
    Provoked severely.

It was a dark and fearful day
When thou held'st sovereign rule and sway,
And all Humanity might say
    Could not avert
The doom that brought thee into play,
    And wrought us hurt!

Ah, Solomon, that dogma wild,
Of sparing rod and spoiling child,
Has long thy reputation soiled,
    And few defend it;
Our teachers draw it far more mild,
    And strive to mend it.

Oh! bitter were the blows and whacks
That fell on our delinquent backs,
When, varying from moral tracks,
    In youthful error,
Thou mad'st our stubborn nerves relax
    With direst terror.

I know 'twas urged that our own good
Dwelt in the tingle of the wood
That scored us as we trembling stood,
    And couldn't flee it;
But I confess I never could
    Exactly see it.

The smothered wrath at every stroke
Was keenly felt, though never spoke,
And twenty devils rampant broke
    For one subdued,
And all discordances awoke —
    A fiendish brood.
    19*

And impish trick and vengeful spite
Essayed with all their skill and might
To make the balance poise aright;
    And hate, sharp-witted,
Ne'er left occasion, day or night,
    To pass omitted.

I see it now : — the whittled doors,
The window-panes smashed in by scores,
The desecrated classic floors, .
    The benches levelled,
The streaming ink from murky pores,
    The books bedevilled.

Small reverence for Learning's fane,
For master's toil of nerve and brain,
They saw Instruction marred with pain,
    And Alma Mater
Was thought of only by the train
    To deprecate her.

'Tis strange to have thee in my grasp,
My fingers round thy handle clasp;
No sense of pain my feelings rasp,
    As last I knew thee ;
Then thou didst sting me like an asp,
    Foul shame unto thee !

But gentler moods suggest the thought —
That still thine office, anguish-fraught,
For my best good unselfish wrought,
    Had I but known it,
And I, with grateful spirit, ought
    To freely own it.

Perhaps — but I am glad at heart
That thou no more bear'st sovereign part
In helping on Instruction's art
    By terror's rule —
That other modes will prompt the smart
    Than this in school.

Thanks, old reminder of the past,
For this brief vision backward cast;
We measure progress to contrast
    Times far and near,
Rejoiced, on summing up at last,
    We're not arrear.

GRAPE-SKINS.

I saw a man of portly estate
Walking the street with regal gait;
Just the man that the eye well suits,
Proper and nice from hat to boots.
So perfect his coat, so neat his vest,
An exquisite taste was manifest,
And every one who chose to scan
Could only say, " What a tasteful man ! "

Alas for the glory of human pride,
As frail and fickle as the tide !
For the polish of blacking and brush and oil
One little spatter of mud may spoil.

E'en as he walked the pave along,
With head exalted and footstep strong,
He trod on a grape-skin in his way,
And a man disgraced in the dirt he lay!

This moral I drew from what I saw :
There are men in the world without a flaw,
Who are in such robes of sanctity found,
And such rare virtues engirt them round,
That we humble ourselves, as we pass them by,
With reverent and admiring eye,
Saying, while viewing such merits rare,
" Bless us, what good men they are ! "

But alas for the glory of human pride,
As frail and fickle as the tide !
In the world of men they exalt their horn,
As though of a better clay they were born.
But there in their path the grape-skins wait,
— Temptations hidden perhaps till late —
One step of the foot — one curvetting lurch,
And down they come from their eminent perch.

In dress or morals 'tis much the same ;
And happy is he who wins his fame,
If he die at its zenith, nor has to wait
Till he slip and fall through invidious fate.
He may dodge the rock and shy the cloud
That threat his step and bearing proud,
But let him not crow till danger's past —
He may by a grape-skin be overcast.

THE LETTER OF DISMISSAL.

MANY years ago there lived in our town two young persons that every one said were made expressly for each other; and that the parties thought so to, was very evident from the way in which they sought each other's society. It was rare to meet one without the other — at church, or on a ramble in the romantic places about the town, on the old bridge that crossed the brook in the meadow, in the forest path that led down by the ruin of the mill where the man was sawn into slabs by a gang saw, at every rustic party where candy and kisses ruled the hour, — they were always together; and a more loving couple never were seen than they. They obtained the sobriquet of "The Turtle Doves," and as they moved along so very lovingly, the young girls would look after them very wistfully, and wish that Heaven had made them such a dear, nice, pretty, agreeable young man as was Walter Rymes, and the young men had a similar wish about Jennie Laurel, who was called the village belle.

And she was pretty. I remember her very well, and before her entire absorption by Walter Rymes, I had what a maiden aunt of mine denominated, very unpoetically, a "sneaking notion," after her myself; had twice escorted her home from singing school, and once had pressed upon her acceptance a large pippin apple, at which she was quite grateful; but Rymes cut me out at the singing school, the gift of the apple was forgotten, and so was I. But like a philosopher I endured to see the attachment strengthen between them without howling about "Revenge!" or enacting any other melodramatic absurdity. I was assured by my venerable relative mentioned above, that there was as good fish in the sea as ever were caught; and rightly applying the soothing remark, I took to smoking, and merely puffed a little more vigorously at the continual evidence of Rymes's triumph.

That she was beautiful I could prove by a daguerrotype of her upon my memory, — not heart, but memory, — which the changes of time and circumstances have not dimmed. The only difficulty would be to get at it, and my powers of description are somewhat limited. She was a fine buxom lass, with flesh enough upon her bones for one and a half of the common sort of women. Her cheeks were of the most unsentimental cast, — red and glowing, — her hair golden. and lay in curls all about her head, and her eyes were bewitching — of an indefinable color, for it was impossible to look in them long enough to detect any thing but the spirit of mischief that dwelt in them — that looked through their half-closed lids like a sword ready to start from its scabbard. Her complexion was white and transparent, and her shoulder! — The attempt were altogether vain that would do justice to charms like hers.

And Rymes seemed like a happy man. He walked the streets gayly, and whistled at his business, which was that of foreman and cutter to the tailor of the village, and was envied and quizzed, and laughed at to any extent, all of which he bore with cheerfulness, because he was the one that had the best right to laugh — the winner.

And thus matters were, when the ambition that plays such havoc with the young, found entrance at the door of Rymes's heart, and he thought to himself that the position of journeyman tailor in a small town was not a very high one, and he thought very nearly right, resolving, very sensibly, that he would leave the " gay and festive," that the village afforded, and, with the hope of winning fortune and Jennie, go to some big city where he could have room for his gigantic energies, and make money, and get married. Jennie was the sunlight that warmed his ambition into life, her smile fringed his future with joyous successes, her voice called him to duty in the big world. And how true they were both going to be! The everlasting hills might melt away like snow-flakes, but their loves should be more substantial than the everlasting hills, and would not melt away.

Thus they parted.

I heard from those acquainted with the parties, that letters, warm, glowing, and frequent, passed between them; that Rymes was succeeding beyond his expectations, and predictions were rife that a wedding would soon take place. About a year after he left the town, I followed him, and by queer chance, found myself in the same city with him, and beneath the same roof. The lady who kept the boarding-house was a towns-woman of ours, and her hotel was the natural resort of people of our place who visited the city. There always are such resorts in every city, where people from all parts of the world meet and smoke, and talk with friends from the old town or the old country. And such associations keep alive our home sympathies and love for early scenes, all a lifetime, which, but for them, might have died out or grown dim in the damps and fogs of earthly care. Those quiet reminders of home — those domestic oases in the great waste of cities — are of much benefit, and the homesick are drawn towards them instinctively by the attractions of common interest, to find there some motherly old heart to confide in, whose counsels and sympathies come to the disconsolate, like the dew on the flowers, giving them new hope and new strength in the encounter of life. There, too, companionship may be renewed, and old joys be discussed, and old hopes be recalled, verified or not in the great arena of Aftertime. There are those, however, who take no pleasure in such places, and have no attraction there — who are hard-faced and self-sufficient, and ask no sympathy from any. Such may be those we have loved as boys, and we feel pained as we find them passing by us in the street without sign of recognition, evincing their forgetfulness of the scenes in which we were sharers, and all because the old boarding-house down in some dark street has been overlooked, where the lamp of loving memory is kept burning, and where the ties of dear companionship remain intact and unbroken.

"Ah! my boy, how are ye?" said a voice in the serene twilight that pervaded the little parlor of the boarding-house on the afternoon of the day that I had arrived by the eastern stage. I had been seized, upon my arrival, by the landlady. and called to answer a thousand questions about the old place, which had been poured upon me with such volubility that I was rather exhausted, when the voice and its hearty tone came with a sense of relief, and turning round hastily I recognized Walter Rymes. But how unlike the old-time Walter was he! He had undergone a metamorphosis, to be sure. He was dressed in the height of fashion, his hair was profusely curled, and a pair of elaborate whiskers adorned his cheeks.

He shook me warmly by the hand, again and again, asked me when I arrived, and when I was going away, — the invariable sequence, — and inquired after the old place very affectionately. I answered the last question first, and assured him that every thing was all right.

"By the way, Rymes," said I, "I saw Jennie yesterday. She's just as charming as ever — blooming as a rose — sweet as a pink. Ah, you're a lucky fellow!"

I really felt that he was a lucky fellow, and enforced my remark with a touch just above the waistband, near where anatomists and fact locate the heart. He colored a little, looked down, drew a line on the faded three-ply carpet with the toe of his glossy boot, but made no reply. I thought this very strange, but imputed it to modesty, and the tender sentiment that allows none to obtrude upon the sanctity of the feelings, and made no further remark upon the subject.

I found Walter a great favorite, especially among the ladies of the house. He was gay and handsome, — two powerful reasons for his popularity, — and I soon saw that if he were not spoiled, he was in a fair way to be spoiled. There was no party to which he was not invited; he was the chaperon of fair damsels to theatres and concerts, to balls and suppers he was a welcome addition, and every Sunday he slept in a fashionable church in the most approved mode. But Walter was lacking, I soon detected, in the substantial element of sound sense, and his intellectuality was not of the order that characterized a Channing or a Story, for profundity. With him show was every thing, and the tinsel and glitter of life were all of its gold.

I was surprised one Sunday morning by having Walter take me by the button in a very mysterious manner, and then, after looking in every direction to see that there were none observing him, he whisked me into his room, and closed his door. At first I deemed there might be some danger, seeing that he removed the key, and placed it in his pocket, hung his hat upon the handle of the door in order to cover up the key-hole, and took other precautionary steps that seemed scarcely called for under ordinary pacific circumstances; but seeing no more than the usual fire in his eye, I ventured to ask, —

20

"What's the row?"

Putting his mouth close to my ear, he whispered, —

"Can you keep a secret?"

I assured him that I positively thought I could, and would give him evidence of it if he confided in me, binding myself by any penalty he might propose.

"Well, then," he began, pulling his chair in front of mine, and bending forward, "you remember my little affair with Jennie; you spoke of her the day we met. 'Twas a pleasant little affair enough when I was there; but faith, there are so many attractions pulling all ways here, that such rustic emotions must change, you know. To tell the truth, I've got tired of Jennie — tip-top girl, and all that; but, you know, she's rustic as the doose."

"Well," said I, somewhat surprised, "what next?"

"Why, the fact is, my dear boy," continued he, "I want to write her a letter, breaking off the little engagement between us; but I don't know exactly how to go about it. I want to express for her the warmest friendship, but to regard the old love passage between us as nothing more than a mere childish whim. I want to do it so that it may not break her heart, for I don't wish to injure the poor thing."

I could scarcely refrain from laughing in his face, but kept my countenance, and answered him that if he wanted such a letter written he had better write it.

"That's just it; I want to, but don't know how. Now I believe you can do it, and if you will, I shall consider myself very much your debtor. You will — won't you?"

I could not resist such importunity; so I drew up to the little yellow painted table, with which every boarding-house is supplied, and he, placing his chair next to mine, glanced over my shoulder, whilst I wrote as follows: —

"Boston, June 1, 18—.

"Miss Laurel: It is a painful task that I have to perform, involving as it does much that is regretted by myself, and much that I fear will be offensive to you, affecting, as it does, essentially, the pleasant relations that have so long subsisted between us. The feeling of attachment that we encouraged, I have found, upon mature examination, to be but a childish sentimentalism, rather than love, which should be rightly understood, in order that we may assume our true position towards each other. I have therefore thought best to write you this, expressing my warmest admiration for you as a woman — the enjoyment of whose friendship I shall always prize as the brightest page of my life's history, and the continuance of which, *as* friendship, I should prize above rubies. Wishing for you the choicest blessings in life, I remain

"Yours, very unworthily,

"Walter Rymes."

I submitted it to him, and he read it over as well as he could, for my chirography was not of the Duntonian school, pronouncing it a very fine letter, and assuring me that he could scarcely refrain from weeping as he read it. But that was all in his eye. He locked it up carefully in the drawer of the little yellow table, and we went down stairs. I saw by the appearance of things that there was some fun afloat. A broad grin rested upon the faces of all the boarders, and several positive winks gave me to understand that there was a secret resting among them somewhere that was aching to get out.

"So Rymes has told you his secret?" said one, when Walter had gone.

"Yes," said I; "but what do you know about it?"

"As much as *you* do," said he ; "he has told it to every one in the house."

Another one coming up, — a jolly dog. — chucked me under the ribs, and in a mysterious manner begged me not to tell *that secret* to any living being ! I found it was really known to all in the house, but said nothing.

Walter copied my letter, adopting his own orthography in many instances, but preserving the phraseology very generally, and with the same mystery that had attended its conception, I was called to look it over. I saw it addressed, and deemed that now my share in the business was at an end. That night I received a letter from our town, calling upon me to come home for a particular purpose, and as the letter had not been sent. I volunteered to carry it. I accordingly became the bearer of despatches, and all the way during the sixty miles that I rode in the stage. I was imagining how the letter would be received, preparing myself for a fainting fit or two, and reproaches, and tears, and the usual scenes attendant, as per romances, on sundered ties and broken vows.

I called upon Miss Jennie Laurel as soon as I arrived, and was received as an old friend should be. She threw her arms around my neck and kissed me with a warmth that gave my conscience a twinge for my complicity in the guilty letter which still reposed in my pocket.

"And so you are a Boston fellow!" said she, feeling of the quality of my coat as she spoke, and inspecting me from top to toe.

"Yes," said I, "and I board with Walter Rymes. I have a letter for you in some of my pockets."

"Oh !" cried she, clapping her hands, "that's prime ; he is such a fool. and we always have fine fun with his letters. I always show them to the girls."

"Indeed !" said I ; "then you must care a great deal for him."

"Care for him! Why, I never cared for him except as a walking-stick."

" Here is his letter," said I, extending the missive.

She took it and began to read, and I could see her eye sparkle as she proceeded; but what the particular emotion was, — whether of grief or anger, — I could not determine. At last she screamed out with a gushing laugh, as musical as a summer brook.

"'Tis a letter of dismissal. Oh! it is delightful — the only sensible letter he ever wrote me in his life."

I thought her cold-hearted, and I found that my former passion had lost its power over me.

" Well," said she, " you must carry my answer back, and I hardly know what to say, either. I wish I could get you to write a few lines for me."

" With pleasure," said I, laughing at the oddity of writing an answer to my own letter, and taking out my pencil, wrote as follows : —

" RIVER BRINK, June 5.

"Mr. WALTER RYMES.

" Sir: Yours received. Such a step as you have taken was quite necessary on the part of one of us, as I am to be married on Wednesday next. Your friendship would be no more agreeable than your love.

" I am, sir,

"JENNIE LAUREL."

She read over what I had written, blushed a little, smiled a little, and whispered, —

" If you had said Sunday instead of Wednesday, you would have come nearer the truth."

" Indeed!" said I, surprised; and then she told me the story of an immense ship carpenter, who had been courting her as powerfully as only a ship carpenter can court, for six months, and that she had consented to marry him on the next Sunday night, the only difficulty in the way being her connection with Walter, and she feared his heart would break to lose her. His letter came very opportunely, and she was happy to be released from the fear of causing him evil, even at the expense of her pride.

She copied the letter, and I carried it to Walter, and he enjoyed the triumph of the dismissing party. Jennie was married at the time she named, moved down east, and became the mother of a large family of good-natured children. Walter left our house soon after, and I lost sight of him for many years. One day, about three years since, while passing up State Street, I heard my name called by a very ordinary looking fattish man, slightly grizzled, whom I did not at once recognize.

"What," said he, "don't know Rymes? — don't remember the letter of dismissal?"

I shook him by the hand, and inquired regarding his welfare.

"All right," said he; "got married, and made money by it — needn't do a stitch of work again as long as I live."

"Are you happy in your marriage relations?" I asked.

"There," said he, in a whisper, "is just where the shoe pinches; and if it wasn't for the confounded relations by marriage, I should get along very well."

"Mr. Rymes!" screamed a shrill voice; and looking in the direction from whence it came, I saw an obese looking woman, very slatternly and last-yearly in fashion, beckoning my friend towards her with a faded parasol.

"You will please excuse me," said he; "my wife is calling me. We live out of town. Come and see us. She will be delighted to get acquainted with you. You will like her — but — have you a mother-in-law?"

Before I had a chance to reply he was again summoned
by the shrill voice, and shaking my hand violently, he
darted away, barely escaping the wheels of a coal-cart that
was going along.

Poor Rymes! I never saw him again, but I heard soon
after that he was dead; and I could not help suspecting
that that mother-in-law was somehow responsible for his
demise.

MY FRIEND'S SECRET.

I found my friend in his easy chair,
With his heart and his head undisturbed by a care;
The smoke of a Cuba outpoured from his lips,
His face like the moon in a semi-eclipse;
His feet, in slippers, as high as his nose,
And his chair tilted back to a classical pose.

I marvelled much such contentment to see —
The secret whereof I begged he'd give me.
He puffed away with re-animate zest,
As though with an added jollity blest.
" I'll tell you, my friend," said he, in a pause,
" What is the very ' identical ' cause.

" Don't fret ! — Let this be the first rule of your life ; —
Don't fret with your children, don't fret with your wife ;
Let every thing happen as happen it may,
Be cool as a cucumber every day ;
If favorite of fortune or a thing of its spite,
Keep calm, and believe that all is just right.

" If you're blown up abroad or scolded at home,
Just make up your mind to let it all come;
If people revile you or pile on offence,
'Twill not make any odds a century hence.
For all the reviling that malice can fling,
A little philosophy softens the sting.

" Run never in debt, but pay as you go;
A man free from debt feels a heaven below;
He rests in a sunshine undimmed by a dun,
And ranks 'mid the favored as A No. 1.
It needs a great effort the spirit to brace
'Gainst the terror that dwells in a creditor's face.

" And this one resolve you should cherish like gold,
— It has ever my life and endeavor controlled, —
If fortune assail, and worst comes to worst,
And business proves bad, its bubbles all burst,
Be resolved, if disaster your plans circumvent,
That you will, if you fail, owe no man a cent."

There was Bunsby's deep wisdom revealed in his tone,
Though its depth was hard to fathom I own;
" For how can I fail," I said to myself,
" If to pay all my debts I have enough pelf?"
Then I scratched my sinciput, battling for light,
But gave up the effort, supposing 'twas right;
And herein give out, as my earnest intent,
Whenever I fail to owe no man a cent.

THE WIFE CURER.

"Been up in the country?" I queried, as I met my friend Burner in the street a few days since. I hadn't seen him for some time, and he looked browned and very rough, as if he had been exposed to the country sun. He informed me that he had, and that he had been to visit Tim Somers, a mutual friend of ours, who had moved away from town many years before. After inquiries concerning his visit, and his enjoyment during the warm months, conversation reverted to our old friend.

"I never was more surprised in my life," said Burner, "than I was to see him in the depot at Ramshead. I had quite forgotten that he was located there."

I informed him that I had also forgotten it, though I believed his wife's relatives were living there.

"His wife's — yes, yes," continued Burner; "singular woman that! Did you know her?"

"Yes," I replied; "she is a little, bustling, talkative thing, full of fun and chat, and making her house merry by the music of her voice. Nice little woman!"

Burner looked at me a moment, and burst into a laugh, to my great wonderment. I requested him, in a tone of chagrin, to inform me what the deuse he was laughing at.

"Talkative!" said he, when he could check in his cachinnatory colt; "I found her any thing but that, I tell you. I never knew the lady when she lived in town; but a more taciturn body I never saw than I found her."

"Indeed!" I remarked; "then there must have been a change, truly. Tell me about it."

I met Somers upon my arrival in the depot, and he

was very glad to see me, inquiring after his old friends, and you with the rest. Through all his joy, however, I saw that there was a vein of sadness; and when I alluded to his family, he appeared embarrassed, and disposed to change the subject. I had no object in view in visiting Bamshead, other than the change of scene, and did not intend to remain there more than a day or two; but meeting Somers led me to think that it would not be a bad thing to tarry there a while, seeing that there was a beautiful pond of water in the vicinity, as I had seen from the car as I came along, and a deep wood, denoting game. Somers used to be great on those things, you know. I hinted at our former sporting practices, and mentioned my half resolution to stay; but instead of manifesting any interest in the subject, he sighed deeply, and replied, —

"Burner, I haven't taken a pole in my hand nor put a gun to my shoulder for five long years, and I never shall again."

I looked at him with astonishment, but I knew that he was sincere. I fancied that I saw a tear in his intelligent eye, and my heart drew stronger towards him than ever. I then quite resolved to stay, and ordered the porter of the hotel to carry my baggage — my valise and gun — up to the house, which was close by. My rod-cane I carried in my hand. Taking Somers on my arm, we followed the porter; and a few moments later found us seated in my room, with a little rummer of claret negus between us — an excellent lubricator for a dusty day.

"Well, how are you prospering, Somers?" I inquired, wishing to penetrate, if possible, the mystery that enshrouded him, deeming that it might be some business difficulty in which he was involved.

"Doing capitally," he replied; "haven't lost a dollar since I came here. People have nicknamed me 'Lucky Tom.' How wrongly people judge in measuring men!"

"What do you mean by that?" said I, as I saw the cloud creep over his face, as you have, while standing on the mountains, seen a shadow flitting across the meadow.

"I mean," said he, "that in measuring us, they take but one feature into the account, and upon that base an hypothesis of happiness, or luck, as the case may be."

"Are you not happy?" I asked, in a tone calculated to win his confidence.

"I am far from it," he replied; "indeed, a more miserable man is not to be found in these parts."

"In what regard?"

"My wife is dumb," he almost sobbed, in answer to my question.

"Dumb?" I repeated; and, thinking to rally him, said, in a jocular manner, "Well, that is a very singular thing to be sad for! I know many husbands who would be too happy to have such a calamity happen to them. Burns says, —

    "'An auld wife's tongue's a feckless matter;'

and there's no contention in a house where a perpetual silence is the bond of unity."

I saw that he was hurt, and hastened to remedy the evil I had done. Taking him by the hand, I said, —

"Tom, I assure you I would not wound your feelings willingly. I am no less your friend than I ever was, and no less worthy your confidence. Now, I wish you to tell me the cause of your trouble, that I may share it with you, or possibly alleviate it."

He hesitated a few moments, and then said, with considerable emotion, —

"Well, Burner, old friendship is stirring within me, and I shall do at its prompting that which I thought nothing could wring from me. You remember how happy I was.

There was not a man in the world who had more friends, true friends, than I had. My home was a happy one — my wife pleasant, my children handsome and intelligent. You never saw my wife, Burner?"

My name in the connection sounded like an imprecation upon his wife, and the Burner a wrathful explosive — "burn her." Somers continued: —

"When we moved up here, things went on in pretty much the same pleasant way, until there came to the village a lady whom I had formerly known, and about whom and myself there had been a little gossip in old days. Our acquaintance was renewed, and I visited her several times ; made no concealment of my intimacy with her, and invited my wife to accompany me, but she declined. She wished to make no new acquaintances, she said. There was a frequent visitor at my house, a relative of my wife's, who poisoned her ears with suspicions that it was not right between May Brennon and myself. She repeated the old gossip, with additions, spoke of my visits to Miss Brennon, and hinted at criminality, as that foul-minded class always will, who, having small virtues of their own, conjure up impure conceits regarding their neighbors, imputing wrong where the strictest purity might not see occasion to blush. I was returning home one summer evening on foot, having spent the day in business at a town a few miles from this, when, by a strange chance, a short distance from town, I met Miss Brennon. It was pure accident that brought us together, and she turned back with me, taking my arm. We walked slowly, as the weather was warm, and stopped a moment on the rustic bridge yonder to look down into the stream, and say a few pleasant words about old times. I saw some one pass by us as we stood there, but was indifferent as to whom it might be, and bidding my companion good by, I went home as happy as a lord, in anticipation of meeting the ones there that I loved so well. I met with a cold reception. My bane was sitting with my wife in council, and I read judgment on the face that had too many times lately turned unkindly towards me.

"So you've come, Mr. Hypocrite, have you?" was the first salutation.

"Certainly, my dear, I have come," I replied, "though I can scarcely see reason for the application of the name to me."

"You cannot! You who have just left that vile creature, on whose account and in whose company you have all day been absent from your home! You cannot!"

"I have been away all day on business," I said, as calm as Socrates. "I was returning home, and encountered Miss Brennon. We walked together a little way, and then I left her for my pleasant home, and certainly did not expect such a reception."

"You did not!" said she, sneeringly; "but you are found out, sir! You stood upon the bridge with your arm around the strumpet's waist, and kissed her!"

I felt aroused at this. I can bear any attack upon myself, but the reflection upon Miss Brennon was too much for me, who knew her pure character and exalted worth.

"It is a falsehood!" I shouted, "and your informant is a malicious and malignant falsifier!"

The relative gathered herself up to go; but before she went, I gave her a lesson on lying and tale-bearing that she has not forgotten yet. She has never crossed my door since. As soon as she was gone, I turned to my wife, and said, —

"As for you, madam, if you cannot make a better use of your tongue, you had better never speak again."

I was heated, in a passion, and scarcely knew what I

said; but the unkind words entered into her soul. I left the house, and did not return for a long time. I found her calmly and undisturbedly sitting where I had left her, but she spoke not. She arose, and performed such duties as were required of her, but she did not speak. Vainly I addressed her: she made no reply. I grew alarmed. I begged her to speak to me, but not one word would she deign me. It has continued thus ever since. Not one word has she uttered to me or any one. My home is dismal as a tomb, or I would have invited you there."

He ceased his story, and I told him how much it had interested me.

"But," said I, "have you tried no remedy to cure this disease? for disease it must be."

He told me that he had not.

"Then," said I, "take me home with you, and if I don't cure her, strike the spurs from my heel as an unworthy knight."

I went home with the poor fellow, and found things pretty much as he had represented. I was introduced to the mistress of the mansion, who received me with a profound bow.

"A delightful home, madam, this of yours?" said I, glancing admiringly out of the window.

I looked towards her, as though expecting a reply. She merely nodded her head.

"Are there many such in this vicinity, among the hills?" I persisted, looking her in the face.

She colored, as though she were confused. I found subsequently that I was the first stranger that he had dared to take home for several years. I saw by her organism that she was not naturally a bad woman, and divined at once that she had vowed perpetual silence at the unkind words of her husband, and that it needed but a single word to break the spell which rested upon her.

I continued my engineering, making all manner of domestic inquiries regarding the children, of whom she appeared very fond, but could not elicit a word from her. I next alluded to her husband and our old acquaintance, and in the course of my remarks made some reflections, in a playful way, upon the slight blemish in one of his eyes — the only fault in his really handsome face. I saw a shadow of chagrin rest upon her brow, and a moment after, when I praised him, a pleased expression effaced the cloud.

"Aha!" said I to myself; "here are pride and affection, at any rate; these springs have not dried up, and I think that language may yet be unsealed."

A day passed, but nothing transpired save manœuvres. I have never tried so hard to make myself attractive as on this occasion, and felt that I had succeeded, when on the second morning she greeted me with a smile, and extended her hand to me as I came from my chamber. I chatted and rattled on about the town and its splendors, told of new improvements, changing fashions, crinoline and lovely bonnets, all of which was listened to with evident interest. Still she wouldn't speak, confound it! I trembled for my spurs. Something must be done.

"Mrs. Somers," said I very suddenly, "will you allow me to look at the palm of your hand?"

She extended her hand very readily, and I gazed upon it as though I were a wizard engaged in some trick of necromancy involving the fate of the household. Looking in her face, I relinquished her hand and sighed deeply. She appeared surprised, and seemed as if expecting me to say something.

"You may well be surpised at my conduct," I said, "but your surprise would be overwhelming could I dare tell you the motive of it. I cannot do this without compromising others. I may say, however, that in your hand

I discern a power that may be employed for immense good. There are lines in it that meet and diverge, and come near together again without meeting. There is a mystery!" I looked at the hand again, rubbed my forehead as though I were much perplexed, and went out abruptly. I saw her face depicted in the glass as I passed out, and it bore the expression of great wonder.

"How far is it to the top of Rattlesnake Hill, Somers?" I asked, at dinner time, as we sat at table.

"About fifteen miles; why?" he replied, and asked.

"Because I am going there to-night. I must be there at precisely midnight. I am going to gather a charm from the old Rattler's cave, through which I hope to obtain a treasure that will compensate for all trouble and danger."

"You cannot go," said he, anxiously; "the way is one of peril. It is full of ravines and pitfalls, and the serpents are very numerous."

I saw that his wife shared in his uneasiness, and her looks said, "Don't go!" plainer than words could speak.

"So much the better for my purpose," said I; "were it not attended with danger, that which I seek would be valueless. I shall go; and more than this, I shall walk."

Somers and his wife exchanged looks, which I interpreted to mean, "Well, isn't he a queer one?" and after a few moments at table I left the house, telling Somers that I should be back by the morning. I accordingly struck out stoutly for Rattlesnake Hill, accompanied by his uttered blessing and his wife's inarticulate benison; but when I reached the first brook, I made my cane into a jointed fishing rod, and indulged till sundown in very fine sport. The trout never bit with more avidity; and having caught a goodly string, I carried them to a farm-house not far away, and had them cooked for my supper. Late in the evening I returned to my friend Somers's, and enjoyed a fine night's rest upon his haymow. At daylight I aroused the family by knocking at the door; but I greeted them with a simple shake of the hand, gazing abstractedly at Mrs. Somers. She looked troubled.

"Somers," said I, "please leave me a moment with your wife. It is a matter that you may some time know, but not at present. Have you not heard of my wonderful development as a seer?"

He said he had not, but, without explaining, I pushed him out and closed the door. I knew that he would listen, however.

"Mrs. Somers," said I, "my mysterious movements are fast growing to a climax. I last night plucked a dragon's tongue from the mouth of the rattlesnake's den; I laughed with the midnight echoes, and stood face to face with the darkness, in order to gain what I sought. Your hand, please; thank you. The lines are brought nearer together, and it needs but one word of yours, in response to an incantation that I shall utter, to make my mystic charm complete. You must say, Yes, or all is as nought."

I looked wildly as I spoke, and I saw that she was, as it were. spell-bound.

"And this is my incantation," I continued; "you swear that you hate Tom Somers."

"No!" she almost shrieked.

Poor Tom had been listening. Fearing harm to his wife from my supposed lunacy, and hearing the question I had put, and the response, he rushed in, frantic with joy, clasped her in his arms, kissed her over and over again, and jumped about the room with the wildness of a madman. She did not seem to comprehend what she had done for an instant, but when she remembered that she had spoken, and divined the meaning of my cabalistic efforts, she came near fainting with her emotion.

21*

"Thank God! the spell is broken!" said she, "the hideous spell that has bound me to silence and sorrow so long."

"The mystical word having been spoken," said I, "that brought the diverging lines together, I am free to tell what I sought at midnight on Rattlesnake Hill."

"What was it?" they both asked in a breath.

"A woman's tongue!" I replied; "and since I have found it, never allow any trifling cause to silence it again."

My theory was correct with regard to her not speaking. She had vowed perpetual silence, and had kept her vow until brought to utter one word, by stratagem, which had unsealed her tongue again. The children were delighted, and ran all around the neighborhood telling everybody that their mother could talk, and everybody rushed in to ascertain what it meant. For a time it seemed as though anarchy and confusion had become installed on Tom Somers's hearthstone, to make up for the silence that had so long brooded there, but he bore it all good-humoredly. I left them a week afterwards, the happiest couple you ever saw, and my midnight excursion to Rattlesnake Hill was frequently alluded to.

"Did you really go there?" Mrs. Somers asked, the morning before I came away.

"No!" said I, imitating her emphatic accent of the same monosyllable in reply to my incantation, and we had a grand laugh about it; Tom Somers swearing that my seership was the best ever known, and my magic had wrought a happier effect than that of all the fairies he had ever seen exhibited at the theatre.

"Good by," said Burner, as he finished his story, and he left me well satisfied with the manner in which he had spent his vacation.

GOUT:

A SUBDUED CASE.

DEAR NANNIE, place my easy chair,
And give my foot the proper square —
Be careful how you touch it! — THERE! —
    That pang, just past,
Might cause an anchorite to swear,
    Nor risk his caste.

And now my pen with acrid sting
And ink of verjuice hither bring,
That I may GOUT's demerits sing
    In limpèd strains;
A theme ignored — a baleful thing —
    It prompts *my* pains.

My muse is no ecstatic sprite,
To lead me, wildered, out of sight,
And breathe ineffable delight
    In bird-like lays;
Than this I try no higher flight
    To win my baize.

But how describe the pain and ache —
The surging, burning, shooting shake;
The wrench, the rend, the twist, the break,
    The anguish deep,
The while dire demons hold a wake
    To murder sleep!

Milton has writ of Purgatory,
And Pollok a more lurid story,
And Dante raised h—eat *con amore*,
    But mine the worse,
Compared with which their highest glory
    'S not worth a curse.

But hold! my pet canary there
Sings from his perch a gentle air,
Regarding me with tender care —
    In fear, 'twould seem,
His looks might fall on me somewhere,
    To make me scream.

Entranced I listen — pen suspent —
To him strange fascination lent,
And his sweet song, the air besprent,
    Thus seems to say —
The while from me his eye intent
    Turns not away : —

"You surely make a great to-do
About this thing that troubles you,
All selfishly forgetting. too,
    The pain you make ;
Be just a bit to reason true,
    For manhood's sake.

"And don't you see, my muddled friend,
Great good from great ill may descend?
And anguish, that the heart doth rend,
    May give a birth,
Of grandest offices the end,
    And priceless worth?

"So this same gout that you revile,
Though painful, doubtless, for a while,
May prove at last the creaming oil
        —The thought is valid—
That makes antagonisms smile
        In life's great salad.

"But for this gout would you have known
The myriad favors to you shown—
The kindly hearts to you have flown,
        Attentions dear,
The atmosphere of love outthrown
        To give you cheer?

"How friends have pressed, with smiling lips,
Freighted with fruits, like orient ships,
To lighten up your joy's eclipse,
        While here you groan;
And, from electric finger-tips,
        Hope's seeds have sown!

"What gives that crutch its magic power
To call more spirits than Glendower?
You'd hammer like a thunder shower,
        I greatly fear,
Did sympathy not ope a door
        Through which to hear.

"A most ungrateful churl, at best,
You will nor reason manifest;
Inside's a demon more a pest
        Than this without;
Disturbance of the spirit's rest
        Is worse than gout.

"Then stop complaint, and be a man;
Be true, and your tormentor scan,
And ask, May it not be a plan
    Your faults to snub?
Perhaps in them it all began,
    And there's the *rub*."

The song here ceased.   I dipped my pen,
But all the spite had left me then,
And simply shouting out, "Amen!"
    I gave it o'er;
Sure ne'er a bird to mortal ken
    Sang so before.

THE VENERABLE SLEDGE.

WHEN the Venerable Sledge joined the Tweedleville
Church there was a sensation.   He had been set down as
one of the hardest headed and hardest hearted among the
inevitably doomed; and though he had done well by the
church, and helped support it, they had long since come to
the conclusion that the Venerable Sledge could not be
pointed to as a living light illustrative of the efficacy of their
labor.   It was told of him that at one time a committee
was appointed to wait on him and expostulate with him
on some practices that would not, they conceived, help him
to any moral elevation.   He met them with a smile, invited
them to take a little something for the stomach's sake, —
which I am happy to say they declined, — listened to all
they had to say, and without replying, asked them if a cer-

tain pew that he named was for sale, sending them back with the assurance that he thought he should buy that pew, which he did.

The Venerable Sledge joined the church, and though those who knew him best did not see any very particular change in him, his new associates were aware of a wonderful transformation. His jokes in which he still occasionally indulged, were no longer the fruit of levity, but of innocent playfulness, and his laugh, which, before his joining, was the outward expression of some unclean spirit, now was the ebullition of a cheerful temper.

There was a picnic in a grove, gotten up for the delectation and benefit of the small fry of the parish, and the old were all invited to give counsel to the young by presence and by word; and they all went, the Venerable Sledge among them. It was delightful to see him trudging towards the depot with his capacious basket, and his coat pockets full to repletion with good things. Even the dogs looked pleased as he went along, and turned and followed him a few steps, as if looking for an invitation, and then ran away, licking their chaps, and undoubtedly regretting that they belonged to some other parish. The picnic was a great affair. The sponge-cake and doughnuts were the lightest that ever were made, but the speeches were very heavy, — at least the children thought so, — and the day passed nominally happy, though in reality all that thought any thing about it, as ever since picnics were invented, said to themselves it was a bore, to be tolerated, however, for the sake of the children.

The Venerable Sledge thought for a long while that he was happy. He promenaded, and swung, and played Copenhagen with a truly delightful temper, but at last his laugh was forced, and his legs were weary; his patience gave out, and a large black ant, crawling up one of his feet handles, broke him down completely. He vowed he never would be caught in a like scrape again. I should like to know one who has not made the same resolution, and I should like to know one who has ever kept it.

In a mood far from placid, with his hands thrust deep down into his pockets, as if he were trying to keep something from jumping out, the Venerable Sledge roamed about like a perturbed spirit, whistling. "Ever be happy"—an injunction in wide contrast with his real feelings. The day had seemed very long to him, but he knew it must come to an end—he had never known one to keep more than twenty-four hours—and the reflection had a touch of joy in it. A voice accosted him.

"Mr. Sledge," said the Seductive Deacon Tung, touching his arm; "we are about taking up a contribution for our Sunday School, and would like to have your name for a five spot."

"Make it ten," said Sledge, in a very demonstrative way.

"Oh, thank you!" replied Tung; "he that giveth, you know, lendeth, and so forth."

"What building is that?" asked the Venerable Sledge, for the first time observing a very long building near, that he had not seen before, with windows all along the sides; "is it a ropewalk?"

"Oh, no!" said the Seductive Deacon, smilingly; "and I am surprised to hear you ask such a question—that is a bowling alley."

"And now I *am* floored," said the Venerable Sledge; "pray tell us what bowling is—is it any thing like this?"—making his hand as near like a wine-glass as he could, and pretending to drink.

"Bless you, no," replied the Seductive Deacon Tung; "it is a very innocent and harmless amusement and exercise, called by many ninepins. There are really ten pins, though originally nine, the tenth being introduced to evade a ridiculous law that proscribed ninepins. Let us see if we cannot get in, and I will show you."

He went to the house near by, and returned with the key, the Venerable Sledge taking a deep interest in the proposed lesson.

"'Tis played with balls — is it?" said he, as he tried to get hold of one of the big balls, which seemed to evade his grasp and slip from his fingers.

"Yes," said the Seductive Deacon Tung, "the pins are set up on the boards yonder. We stand at this end of the alley, and, throwing the balls, knock down as many of the pins as we can, and those who knock down the most win the game."

The Venerable Sledge looked at the Seductive Deacon and the man that owned the alley, who had come in hoping to get a quarter, and then at the board, and then he tried to lift the ball again, making awkward work of it.

"If you think there'd be nothing wrong in it," said the Venerable Sledge to the Seductive Deacon, "I think I should like to roll just once; not if there's any harm in it, you know. I believe I could knock all the pins down at a lick."

They did look tempting, for the man had stood up the pins like a little army, and there they were as if challenging the prowess of the Venerable Sledge and the Seductive Deacon Tung. The deacon said he did not consider there would be the least harm in it, and proposed that they should roll just for sport, the one who knocked down the least to pay twenty-five cents for the use of the alley.

The Venerable Sledge selected a ball, at first spitting on his hand; then he moved first one way and then the other way, stooping down and standing up, closing one eye and opening the other, thrusting out his tongue, and showing all signs of nice calculation. At last he drew a line on the pins; but the ball sheered, and he made a positive failure of it, much to his mortification; the next time he hit the outside pin with such vehemence that he came nigh driving it through the end of the building; the next time he succeeded in bringing down two.

"My eyes!" said he, when he had done; "it looked easy enough."

The Seductive Deacon carefully selected his ball, took his position, gave a short run, and a large portion of the pins went by the board; the other throw was alike successful, and the third as much so, proving the Seductive Deacon the winner.

"You are an old player at it, I guess," said the Venerable Sledge, paying the man the quarter, with evident mortification on his countenance.

"I have played some," replied the Seductive Deacon.

"Well," said the Venerable Sledge, "I believe I can do better next time. Now, if you will roll to see who shall pay the whole that we have subscribed to the Sunday School fund, I am ready to do it. What say?"

The Seductive Deacon smiled, for there was a strong temptation in the proposition. It would be an easy way to liquidate his subscription, and secure the same benefit to the school as though he paid it himself. Besides, it would be a transaction between themselves, and it would teach the Venerable Sledge a lesson. He would see by his loss the truth of the Orphic saying, —

> "Children and fools
> Mustn't play with edge tools."

"I'll do it," said he after a little hesitancy, "though I am afraid you risk a little too much. Shall I roll first?"

" Yes," said the Venerable Sledge ; " and then I can see how you do it."

They took their stand — the Seductive Deacon still smiling in a very self-satisfied manner, justifying himself on the plea that the end sanctifies the means. He made three excellent hits, bringing down nearly all the pins every time. At last it came the turn of the Venerable Sledge. He took up the ball awkwardly, poised it as though it were a hundred pound shell and he were afraid of its exploding ; then his muscles grew very rigid, his lips compressed, his eye was wonderfully clear, and the ball went from his hand like an arrow to its target, sweeping down every pin at the first sweep.

" A ten strike ! " said the Venerable Sledge with wonderful familiarity with the terms of the alley : " Two spares."

He looked at the Seductive Deacon, who stood in blank astonishment, as though he were floored as completely as the pins had been.

" I think," said the Seductive Deacon, faintly, " you must be an old player."

The Venerable Sledge only replied by throwing another ball with the same result, as if to clinch the matter, and then they rejoined the picnic — the Seductive Deacon Tung satisfied that he had made an ass of himself. He paid the subscription, but never thought the Venerable Sledge's moral quality was any better than his own, though he never said much about it.

A HORSE-CAR INCIDENT.

No matter what horse-car, but it happened that I had to go a mile or two, and held up my cane to attract the attention of the driver or the conductor of one of them, which I did after some difficulty. I am bound to say it was not on the Touchandgo road, for the officers employed there have an instinctive knowledge whether a man wishes to ride or not, and indeed often by the magic of the up-raised finger they draw people in to ride who had hardly any previous intention of it. I have been attracted in this way, and found myself to my astonishment, seated in the car, confident that I had signified no disposition to do so. In this instance, however, I would ride, and got in.

There were the usual passengers in the car — the respectable people going out of town, who were reading the last editions of the papers, the women who had been shopping, the servant girls who had been in to visit their friends, feeling no interest in one another, and all absorbed in their own reflections, as I was. I was thinking seriously, when — my eye was attracted by some glittering object on the floor, beneath the opposite seat.

Of course everybody is attracted by glitter. A piece of glass in the moonlight may be a diamond, and show is far ahead of substance in influencing men, from the illusion which affects short-sighted vision. Thus this glittering object. What was it? — a diamond pin dropped by a former passenger? No, it could not be this, because it appeared to be round, and bigger than a pin stone could be. Could it be a bracelet? No, for it was too small. I directed my gaze more earnestly towards it in my doubt, and saw that it was a QUARTER, bright and sparkling with the freshness of new mint about it, so it seemed.

This I determined to make mine at the first chance, for a woman was sitting very near it, and I dreaded any confusion I might cause, by a sudden plunge, through the motion of the cars; so, whistling at a low breath, as if indifferent, but keeping my eye upon the prize, I awaited the opportunity that should insure me the coveted one-and-sixpence. It soon came : the bell rang, and the lady opposite, with her arms full of bundles, walked out, leaving the object of my ardent regard more distinctly in view. It seemed to me that every one in the car had an eye on that quarter, which I felt was mine by right of discovery, and which I was determined to have.

As the coach started I rose and fairly tumbled over into the just-vacated seat, taking care to drop in such a way as to screen the glittering bait. I looked at my fellow-passengers, and found that all were staring at me, as though they were reading my secret. The conductor had come inside the door, and was looking at me, and a heavy gentleman on the same seat with me leaned far out on his cane, so that he could take in my whole person with his glance, as though I were a piece of property on which he had to estimate. I felt my face burn, and a general discomfort seized me, as a man sometimes feels when he has done a wrong or a foolish act; though I couldn't think the act I was about to perform was wrong, and no one could say it was foolish in one to try to get a quarter of a dollar in this day of postal currency. At length I stooped down as if to adjust something about my boot, and slipped the object of my solicitude into my hand, unseen, as I believed.

" What is it ? " asked the conductor.

" What's what ? " said I, with affected smartness.

22*

"What you just found," he persisted.

"I was pulling my pants down over my boot," I prevaricated.

"That's all humbug," said he; "you found something in the car, and it belongs to the company."

"Prove that I found any thing," said I, angrily.

"Young man," said the voice of the big man who was leaning on his cane, still looking at me, "it is as bad to lie about a thing as it is to steal. I saw you pick something up, and to me it had the appearance of money." He struck his cane on the floor as he spoke, and grasped it firmer, as if to clinch his remark.

"Yes," said the conductor; "and we don't want nothing of the kind here, and what's more, we won't have it; so hand over."

"My fine fellow," said I, prepared for a crisis, "I know my rights, and, without admitting that I have found any thing, I contend that if I had, in this public conveyance, which is as public as the street to him who pays for a ride in it, that which I find in it is mine after I have made due endeavor to find out its owner. Money being an article impossible to identify, unless it is marked, if I had found it, it would have been mine — according to Whately, Lycurgus, and Jew Moses."

"Hang your authorities," said he; "I don't know any thing about 'em, but this I know, — that money belongs to the Touchandgo Horse Railroad Company, and I'll have it. Ain't I right, Mr. Diggs?" addressing a gentleman with glasses on, reading the Journal.

"I think you are," replied he, looking at me over the top of his spectacles, as though he were shooting from behind a breastwork; "I think the pint is clear, and that it belongs to the company to advertise it and find out the owner."

"Well," I put in, "suppose they don't find the owner; who has it?"

"The company, I should think," said he, folding his paper preparatory to getting out.

"That's it," said the conductor, taking up the thread as he put the passenger down; "and now I want that money." He looked ugly.

"What money?" I queried.

"The money you picked up on the floor."

I saw that I was in a place of considerable difficulty, involving a row on one side and imputation of villany on the other, and studied how to escape.

"Well," said I, "if, in spite of the authorities I have quoted, you insist upon my giving this up which I hold in my hand, — the value of which I do not know,— I shall protest against your act, and hold the company responsible."

"Responsible be —— blowed," replied he, severely; "shell out."

The people in the car were much excited. The fat man on the seat had risen up, though still in sitting position, and balanced himself upon his toes to get a better view. I unclosed my hand and deposited in the conductor's a round piece of tin that had been punched out by some tin-man and hammered smooth, bearing a close resemblance to money!

The disappointment of every one was intense. The conductor intimated that if he met me in society he would give me my money's worth, the fat man muttered something about my being an "imposture," several lady passengers looked bluely at me, and only one laughed heartily at the whole affair, as I did. It was a queer incident.

THE OLD RED EAR.

Thou 'mind'st me of the festal night
When, though the stars were shut from sight,
The fleet hours winged with footsteps light,
    To pleasure's note,
And mirth and song put care to flight
    To realms remote.

Ah, sweet the picture thou dost bring!
Reseated in that magic ring,
We round the circle deftly swing,
    As then we swung;
While every way the husks we fling
    The crowd among.

And merry joke and repartee
Dart to and fro with noisy glee,
And speech unloosed finds accent free
    From mirthful lips,
As sweet as roses that the bee
    Delighted sips.

Dim is the lantern's dusky glow
Upon the cereal heaps below,
But bright the wit in ceaseless flow,
    And bright the gleam
Of eyes, above the gloom that throw
    A brighter beam.

The old grow young again to mark
The sounds that shatter in the dark,
Where boys and girls in playful lark
    Their bent attain,
And fun, like an electric spark,
    Smacks out amain.

Ah, crimson ear! thou led'st me through
A scene I'd fain again renew,
That e'en to ponder in review,
    By memory's beam,
Enchants me till I sadden to
    Dispel the dream.

What precious rights didst thou impart!
How soon I learned them all by heart!
How did my pulse in tumult start,
    As thou, revealed,
Didst prove a key, whose dexterous art
    Rare sweets unsealed!

Ah, every kernel is a tongue
That speaks me back those scenes among;
Through Time's back door, wide open swung,
    A sight I see,
Of flowers of joy, at random flung,
    No more for me.

But such is doom, and such is best;
And older hearts should seek for rest,
Nor in such fancy stocks invest
    As husking bouts;
They are for youth, 'tis manifest —
    The elders " outs."

EXPERIENCES OF A LAME MAN.

My fall on the ice last winter and the dislocation of my hip were attended by evils of a serious nature, and they have followed me ever since — the great pain that attended the hurt being followed — as my wife who is a joker has it — by the great payin' of the incidental bills that seem to grow stronger every day, though it is now the mosquito and fly season, when the seasonable bills are superadded. I but yesterday received one from Dr. Bolus to this effect, written in a style of calligraphy unsurpassable for its obscurity : —

Mr. Doubledash to Dr. Bolus.	Dr.
To setting one hip	$15.00
" two months' medical attendance	50.00
" medical attendance at office	10.00
Received Payment,	$75.00

The bill was handed in by the doctor's collector, and after some trouble we deciphered it. The setting a hip was at first construed to mean setting a hen, the medical attendance musical attending, and the third charge, appearing to be a frantic attempt at Sanscrit, was too much for us, saving the amount, which was remarkably distinct. The luxury of disease has to be very severely paid for — the immediate need of a doctor shutting out all idea of after payment, and the bill comes in upon our convalescence like an Alpine avalanche of snow upon a summer valley. In war as in sickness the same rule holds. We need armies, and ships, and munitions, and we order them regardless of the bill that will one day come in for them, that is to be paid.

I said at the outset that the evil thus begun has ever since followed me. Though every one of my friends knew very well how I became lame — that with my customary gallantry I turned aside from the icy path to admit of the passage of a crinoline of nearly the diameter of a load of hay, and slipping fell, as Cæsar fell at the base of Pompey's statue — still insinuations were rife, and nods and finger ends made mischief whenever the affair was mentioned, subjecting me to great annoyance. I was beset with importunities to sign the pledge, grave people with white chokers stopped me in the street on very slight acquaintance, and cautioned me as to the tendency of habits whose indulgence was unworthy a Christian gentleman, and a tract entitled the "Drunkard's Doom," was put into my hands as I stood at the door of my own hired house, by a woman with a blue nose and red spectacles, or vice versa, as I was too much angered to remark distinctly which. It was in vain I repelled the insinuations. I was met with a sickly sort of pitying smile, and the remark, "Yes, yes, we know — they all say so," and in their minds insincerity was added to the original offence. It has always been a proud stand for me, and which I have taken in a spirit of moral defiance, that a name not well enough grounded to be proof against malicious attacks was not worth maintaining; but here I have found myself emphatically floored.

And these annoyances have been more than counterbalanced by the sympathy I have excited in the minds of tender-hearted people who have jumped at the conclusion that I am a wounded soldier. Many a sympathetic look have I received, many a sympathetic word, on this supposition, and have felt all the while as a conscientious scoundrel might be supposed to feel who is receiving goods under false pretences. One lady in the horse-cars one day asked me, in a very tender tone, where I received my wound. I felt some delicacy about answering the question, not knowing whether she meant the particular battle where it was received, or the locality of the wound. I came to a consciousness of her meaning in time to say "Hackmetack Court," when she made a note of it in order to consult some map.

I have been consulted repeatedly regarding the construction of ambulances, and the location of hospitals, from my supposed familiarity with them; and with that weakness, if I may call it so, that desires consideration, I have given my opinion with some freedom, involving no confession of how my wound was received, it being taken for granted that it was in gallant service, as it undoubtedly was. I have been an object of unbounded admiration to the boys, who have invested me with all sorts of dignities and indignities, and I have overheard remarks — as boys are not over and above troubled with caution, or regard for the feelings of others — that have made my blood tingle, and my hand grasp my cane with the impulse that I would like to beat the young rascals — "Go it, yer cripple !" being a favorite objurgation from their indecent lips. I was invited, by the authorities of a city I visited on the Fourth, to sit on the platform as one of the Union soldiers. I could scarcely persuade them that I had no claim to such distinction.

But the greatest annoyance that has happened to me in consequence of my limp, was while I was on a visit to Spunkville, remarkable for its patriotic proclivities. It was late in the afternoon when I got off at the station, and I became aware of the presence of a large crowd of people — larger by far than was to be expected in so small a place — and immediately, as I limped along the platform, I was the observed of all observers. Something which I

could not understand was said by some one, when a shout
went up that made the welkin ring. The crowd surged
towards me, shouting in a most boisterous manner, and
then I got it through my head that the shouting and the
crowd were for me. Could it be possible, I thought, that
my humble name had attained the degree of celebrity to
entitle me to any such consideration? It was explained
a moment after by a little gentleman, who bustled before
me and taking a manuscript from his pocket began to read
a welcoming address, styling me " Colonel Frink," and assuring me that my deeds had preceded me, and my name
associated with patriotic daring had endeared me to the
land, therefore the people had come out to receive me and
give me a heart-offering of grateful regard. He beckoned
to the people as he spoke, and they responded by a shout
that eclipsed in volume and unanimity all their other
shouting. Before he had a chance to begin a new paragraph, I begged to assure him that I was not Colonel
Frink, that I never had been in battle, though I greatly
regretted that I had not been, in order to be entitled in
some small degree to the ovation which had greeted me.
A voice in the crowd at this cried out, " Where'd you get
yer game leg, then ? " to my horror and disgust. I saw in
an instant where the mistake lay, and felt that I was in a
hobble. The little man who had addressed me turned
coldly away, and the people who gave me so warm a reception grew instantly cool, regarding me evidently as an
impostor, and, as I thought, meditated some personal violence for the part in deceiving them that I had innocently
taken. I overheard the remark of one sturdy citizen that
I was " an infernal humbug ; " and as I thought I saw in
the eye of the multitude any thing but a kind spirit, I
left as speedily as possible for the hotel. The arrival of
the real colonel by the next train diverted attention from
23

me, and I escaped with merely my alarm. I subjoin the local item from the Spunkville Bayonet, that chronicled my advent in the article describing the "Reception of Colonel Frink:" —

"At this point [the arrival of the train in which I was] when expectation was at its height, a tall, gaunt, weasel-faced individual stepped upon the platform, whose limping gait attracted the notice of the crowd, that cheered boisterously for their supposed guest. The impostor received the attention with all the impudence in the world, and displayed brass enough to supply any demand for that article. Our respected fellow-townsman, Stubbs, laid bare the deception, and the swindler sneaked away with the execration of the crowd. A more flagitious attempt to delude a patriotic people never was practised, and the disgraceful perpetrator may be sure that he is marked for a warm reception the next time he visits Spunkville."

This is very pleasant under the circumstances, and, in addition to my present burden of ill, resulting from my lameness, here is a fine prospective deposit to be drawn upon in anticipation. With which lame and impotent conclusion allow me to close.

————◆◆————

BLESS YOU!

There is a prayer of simple art,
  That from the tongue the readiest slips,
Which springs spontaneous from the heart,
  And breaks in blessing on the lips :
    Bless you !

When joy's bright beam about us rests,
  As some dear hand our cup o'erfills,
In this our gladness manifests,
  And with love's fondest cadence thrills :
    Bless you !

The sympathy with others' woe
  That melts the heart to loving tears,
No sweeter form of speech may know
  Than this the sorrowing spirit hears:
    Bless you!

When weary limb and aching brain
  Attest the weight of busy care,
How lifts the dulling cloud of pain
  To catch the accent of that prayer:
    Bless you!

In love's pure sacrament of bliss,
  When lip meets lip in fond embrace,
Rises with blest approval this
  To give the chrism a holier grace:
    Bless you!

As failing pulse and dimming eye
  Proclaim some loved one's exit near,
How like a whisper from on high
  Comes the faint murmur to our ear:
    Bless you!

But yet no language it may need;
  A glance, as well as words, may pray;
All speech kind action may exceed,
  A smile a deeper sense convey:
    Bless you!

Oh! may our hearts be tuned aright,
  Unselfishly this prayer to feel,
And fill *our* measure of delight
  By supplicating *others'* weal:
    Bless you!

SALT-WATER TROUT.

The following reminds one very much of stories we have read of the Adirondacks : —

"Ben and I rose at early morn, when the dew was on the grass, and snuffed the air with satisfaction, as we pulled on our boots. The river (Piscataqua), sparkling and bright in the early sunlight, flashed by, before us, on its way to the sea, for it was flood tide, and promised excellent sport.

"'Ben,' said I, ''tis a fine morning for fish.'

"'Yes, sir,' replied he, as he looked over towards Eliot, and his eye took in the clear outline of Mount Agamenticus and a woman in a red dress on the opposite bank, 'good fishing to-day; and there's more fish in that river than in any stream of its size in this country.'

"'Take the clams, Ben,' said I, 'and we'll try 'em.'

"I had the flexible rod I had bought of Banfield, charged to my account, that I knew would tie up in a hard knot before it would break, and lots of cunner hooks.

"'Ben,' said I, 'where's the canteen ?'

"'All right, sir,' replied he, slapping his off side, and bringing the article round to view.

"'Nuff sed ; now for it,' as we reached the small wharf that jutted out below the bank. Opposite was Boiling Rock, now quiescent in the high tide, the full stream, like a man after dinner, moving as if reluctantly. There was a ripple of eddy in the water, that swirled away coquettishly, while a kingfisher chattered overhead on the limb of a tree.

"'My gracious !' said Ben, as he seated himself on top of a stone post. 'If I only had a gun, I'd stop that fellow's music.'

"'And wherefore, O Ben?' I remonstrated, while adjusting my line, that kinked terribly, so that I found some difficulty in getting it through the rings. 'Has he not a right to sing?' Indeed, he cannot help it. It is his nature to. Don't let any profane wish interpose here to mar the ecstasy of this glorious morning. D—— the line!' I said, in my vexation; whereat Ben laughed.

"'Don't profane it, sir,' he said; whereat I did not laugh, while the kingfisher flew away with a long shout of ornithological delight.

"All right at last, after half an hour's sweating, and throwing over the hook, baited with the seductive clam, I bobbed and bobbed for a bite. There came a positive nibble, at which I jerked.

"'Let 'im have it, sir,' said Ben, from the post.

"This was needless advice, for the fish, whatever it was, took it itself. I baited again, and threw over, with the same result.

"'If you jerk in that way,' said Ben, 'you'll pull his in'ards out, sir, afore you ketch him. Try him gently, sir.' Ben lighted his pipe as he spoke, and smoked away like a philosopher.

"I was made happy a moment after in landing a three ounce perch on the wharf; and another and another followed, all of the same gigantic mould, whereat Ben laughed heartily.

"'My gracious!' said he; 'you beat Parson Murray, up in the Highdrowndicks, higher'n a kite. He never see fishin' like that, you bet.'

"I fancied Ben was slightly sarcastic.

"'Now,' said I, as I put on a whole clam, 'I'll show you fishing that will astonish you.'

"'I dessay,' said Ben, from the post, blowing out a cloud of smoke.

"Down went the morsel to the bottom, which it no sooner
23*

touched than I had a bite. And such a bite! The rod in my hand bent like a withe, and the line whistled through the water as the struggling fish essayed to escape, now this way, now that way — now up, and then plunging heavily down.

"'Hold on!' cried Ben, from the post; 'you've got him, sure. He must be a halibut!' He was very much excited, but stuck to the top of the post. 'Give him play, sir, and you'll tire him out.'

"I made a feint to pull him, and he again started, coming to rest again speedily in six fathom of water, from which I in vain endeavored to start him, my pole bending double as I tugged to draw him from the bottom; but he held on most tenaciously. At last, after a violent struggle, grown weary with the effort, the sweat streaming down my face, I laid down the rod and pulled the victim in, to Ben's great delight, hand over hand.

"'You've cotched him, sir, as sure as eggs!' said Ben from the post, who had not, I was sure, as I certainly had not, breathed for fifteen minutes, as I drew upon the wharf a splendid river trout, weighing, I should judge, three pounds, that, as I threw him down, flapped a half handful of gravel into my eyes with his tail. He was a noble speckled fellow, with horns on his head, and a mouth four inches wide, with which he had swallowed my hook. Such a pair of expressive eyes I never saw in a trout before; and as he turned them up to mine, there seemed almost a human reproach in them, that melted me.

"'Ben,' said I, 'isn't that a monstrous trout?'

"'That's the king of 'em,' said Ben; 'but they don't call 'em trout down here.'

"'What do they call 'em?' I asked, with much interest.

"He gave a name.

"'Well, a fish is a fish, anyhow, whatever may be said to the contrary; and if any one wishes to know what I caught, let him ask Ben.''

THE POOR BLIND MAN.

A poor blind man besought my aid,
   Feeling his way with a crooked stick,
Stepping as if of the earth afraid,
   And touching the pave with pensive lick.

I held a penny before his eyes;
   He could see no more than a dead man can,
And I felt my pity within me rise,
   For such a very·unfortunate man.

I took his hand and led him o'er
   The crossing where the mud was deep,
And guided his steps where a bit before
   An Irishman had tried to sweep.

He thanked me kindly, with rayless eye,
   And a tearful tone of cadence sweet;
Just then a dog, that was going by,
   Smelt him to know were he good to eat.

I could but mark the blind man's look
   As the canine smelt his brogans thick;
And I marked the capital aim he took
   As he gave that canine a damaging kick.

Then the blind man chuckled in merry mood,
   As the dog yelped out his agony;
But how he knew where the canine stood
   Was more than I, with both eyes, could see.

Just then came along a street horse-car,
   And the blind man hailed it, and off he rolled,
And I felt it on my consciousness jar,
   That I had been infernally sold.

MR. SPOTGAM'S TREAT.

IT was a habit that Mr. Spotgam contracted at Saratoga. He came home full of it, and used to make his brags that he drank, at times, ten tumblers at a single standing! What, in Heaven's name? the reader asks. The answer, Empire Spring Water. It was his weakness, — his weakness literally, — and he left, with the little strength he had, in three days. But his visit to Saratoga was an epoch in his life, and "when I was in Saratoga" became a "chronic affectation" with him, as Mrs. Partington might say. Those who heard him tell the story of the ten tumblers of Empire Spring Water invariably knocked with their knuckles on a table. or other sounding-board that might be near, which implied a measure of unbelief; but he stoutly persisted in the ten-strike. Bless you! why, he was so fond of the water that he has gone to the spring twenty times in a day, till the little boy who drew up the drink learned to know him, and always had two tumblers ready drawn for him when he arrived, and stood ready to draw more should he want it, which of course he did. He never drank less than six tumblers. It was marvellous to him that some didn't like it; but he had actually seen some make up faces at it, and others spit it out. It was mother's milk to him, and if he lived in Saratoga he should have his tea made of it.

Spotgam boarded out. His salary was not large, but he managed very respectably with not very extensive means. He kept cigars in his room, and had wherewithal to regale his friends when they came to see him. He was an oracle at table, and his visit to Saratoga had made him a man to be looked up to. He quite put out the pipe of the ex-colonel, and the foreman of No. 27, who also boarded there, was nowhere. There was a constant rivalry among the seven young lady boarders for his chaperonage, and the one who succeeded in securing him for an evening to the theatre, or other place of amusement, was an object of envy with the rest for a week afterwards.

After the fall cleaning was all done up, Spotgam and the young ladies put their heads together,— they were always putting their heads together in one way or another, — and a party was soon announced, by cards and compliments, to take place on Spotgam's twenty-first birthday, the twelfth of September. The ladies at once were installed a committee of arrangements, with occasional conferences with the giver of the entertainment, who, of course, left it entirely with them. There was subsequently a great deal of stir in the house, and Mrs. Miles, the landlady, who was an excellent cook, was early and late at work preparing for the treat. The invitations were sent out, and the various essentials sent in, and the bill amounted to a formidable figure. But a man's twenty-first birthday doesn't happen more than once in a lifetime, and Spotgam contemned the expense.

He was considerably anxious as the day approached, as he wished the matter to go off well. The Wiggins and Trotts had given treats that had set the neighborhood agog, and proved vital themes of conversation for many moons, and he wished the Miles party to eclipse them all. He set his wits to work to devise something in which to excel them, and procured many delicacies they had not possessed. It was really no common corn-ball affair, but one that the papers would call *recherché*.

Passing along through a street the day before the party, Spotgam saw a label hanging over the neck of a bottle by a window, "Saratoga Water — Empire Spring — for sale here." He immediately said to himself, " I must have some of that, sure;" and, going in, he ordered that a half dozen bottles be sent up. "There," said he, chuckling to himself, "there is a matter in which the Wiggins and Trotts will be outdone. They know nothing of Saratoga; and with a little Hock wine, hey!" He almost capered at the idea; and it was an eclipsing feature for the rivals of Deal Court, so called because it was chiefly devoted to boarding-houses.

When Spotgam came home in the evening, his first business was to see Bridget, the maid of all work, and ascertain if the water had come, as an anxious housekeeper might concerning a pump that had long been dry. She told him that it had, and that she had put it in a safe place in a closet which was not much used, that he well knew, and he went up stairs delighted. He would take them by surprise; and when he sprung his Empire Spring Water upon them, it would strike them, he thought, as the spectator was struck at the engine trial, who received the whole stream of No. 11 with astonishment. How the Wiggins and Trotts would feel when they came to hear of it!

Well, the fussing, and fuming, and inviting, and preparing all ended in the grand climax, — the treat, — and Spotgam, in white kids and great affability, backed by his charming coadjutors, received his guests like a prince; and Deal Court wore a lively aspect on the eventful night of the twelfth of September. The entry-lamp had an additional lustre, and the wax candles upon the parlor candelabras brilliantly reflected back upon each other, like two wits at a party disposed to be personal. Mrs. Miles's red face in the kitchen looked immense with anxiety and heat, for that night was to be an eventful one in the annals of her house, and she felt its importance, to say nothing of a five-dollar bill that the giver of the treat had thrust into her hand, eliciting the remark from her that he was the " generousest creetur." Even Bridget looked luminous in new calico, with flowers as big as your hand, that she had lately received as a present. In short, every thing was as it should be, and, like Saxe's briefless barrister, Spotgam said, " 'Tis well."

The party was a delightful one, composed of the most judicious materials — a human punch, with just enough of the acid of sarcasm, and the spirit of wit and repartee, and the sweet of femininity, and the ice of etiquette, and the water — well, we haven't got to the water yet — nothing will do for such a compound but Empire Spring Water; and Spotgam smiled to himself as he thought of the black quart bottles that waited almost impatiently for his summons. Every one seemed pleased, and such a clatter of delightful tongues had never been heard in Deal Court before. The spirit of the scene blazed in musical execution to the melodies of Du-dah, Du-dah, and Nelly Bly, and smacked like champagne in the delicate manœuvres incident to Copenhagen.

At length, wearied with pleasure, having exhausted all expedients and resources of fun, the party adjourned to the supper table, that groaned, as is customary with tables, with the weight of good things that oppressed it, like an alderman after a public dinner, where every one was invited to partake, and Mr. Spotgam did the honors of the table. The Wiggins and the Trotts were really nowhere. The variety, quality, profusion, all operated to place the treat in brilliant and exalted comparison with all other treats that ever transpired in Deal Court. Everbody was delighted, and Mrs. Miles's boarders must thereafter take higher rank.

At last Spotgam asked to be excused for one moment.

He wished to introduce to the company a friend, of whom many of them had heard him speak, whose acquaintance he had made at Saratoga last summer, a sparkling, pungent fellow that he believed they would all like. He would bring him in immediately. He retired, and a very quiet smile flitted over the features of those who were in the secret as he left the room. He came back very soon, bearing two black bottles under each arm and one in each hand.

"Gentlemen and la'lies," said he, applying a corkscrew to the bottle before him, "this is the friend of whom I spoke, and I mistake in my guess if you do not regard him as a jewel of the first water, and this lesser individual is his companion. Ladies and gentleman, this is Empire Spring Water, Esq., and this General Hock."

When the bottles were all uncorked, he gave Bridget, who waited upon the table, the task to fill the glasses around the board with the fluids, which she did; then he proposed a toast to be drunk in the water, in order that he might witness the pleasure he was confident they would experience. He raised his glass to his lips, and quaffed it all off. His guests sipped, but none could accomplish more, immediately "dipping their nose in the Gascon wine," as if the other were unpleasant.

"You will find the second drink far more pleasant," said he, filling another tumbler. "I found it so at first when I was at Saratoga. I always found the tenth tumbler," — here there was a slight knock on the table, — "yes, I said the tenth tumbler, — the sweetest of any;" he raised the tumbler to his lips, and tossed off the second. "I confess," continued he, "that it tastes better at the springs, but still it is very palatable."

No one else dared venture upon the second, and Spotgam saw the one grand hope of the occasion expire. It was to be the skeleton at his feast. He therefore ordered that Bridget clear away the glasses. The treat ended, and the party broke up, after more Copenhagen, and more twirling the platter, and more "Du-dah, Du-dah," at a late hour in the morning.

"And, indade, 'twas a quare thing you did with the wather, sir," said Bridget to Spotgam next day, and her mouth retreated on both sides to a point beneath her ears; "mighty quare!"

"Ah, why?" inquired he, with a slight tremor in his voice.

"Indade, 'twas the forge wather, sir," she said, the expressive mouth reaching some distance behind the ears.

"The forge water?—spurious, eh?—counterfeit?" eagerly queried Spotgam.

"'Twas the forge wather the young ladies got from the blacksmith's shop, sir," said she, to wash their purty faces in, and you got howld of the wrong bottles, sir."

"That accounts for it, by Jove!" said he, slapping his knee. "I thought it tasted infernally nasty. I guess you'd better not say any thing about it."

Bridget, however, who had a keen relish for fun, found it a hard thing to keep. She had, unfortunately, a cousin living with the Wiggins, who was intrusted with the story under an injunction of secrecy, who in turn told it to a servant that lived with the Trotts, under the same charge, and the result was, that in a short time the whole of Deal Court knew it, though no one could tell how it transpired. To be sure there was a grand laugh at Spotgam's expense, and "*Mr. Spotgam's Treat*" became a proverb. The worst of it was, that his reputation as a connoisseur in Saratoga water died out from that time, and he is very careful to whom he tells the story about the ten tumblers of Empire Spring Water, though at the mention of Saratoga he always looks as if he wanted to.

24

HOME IN VACATION.

How still the house is!   All the noise and riot,
   That late our ears with fearful din distracted,
Are now submerged in overwhelming quiet,
   And order reigns where chaos was enacted.

Ah, blessed order! we thy peace enjoying,
   Forget the recent source of our vexation,
And while the tranquil time we are employing,
   We bless the happy season of vacation.

No voices by the chamber stairs are calling;
   No lawless hands on the piano drumming;
No teasing Ike his sisterhood is hauling;
   No screams for "Father!" to his ear are coming;

No boisterous lungs in disputatious fretting;
   No tart remark, no sharp recrimination;
No little rebel duty's claim forgetting;
   No broken rules for stern examination.

The books are on the shelves in nice condition,
   The music piled up in the proper places,
The table-cloths are in exact position,
   And just the angle are the shells and vases.

It is *so* quiet!   Not an echo hearing
   In all the rooms, from basement to the attic.
We smile to realize the comfort cheering
   Of stillness so profound — bliss so ecstatic.

But yet, amid the turbulence and clatter,
  There mingled strains that filled the heart with pleasure,
Kernels of love mixed with the idle chatter,
  Bright grains among the dross we loved to treasure.

Glad glances met our own each day returning,
  And faces with the soul's young sunlight glowing,
And hearts with warm, impulsive fervor burning,
  Spoke out from lips with youth's own language flowing.

Sweet melodies upon the air of even
  Woke the heart's tenderness to fondest dreaming,
And lost in notes that seemed like those of heaven,
  Forgot were cares with which the earth is teeming.

Although we prize the luxury of order,
  And think ourselves enriched the boon possessing,
The ripless calm that overhangs our border,
  Purchased with loss of these, is not a blessing.

We sigh regretfully the past recalling,
  And crave disorder with the joys attending,
For quiet wears to us a garb appalling,
  And peace thus gained is not worth the defending.

Then welcome once again the wild commotion,
  The song, the shout, the dance, the roguish actions,
Breaking to life the dull domestic ocean,
  By order's oft allowable infractions.

DISPOSING OF A CASE.

There was a case in court wherein Mr. F. M. Pinto was to appear as a witness. He put on his best clothes, and brushed up his hair in order to give him an external semblance of purity consonant with the inward integrity that filled his soul. His testimony was to fix the fact definitely whether the defendant was at a certain point at twenty-five or thirty minutes before or after a certain hour. Those who know Pinto's disposition to exaggerate gave him advice enough to have guided any ordinary man, but Pinto was not an ordinary man. He was a little out of place, however, in a witness box, but put an excellent face on it.

"Pinto," said one, as his name was called, "now be sure and tell the truth."

"Don't do it, Pinto," echoed another; "if you do they will be sure not to believe you."

But he went on the stand, took the oath, and then looked down at the counsel awaiting the questioning.

"Do you understand this case, Mr. Pinto?" asked the counsel.

"I think I do, sir," replied Pinto; "I was present when it was opened, and can testify" —

"Not yet, sir; not yet," said the counsel.

"When the incident occurred on which it is based, were you present?"

"Of course I was; Jim asked in half a dozen of us. There was Tom Grover, and Bill Jewett, and" —

"That is not to the purpose, Mr. Pinto. Now tell the jury the exact time when this happened."

"As nearly as I can remember, it was about eleven o'clock, because Tim Grover" —

"No matter about Tim Grover. May it not have been twenty-five minutes past eleven?"

"Yes, perhaps it might; but Bill Jewett" —

"We will dispense with Jewett. What we wish to know is, whether Muggs, the defendant, was present at Jones's, at twenty-five minutes past eleven, or not? Can you swear that he was there at that time?"

"Of course I can. Jim said" —

"No matter what Jim said. You can sit down."

"Stay," said the counsel for the defendant, and he staid.

"Mr. Pinto," said the counsel, "were you at Jones's, on the twentieth of March, at twenty-five minutes before eleven o'clock?"

"Yes, sir."

"Are you sure about the hour?"

"Yes, sir."

"Now tell the jury what you know about this case."

"Jim Jones said he had a case of rare old gin, and asked us in to try it; and so Tim Grover and Bill Jewett" —

"And Muggs?" said the counsel for the plaintiff.

"No, Muggs wasn't there then."

"Well, when did he come in?" asked the counsel.

"He didn't come in at all."

"But you were there at twenty-five minutes before eleven?"

"Yes."

"And twenty-five minutes past eleven?" said one of the jurymen, waking up.

"Yes."

"Explain yourself," said the court.

"Why, your honor, Jim Jones had a case of gin, and

24*

Tim Grover, and Bill Jewett, and I went to his place about eleven o'clock "—

"You said twenty-five minutes past, Mr. Pinto," said the judge, sternly, consulting his notes.

"Twenty-five minutes before, your honor," said the counsel for the defence.

"Well, gentlemen," said Pinto, "I was there from ten o'clock till twelve. 'Twould be impossible to open and dispose of a case in half an hour "—

"But was Muggs there at all?" asked the counsel for the defence.

"Not that I saw."

"Then what is the case you are trying to prove?" asked the judge, severely.

"The case of gin," said Pinto.

"You may sit down, sir," said the judge.

———◆———

VAIN REGRETS.

A seedy old beggar asked alms of me
As he sat 'neath the shade of a wayside tree.
He was beggared in purse and beggared in soul,
And his voice betrayed a pitiful dole,
As he sang a song, to a dismal pitch,
With the burden, "IF THINGS WAS ONLY SICH!"

"If things was only sich," said he,
"You should see what a wonderful man I'd be;
No beggar I, by the wayside thrown,
But I'd live in a palace and millions own,
And men would court me if I were rich—
As I'd be if things was only sich."

"If things was only sich," said he,
"I'd be lord of the land and lord of the sea;
I would have a throne and be a king,
And rule the roast with a mighty swing —
I'd make a place in Fame's bright niche;
I'd do it if things was only sich."

"If things was only sich," said he,
"Rare wines I'd quaff from the far countree,
I'd clothe myself in dazzling garb,
I'd mount the back of the costly barb,
And none should ask me wherefore or which —
Did it chance that things was only sich."

"If things was only sich," said he,
"I'd love the fairest and they'd love me;
Yon dame, with a smile that warms my heart,
Might have borne with me life's better part,
But lost to me, here in poverty's ditch,
What were mine if things was only sich."

Thus the old beggar moodily sung,
And his eyes dropped tears as his hands he wrung.
I could but pity to hear him berate,
In dolorous tones, the decrees of Fate,
That laid on his back its iron switch,
While he cried, "If things was only sich."

"If things was only sich!" — e'en all
Might the past in sad review recall;
But little the use and little the gain,
Exhuming the bones of buried pain,
And whether we're poor or whether we're rich,
We'll say not, "If things was only sich."

EXTRACT FROM AN UNWRITTEN ROMANCE.

"It was about seven bells when the true character of the corvette was discovered, and there was immediate alacrity on board the privateer (Lively Bug) to get out of the way. All sail was made, and the canvas was wet, but to little advantage, for the corvette gained upon us, and soon her black hull, almost within howitzer range, loomed up behind us. She had the British ensign at the peak, and presented a formidable appearance. She had not as yet fired a gun, but seemed bent on making an easy conquest by boarding us.

"'Oh for a breeze!' cried Captain Jo. Hatch, nervously walking the deck, and turning his eye towards his approaching foe.

"But the breeze did not respond to his asking, and the Lively Bug did not move at a pace in keeping with her name.

"'Mr. Cinder!' shouted the captain. 'Call Cinder, some of you;' which was done.

"Cinder was the armorer, who thought the scene of his labors was below just then. As he put his head above the hatch, the captain sung out, —

"'Cinder, I want the shank of the old anchor on deck in five minutes.'

"'Ay, ay, sir,' said Cinder, as he disappeared, and in the time specified the shank, a heavy mass of iron, borne by four men, was on deck.

"'Mr. Tompion,' said the captain to the gunner of the Long Tom, 'I want three powder cartridges put into the gun.'

"'Twill bust her,' said Tompion.

"'Do as I bid you,' said the captain, sternly, and it was done, the crew instinctively drawing back, and Old Tom Trunnion saying, as he sat down on the windlass, ''Tisn't my ship, and the underwriters'll have to suffer.'

"To our surprise, the captain then ordered the gunner and his men to hoist the shank of the anchor into the cannon, and then we thought the old man was mad, sure enough; but he appeared perfectly self-possessed. He called us aft.

"'Boys,' said he, 'I am not going to be taken by that vessel if good gunnery will save us. Be ready to obey all my orders. Point the gun to windward.'

"We did so, and awaited the result with suspended breath. The corvette came up with us, till we could see the color of the shirts the men wore, when we heard our captain's voice say, —

"'Port your helm!'

"He stood sighting the gun, and as the Lively Bug swung round, bringing the three masts of the corvette directly in range, he pulled the lanyard.

"'Bang!' went the gun, with a crash like thunder, and the captain was seen going rapidly aft as the mass of iron darted from the muzzle of the gun. The Lively Bug trembled in every joint, and keeled over to the water's edge. An instant, and a terrific crash and yell on the corvette revealed what had been done, as all three of her masts fell over her side into the sea, and the single shot of her bow chaser whistled between our masts.

"The wind began to freshen at this instant, and the Bug began to move rapidly through the water. For a few moments we forgot the captain; but on searching for him we found him on the cabin table, having been blown through the skylight. He was insensible for a time; but when he came

to and saw the effect of his shot, he ordered an attack on
the corvette, and, with the wind now in our favor, we so
manœuvred that in fifteen minutes the British corvette
Snapdragon, of twenty-four guns, was prize to the Yankee
privateer Lively Bug!

"The medal awarded by Congress for this gallant exploit is in existence, and at present in possession of an uncle of the narrator, to be seen by any one who desires."

TRUE FAITH.

Old Reuben Fisher, who lived in the lane,
Was never in life disposed to complain;
If the weather proved fair, he thanked God for the sun,
And if it were rainy, with him 'twas all one; —
" I have just the weather I fancy," said he,
" For what pleases God always satisfies me."

If trouble assailed, his brow was ne'er dark,
And his eye never lost its happiest spark.
" 'Twill not better fix it to gloom or to sigh;
To make the best of it I always shall try!
So, Care, do your worst," said Reuben with glee,
" And which of us conquers, we shall see, we shall see."

If his children were wild, as children will prove,
His temper ne'er lost its warm aspect of love;
" My dear wife," he'd say, "don't worry nor fret;
'Twill all be right with the wayward ones yet;
'Tis the folly of youth, that must have its way;
They'll penitent turn from their evil some day."

If a name were assailed, he would cheerily say,
"Well, well; we'll not join in the cry, any way;
There are always two sides to every tale —
And the true one at last is sure to prevail.
There is an old rule that I learned when a lad, —
'Deem every one good till he's proved to be bad.'"

And when in the meshes of sin tightly bound,
The reckless and luckless mortal was found,
Proscribed by every woman and man,
And put under rigid and merciless ban,
Old Reuben would say, with sympathy fraught,
"We none of us do half as well as we ought."

If friends waxed cold, he'd say with a smile —
"Well, if they must go, Heaven bless them the while;
We walked a sweet path till the crossing ways met,
And though we have parted, I'll cherish them yet;
They'll go by their way and I'll go by mine —
Perhaps in the city ahead we shall join."

There were sickness and death at last in his cot,
But still Reuben Fisher in sorrow blenched not:
"'Tis the Father afflicts: let Him do what He will;
What comes from His hand can mean us no ill;
I cheerfully give back the blessing He lent,
And through faith in the future find present content."

Then he lay on his death-bed at last undismayed;
No terror had death at which he was afraid;
"Living or dying, 'tis all well with me,
For God's will is my will," submissive said he.
And so Reuben died, with his breast full of grace,
That beamed in a smile on his time-furrowed face.

A BIT OF OBITUARY.

THE LATE EVERMORE SMOOTH.

THE demise of this distinguished man affords me opportunity to speak of his many virtues. He had for seventy years occupied a prominent place in the popular eye, during which time he had never refused to serve the public in any capacity that promised to pay. When any great question came up on which the people divided, his decision was marked, because it had been arrived at by the slow process of culling the opinions of others, and selecting those which would be likely to prove successful, and therefore he was a safe man to follow. In politics he forever sought to be on the winning side; and when, as sometimes happened through the fickleness of public opinion, that the weaker became the stronger, he ever had the candor to admit his error, and exert as much haste as possible in getting again with the majority, making up by his zeal the mistake of position. He was zealous as a politician, and though he never attempted to coerce a voter, it was always understood that if any in his employ voted against him, their places were vacant, thus leaving their fortune in their own hands and silencing all claims of injustice. When the war of rebellion broke out, he was one of the first to volunteer, as a contractor, and did distinguished service in that field of duty. Before the close of the war, having made all he could out of it, he retired from the field, sick of violence. His health was impaired, and deeming that safety lay in the church, he joined a respectable organization of that description, the stock in which immediately went up fifty per cent. He was inspired by feelings of the grandest benevolence, and his name was always mentioned when he gave away any thing, as an inducement to others. His mission was to visit the widow and the fatherless, which he strictly fulfilled, generally after the fatherless were in bed, as he did not wish to make his virtue too ostentatious by going in the daytime. He loved to take the widows by the hand and listen to their wants and relieve them; but as there were a good many widows in his society, the fund for each was small. He was an uncompromising opponent of sin and sinners — never forgiving either. When he read the injunctions regarding forgiveness, he always read them with a reservation, and insisted that the forgiveness *as* we forgive, in the Lord's Prayer, was wrongly translated. Being a person of influence, this was the view taken of it by nearly everybody in the parish, except the infidels. So with the golden rule: "Do as you are done by" was adopted as the proper translation, at the suggestion of Mr. Smooth, the sentiment of which he faithfully exemplified in his life. In his business dealings with his fellow-men, this was especially his creed. He bought and sold, and was never known to make a trade that did not turn in his own favor; hence he made much lucre, and illustrated in his case the truth of the scriptural assurance regarding the love of money. He made no new friends, and as he never had any old ones, his list of visitors was not troublesome. His poor relatives were not tolerated; he regarded poverty as a crime, and washed his hands of all complicity with it that might attach by recognizing them. He was a patron of letters, and gave a Webster's Unabridged Dictionary, that he had bought at auction, to his native place, on condition that the town clerk should read a chapter from it each town meeting day; but the gift was declined. As a connoisseur of art he stood high, and gave his preference for Jones, the house dauber, over

Raphael as portrait painter. Mr. Evermore Smooth, though removed from our midst, we shall long recall by his majestic presence and the peculiarities that distinguished him. He was about five feet three inches in height, and was wont to make his presence felt by the terrific manner in which he blew his nose. Alas that we shall hear those echoes no more! Peace to his ashes; and that they may not be lost, which would greatly grieve him if it should happen that they were, his heirs have erected a granite obelisk above them.

----♦----

A COUNTRY RAINY DAY.

Up from the river * sweeps the rain,
   Over the field and over the wood,
And the fretful wind, with a note of pain,
Sobs and murmurs a sad refrain,
   Responsive to the angry flood.

Oh the sight for impatient eyes,
   Scanning the desolate, dreary day,
With its drenchèd earth and leaden skies,
To see the misty clouds arise
   That shroud the hills there far away!

I hear the plashing torrent pour,
   And listen with a sense of dread;
There's bodily misery in the roar,
That wakens mental torture sore,
  Till all of sweet content has fled.

* Piscataqua, at Newington.

Drip and drip from yonder eaves —
  The whole day long 'tis dripping there.
There's a shivering sound in all the leaves,
And the feeling the wakeful soul receives
  Is one akin to deep despair.

The poultry in the barnyard stand,
  Damp and cheerless, with drooping quills;
They see no promise in all the land,
Or joy that they can understand
  Through this grand culminate of ills.

That crower never will crow again,
  That hen never exalt her lay;
Their ardor is damped by the falling rain,
And they seem to feel, it is very plain,
  Disgusted with the sloppy day.

The swallows seek the sheltered place,
  High up there on the beams of the barn,
And "touch and go" they flit their race,
Showing their young, with tender grace,
  The useful lesson they must "larn."

The cattle on the barn-floor smoke,
  — A practice they are here allowed —
While all the boys, unhindered, joke,
And "Uncle George"* puts in his spoke,
  The jolliest among the crowd.

He cares not though the day be wet;
  "What is the use," he says, "to cry?

* A true country philosopher, who, when the skies are the blackest,
always predicts that it is "coming off."

'Twill be fair weather, some time, yet —
'Tis not a bit of use to fret,
    Let the weather be wet or dry."

The croakers indoors sadly growl
    At hopes thus gloomily overcast;
The answering wind sets up a howl,
And the rain comes down like a water-fowl,
    Struck by the north-east chilling blast.

I hear the struggling of the spout,
    As it outpours its yeasty flood;
I hear the hay-press workers shout,
And see Hodge driving the cattle out
    Through pools of liquefying mud.

O Patience! what a virtue thou!
    I feel thy need in all my bones;
John Bunyan yonder in the slough
Was no worse off than I am now,
    Hearing these angry tempest tones.

Roar out, ye children on the stair,
    And let your voices do their best;
We'll make believe the day is fair,
And try to mitigate despair,
    Though all our trying prove a jest.

Alas! alas! 'tis even so;
    We cannot banish this one pain;
The frisky winds must have their blow,
And all the racks must overflow,
    That hold the bottles of the rain.

SIDEWALK OPERA.

It is wonderful how infectious opera is. Whole neighborhoods will be bewitched by it; and men and women, in pursuing the quiet avocations of life, will become operatic in spite of themselves. Men ask the price of a beefsteak with a *bravura*, which is replied to by a *cavatina;* the morning salutation becomes a *duet,* and *arias* and *romanzas* are common things. Thus an opera of householders, compelled to shovel off in front after a snow-storm, was quite amusing.

SCENE, *Sidewalk. Snow mountains high.*

SMITH, BROWN, JONES, *and* ROBINSON (*queerly costumed, armed with shovels, prepared to level the drift*). *Quartette.*

> Here we are to stand the brunt :
> We must shovel off in front.
> Now with blades to cleave the snow,
> In we go, and in we go,
> Throwing the invading drift
> Far as human nerve can lift.
> In, boys, in, and do not stay ;
> It will be as good as play.   [*They pitch in.*

SMITH (*resting on his shovel*).

> Whew ! 'tis rough and tough enough :
> I'm not made of seasoned stuff.
> I can't stand this fierce employ :
> I'll knock off, and find a boy.

25*

Brown, Jones, *and* Robinson (*resting on their shovels*).
Trio.

> Ah! peccavi do you cry?
> So soon from the toil to fly?
> Can you thus the joy forego
> Of this fresh and healthy glow?
> Stay: think better of it, Smith,
> Be a man of nerve and pith.

Smith (*shouldering his shovel, and beckoning to a boy
about forty years old*). *Bass.*

> My hope to feel the glow is dim;
> Therefore I resign to him.   [*Exit.*

[Brown, Jones, *and* Robinson *resume shovelling.*]

Brown (*resting on his shovel, and wiping his face*).

> By George! this'll try the back:
> I thought I felt a muscle crack;
> And, though I feel all right and brisk,
> I don't dare too much to risk.
> Therefore I conceive it best
> To call a boy to do the rest.

Jones *and* Robinson (*resting on their shovels*).   *Duet.*

> Ha, ha! thus the toil you shirk,
> While we stick and do the work.
> Men of pluck, we'll trophies show
> Of our struggle with the snow.

Brown (*shouldering his shovel, and calling another boy
of some fifty summers and forty-nine winters*).   *2d Bass.*

> I will leave you all the fun
> Of hope achieved and victory won.   [*Exit.*

[JONES *and* ROBINSON *resume shovelling.*]

JONES (*resting on his shovel, and putting his hand wildly
to his head*).

> Ah ! that horrid vertigo !
> I was fearful 'twould be so.
> Round and round things seem to spin :
> I declare I must cave in.

ROBINSON (*resting on his shovel*).   *Solo.*

> Thus they drop from out the ring,
> Tender as the buds of spring ;
> Leaving me here all alone
> To shovel on, while they have flown.

JONES (*shouldering his shovel, and calling a boy of about
thirty-five years*).   *Tenor.*

> 'Tis rather " going back," I know ;
> But vertigo now makes me go.   [*Exit.*

[ROBINSON *resumes shovelling.*]

ROBINSON (*resting on his shovel, and looking at about
twenty feet of drift he has got to work through*).

> Faith, I think I'd best give o'er,
> My dexter hand is very sore,
> My hair and eyes are full of snow, —
> I guess I'll have the verti-*go.*

ROBINSON (*shouldering his shovel, and calling a boy about
twenty-five*).   *2d Tenor.*

> Here, my lad : just put this through ;
> I'll leave the glory all to you.   [*Exit.*

Quartette by PAT, PHELIM, TERENCE, *and* MICK, *with
shovel accompaniment.*

Ah, begorra! but this is a good job for us, onnyhow:
Blessings on the shnow-storrum that kicked up sich a
      lovely row!
With the worruk half done by the gintlefolk, who broke
      down 'fore they did it,
Laving us to charge what we're a mind to, by the same
      token; and we'll do that, you'd better belaye,
      before we've done wid it.   [*They shovel.*

MY FIRST FUDDLE.

DON'T smile, readers, and look at each other, and touch
elbows, and wink, on reading my title, as though it were a
nucleus of infinite "fuddles" that followed it like the train
of a comet, for it was not so.   I received that day a lesson
which I have always remembered — a lesson that came to
me through pain and mortification and sorrow, and wrought
deeply into a heart not much depraved then, however the
world has hardened and corrupted it since.   Practical lessons are the best, if rightly applied.   Were the first lesson
in tobacco-chewing cherished as it should be, there would
be few tobacco-chewers, as it is only by persistence that
human repugnance to the weed can be overcome.   So
would it be with drinking, were men wise.   My first lesson
in "fuddle" was my last.   And this was the way it happened.

"Penhallow's Field" was a great resort for ball-players,
in old times, in our town, and every half holiday and

Fast Day a band of merry players were very certain to be there. Penhallow's Field lay just before our door — a fine turfy plain at that time, though now streets and houses profane the precinct once sacred to athletic exercise and roistering mirth. At times, older boys would bring to aid the spirit of base a baser spirit, that would have a contrary effect to that intended, for instead of the healthy glow and animation imparted by the sport, the languid eye and lagging gait betokened a dulled spirit and physical prostration; or else the flushed cheek and fierce glance bespoke the presence of an unclean demon — lacking but the power to rend the possessor, like the spirits among the tombs — that even then showed signs of turbulence and wrath, and wakened quarrelsome echoes upon the peaceful air of Rock Pasture, of which Penhallow's Field formed a part.

I have since looked with much interest for these latter individuals, but they have passed along life's highway and gone beyond, leaving no sign. The habits of their youth probably foreshadowed the habits of their maturity; they died, and that was the end of them, so far as earth was concerned. Good fellows they were, all of them, full of life, and generosity, and warm-heartedness, and my heart took to them; I watched their older words as they fell, in not very choice form, and learned them for repetition, till I saw their folly.

But to my "first fuddle." I never shall forget the Fast Day afternoon when it occurred — warm, glorious, and green — as *I* was, in the verdancy of ten summers. It comes to me, a commingling of base, big boys, molasses candy, gingerbread, hard-boiled eggs, egg-nog, and peppermint cordial, the latter largely preponderating. The egg-nog had all been drunk, and most of the eatables disposed of, when a new expedient was devised for a finale to the hallowed day. Such small boys as were near were summoned, and the proposition was made to them that they should have all the candy there was left if they would drink the balance of the peppermint cordial. Tempting bait! No wonder there was a fall about that time, because human nature was weak, and the cordial sweet and very strong.

This first step in the lesson resulted in many irregular steps thereafter, before night. The insidious cordial found its way through every vein of my body, with overwhelming power, darting with a lambent fire over nerve and brain, and making my young head unsteady with half-delirious dreams and diabolical hallucinations. I remember the whirl of excitement that every thing seemed to be in. The grass had become very irregular in its surface, and I found myself stepping up often to surmount the hillocks that were rising before me; the fence in front of our house had become suddenly serpentine, wriggling along its entire length, like a big snake, and I remember that the gate had contracted, because I struck both sides in subsequently attempting to pass through it. I saw more than fifty grinning faces around me, though they could have belonged to but eight boys; and they seemed all dancing an infernal measure in a cabalistic ring, with me for a centre, and bony fingers pointed at me with horrid derision, till in the whirl I fell down. But I had no suspicion of what was the matter with me, and got up again. Then came the experience of the gate mentioned above. I saw my brothers, as I entered the door, look at each other and laugh. They knew what it all meant, but they said nothing.

Amidst it all I retained a self-consciousness that subdued the delirium, and a sense of duty ran through my wildest vagary. Above all was the impression that I had to go about a mile away, around the old North Mill Pond, and get a pair of boots that had been left there to be repaired; and I started off to perform the task, with a decided idea that a more rough and uncomfortable road I had never travelled. This was before Jordan had put in its claim for special severity. How I got over it I never really knew, but found myself, some time after, seated on a shoemaker's bench making free with the hammers of the workmen, pounding upon lapstones, and taking great liberties with awls, lasts, and knives, that lay within reach, kicking the bucket containing the wax, and committing other. outrages, as the auctioneer says, " too numerous to mention." The men touched their noses significantly, and winked at each other, and looked, as I thought, very silly; and I remember that I, with more than ten-year-old wisdom, told them they were acting like "infernal fools."

I got up to go home, and took a path straight for the pond, with a vague impression that I was to ford the stream. As I reached it, however, my knees failed me, and I fell pronely upon the shore, in ignominious helplessness. Were any being to have stood by my elbow and urged my acceptance of the universe, or any other tract of territory, on the condition that I got up and walked, I should not have been able to do it. Utterly helpless; and yet amid it all a light broke upon me that revealed the true state of the case, so that when the men who had watched me from the window came down to me, and asked what was the matter, I responded with an honesty worthy of an older head, " I'm drunk ! "

They took me up very tenderly and carried me to the house where they lived. And here memory recalls a benevolent face encircled by a white cap border, a blazing wood fire over which a tea kettle is simmering, a Dutch oven containing a quantity of bubbling hog's fat, and a large milk-pan full of doughnuts by the side of the nreplace. I remember that venerable figure standing by my side as I sat by the fire, with kindness and sympathy upon her face, and a cup of warm water in her hand, which she urged me to drink. I remember, too, what followed — a nausea — a spasm — and a milk-pan full of doughnuts spoiled forever!

My brother Bob came across the pond in a boat and ferried me home, and still before me is the scene that awaited me — my mother's and sister's tears, my grandmother's pitiful gaze, as if an angel looked through her beautiful eyes, my father's grave and sorrowful earnestness, my brother's mirth. He had got over *his* first fuddle some time before.

Well, there I sat, when I got home, the centre of interest. Never was a little fellow of ten, clothed in no very sweet habiliments, an object of more consideration, and never did shame weigh more heavily on mortal conscience than on mine, with the *feel* of those eyes upon me. I braced myself up with a tipsy resolution that I would brave it out. The silence was painful, and I essayed to break it with a remark; but the remark, like Macbeth's amen, stuck in my throat. My tongue seemed as big as two ordinary beef tongues, and filled my mouth full. I couldn't articulate for the life of me. I gave that up, but attempted to look unconcerned. It was a lamentable failure; for the first thing I saw was my father's benign and sorrowing look, — sorrow without reproach, — that sank into my soul, and remains there till this day, more permanently than though enforced by a hurricane of words. His was no temper to storm. The elements of gentleness and kindness were so developed in him, there was no room for anger, or for any harsher feeling than sorrow. That look was so full of disappointment, and regret, and grief, that encounter it again I would not for the world; and gathering myself up the best way I could, I crawled off to my little bed in the attic to sleep off my first fuddle, and, if possible, a remembrance of the mortification I felt. The first I accomplished, but the latter I have never succeeded in doing, though more than forty years have since swept over me their fates of good and evil. That old man's gaze has never left my mind, and even as I write I recall it. He gave me no lecture besides this — no homily on sobriety, no expostulation, no threatening. As the eye of man is said to be able to check the fiercest madman, so was the unclean spirit in me subdued by a look, and was from that moment dethroned.

I tell this in no vain-glorious spirit of boasting, I tell it in no " I am holier than thou " mood, but give it as a single example of the good effect of a good influence timely exerted. I do confess me to a liking for fluids, however, and when my friend Colonel ———— levelled his glass to me at the Ancients' dinner, and smiled in the urbane manner usual with him, I could not avoid sipping a little response ; besides, I have not entirely conquered my tenderness for cider, especially when it comes commended as a legal beverage by the solemn enactment of the state.

—◦◦◦—

LITTLE WINNIE, with his cheeks red and glowing, was met by a kind old clergyman, who stooped down and patted him on his head, saying, " Well, my little man, what makes your cheeks so red ? " The bright eyes looked up laughingly. " I s'pose," said he, " 'tis 'cause they are red hot."

26

SAN GAREE'S RIDE.

I'll tell you a tale, if you'll list to me,
Of the ride that was rid by San Garee,
On a night in the K. N. Fifty-Five:
There are many witnesses alive
Who were on the spot the thing to see.

He said to his friend, " The constable's come,
But as you'll see, I'm up to trap;
They think they've wholly stopped our rum
By cutting off the tavern's tap.
I'll show 'em a trick worth two of that,
For I'll away to the opposite flat,
Ready to ride to Medford town
And bring the real 'critter' down,
In spite of the tyrannous Maine law's frown !"

Then he said good night. and a jug he took,
And crossed the bridge that spanned the brook,
Just as the moon. half over the bay,
Shed its beam where a hay-cart waiting lay —
A phantom cart, with slats upright,
Through which the moon shone still and bright,
And a huge black hulk of a shadow was cast
On the fence, as San Garee hurried past.

．　　．　　．　　．　　．　　．　　．

A clatter of hoofs rang through the town,
Lickity-cut. at a terrible pace,
And the oldest stagers in the place
Vowed that such riding they'd never known :
That was all ! and yet from his mission that night,
A dozen men ere morning were tight !

．　　．　　．　　．　　．　　．　　．

SAN GAREE'S RIDE.

It was ten by the village clock
When he crossed the bridge into Medford town.
He smelt the fragrance of the dock,
And heard the hum of the 'stillery dam.
And the sound of a distant front door slam,
As folks to their naps were settling down;
And he was fast asleep in his bed.
The one on whom San Garee did call,
Who filled his jug with the fluid red,
And didn't mind the law at all.

The rest is soon told.   He came as he went,
With no policeman on the scent,
His prize securely lashed to his side,
That ere he started he twice had tried,
Dashing along through road and lane
With eager heart and urgent rein;
And under the trees, by the river's brink,
Stopping only to take a drink!

So on that night rode San Garee,
And so through the night his horse's heels
To wakeful ears made noisy appeals, —
Appeals that mocked curiosity; —
A clatter in darkness that passed by the door,
As homeward his trophy the night rider bore!
Now, 'mong the rummest things that are past,
Recounted often in circles fast,
In hours of sport, and mirth, and fun,
They tell the story with shouts of glee
How the Maine-law people were done
By the midnight ride of San Garee.

THE VICTIM OF INVITATIONS.

Mr. Tott was a very excellent man, so everybody said; was largely social and capable of much enjoyment, loved the good things of the world, and had a thousand friends; but he was unhappy. He was haunted by a demon. Not by a thing of "gristly bone," but a shadowy demon that ran in and out of his mind like the worms in the brain of "Alonzo the Brave," sung in the ballad, but not so visible as were those interesting reptiles, working the very mischief with him. This was exceeding sensitiveness. He not only shrank from putting himself forward, but would not allow others to do it for him. He hung back continually and became a man with timidity, like a garment, clinging to him. He was in a constant dread all the time, lest he should be singled out for some distinction. Particularly he dreaded invitations to dinner. He was glad when others got invitations, and loved to hear the music of knife and fork that came to him from a distance, and it gave him pleasure to look in through open doors revealing long lines of pleasant faces by the table; but he was never to be found where men met to meat. He was social, but couldn't mingle with his fellows except in the street, or in places where eating was not involved. He once came very near being seduced by an invitation to a lobster salad; but though, next to virtue, he loved lobster salad, he gave it up just as he had made up his mind to go. He couldn't account for this timidity — nobody could — and he was very miserable.

It is always the case that that which we most dread will happen to us. A man that dreads fire is more apt to have his house burn than one who cares nothing about it; one who dreads dogs always has a regiment of them to annoy him around his house; and I knew a man who had a mortal antipathy to bears, that was chased for three days in State Street by the brokers.

This is a very queer fact. So, as poor Tott dreaded invitations to dine out, did they come upon him. Everybody invited him to dinner, and ten thousand lies did he invent in the course of the year to evade these invitations. Many of his inventions were ingenious and original. With one he had "just eaten," when he was as gaunt as a famished wolf; with another, a "previous engagement" prevented him; and with another, a friend "was coming to dine with him." Like all liars, he at last got found out.

"Tott," said Smith, one day, meeting him in the street, "come and dine with me to-day. Got some fine birds, — woodcock, — I know you like 'em; and, look here, some of the best wine you ever drank."

Tott's mouth watered at the bill of fare; but his diffidence came over him, and he replied, —

"Can't think of it; I'm engaged to dine with Brown. Thank'ee for your invitation, though, just as much. Good by."

Tott turned away, vexed with himself for refusing, when, just as he had turned the corner, he met Brown.

"Tott," said Brown, shaking him warmly by the hand, "glad I've met with you. I want you to dine with me to-day. Banfield, up in New Hampshire, has just sent me down some salmon trout, — prime fellows, — fresh and clean — eh, boy! — that's your sort. Will you come? Say yes."

Tott trembled. It was a proposition sufficient to tempt an anchorite. It was hard to resist; but his old habit came over him, and he replied, —

26*

"Faith, Brown, it's unfortunate, but I've just engaged to take dinner with Smith. Devilish unfortunate to have two such chances at once. Hope you'll have a good time. Farewell."

They parted. Later in the morning Tott dropped into the office of a friend.

"Ah, Tott," said he, "'tis getting near dinner time; I should be glad to have you take dinner with me."

"Can't possibly," replied he; "I expect a friend from New York to dine with me to-day."

At this moment Smith entered.

"My friend Tott, I must insist on your going home to dine with me. Wife and the girls will be glad to see you Come!"

"But," said Tott, "you remember my previous engagement" —

"What, to dine with Brown? Nonsense! Come along."

"He just told me he expected a friend from New York to dine with him," said the friend, winking at Smith.

Poor Tott was cornered; but putting a good face on it, he insisted upon it that he was to dine with Brown, and that Brown had just returned from New York, and so of course he was all straight.

At that moment the door opened, and Brown entered.

"Halloo!" said he; "all right; now, Smith, just release him from his engagement, will you. and let him come and dine with me? Do, there's a good fellow."

"Why, he told me he had engaged to dine with you."

"Gentlemen," said Tott, in despair, "you must both excuse me, as I am engaged to a sit-down with a friend at Parker's."

He went out, and that day dined on clam chowder and a doughnut at Learned's.

Poor fellow! thereafter he was spotted, and every one invited him ten times more pertinaciously than ever to dinner. He was in constant dread, and at times became very nearly drawn into a dinner.

A pale-faced, grave-looking gentleman, holding a position under government, came in one day about dinner time, and approaching Tott, asked him if he would go with him to be a witness in a case that affected him vitally.

"You know," said the grave gentleman, "that I was sick last winter, and a word from you will substantiate a matter that is now involved in a little doubt. Will you go?"

"Certainly," said Tott, putting on his coat; "where are we to go?"

"To City Hall," was the reply.

Soon they arrived at a point near that locality, when the grave gentleman conducted Tott into Hall's eating-house, redolent with the odors of turtle soup, and turning to Tott, he said, —

"What I want you to witness is the excellent quality of this turtle soup and my own excellent appetite. Sit down and take some. Mr. Hall, my friend Tott."

"I vow," said Tott, "it is very unfortunate, but I dined at Parker's not more than fifteen minutes ago, and couldn't eat another mouthful if I should die."

His mouth watered as he spoke, and the tears gathered in his eyes; but he had spoken, and wishing the grave gentleman a good appetite, and bidding Hall an affectionate farewell, went back to his tumbler of cider and piece of pie at Loring's.

Tott grew emaciated and weak daily under his invitations, and so nervous that he sometimes refused before he was asked. Every one who approached him he thought was about to invite him to dinner. One day a stranger met him in the street and inquired the way to the Tremont House.

"Thank you kindly, sir," said he; "but I am positively engaged to-day, to dine with my friend Everett. Oh, ask pardon! Tremont House? There it is, sir."

There was a vacant chair, not long after this, in Tott's domicile, and a jury of twelve grave men sat on a coat and hat found on Charlestown Bridge, who brought in the verdict that as Tott was not to be found, it was inferable from the vacant hat and coat that he had slipped away, by water or otherwise, to avoid being invited to dinner.

——•••——

THE GREEN GOOSE.

Mr. Bogardus "gin a treat,"
And a green goose, best of birds to eat,
Delicious, savory, fat, and sweet,
Formed the dish the guests to greet;
    But such, we know,
    Is small for a "blow,"
    And many times around won't go;
So Mr. Bogardus chanced to reflect,
And with a wisdom circumspect,
He sent round cards to parties select,
Some six or so the goose to dissect,
    The day and hour defining;
And then he laid in lots of things,
That might have served as food for kings,

Liquors drawn from their primal springs,
And all that grateful comfort brings
    To epicures in dining.

But Mr. Bogardus's brother Sim,
With moral qualities rather dim,
Copied the message sent to him,
    In his most clerkly writing,
And sent it round to Tom, and Dick,
And Harry, and Jack, and Frank, and Nick,
And many more, to the green goose "pick"
    Most earnestly inviting;
He laid it on the green goose thick,
    Their appetites exciting.

'Twas dinner time by the Old South clock;
Bogardus waited the sounding knock
Of friends to come at the moment, "chock,"
To try his goose, his game, his hock,
    And hoped they would not dally;
When one, and two, and three, and four,
And running up the scale to a score,
And adding to it many more,
Who all their Sunday fixings wore,
Came in procession to the door,
And crowded in on his parlor floor,
Filling him with confusion sore,
Like an after-election rally!

"Gentlemen," then murmured he,
"To what unhoped contingency
Am I owing for this felicity,
    A visit thus unexpected?"

Then they held their cards before his eyes,
And he saw, to his infinite surprise,
That some sad dog had taken a rise
On him, and his hungry friends likewise,
    And *whom* he half suspected;
But there was Sim,
Of morals dim,
With a face as long, and dull, and grim,
    As though *he* the ire reflected.

Then forth the big procession went,
With mirth and anger equally blent;
To think they didn't get the scent
Of what the cursed missive meant
    Annoyed some of 'em deeply;
They felt they'd been caught by a green goose bait,
And plucked and skinned, and then, light weight,
    Had been sold very cheaply.

MORAL.

Keep your weather eye peeled for trap,
For we never know just what may hap,
    Nor if we shall be winners;
Remembering that one green goose
Will be of very little use
    'Mongst twenty hungry sinners.

MISSING.

On the morning of August 20, 18—, the following paragraph appeared in the columns of the Elmwood Advertiser: —

"MISSING. — Mr. George Wayne, of this town, has mysteriously disappeared from his home, and his friends are plunged into the deepest anxiety regarding him. The last seen of him, he was on his market wagon, proceeding towards this place from Centre Hebron, where he had been with a load of produce; and, as he had received considerable money, it is feared that he has been the victim of foul play. The team reached home without him. Every exertion has been made to ascertain his fate, but all have been fruitless."

People might well be startled, as they were, to read this, for George Wayne was widely known as the most successful farmer in the valley of Sedge River, that ran through Elmwood, and was much esteemed for his many estimable qualities. His energy and prudence had secured for him a competence; and he had a worthy wife and two fine boys, with whom he lived very happily. He had no encumbrances, no troublesome obligations to meet, and, with pleasant domestic relations, no other reason for his disappearance than that of " foul play " could be entertained. The grief of his family was intense, and excited the sympathy of all for many miles around, who were ready to join in any effort that might be made to obtain a solution of the mystery.

Accordingly advertisements were despatched in every direction, describing the missing man, and offering a large sum for the recovery of his body, if dead, or information regarding him, if living. The town authorities also took the matter up, and increased the amount of the reward offered by the friends of Wayne. The promptness with which all this was done attested to the estimation in which he was held; and there was, besides, a desire to free the vicinity from the stigma that attached to the fact that a prominent citizen should thus disappear at mid-day, and no clew be had thereto; for no like event had transpired there before, and the people were jealous of the reputation of the place.

The traders with whom Wayne had last dealt at Centre Hebron were found, who gave an account of all that had happened up to the time of his parting from them on the day of his disappearance. They certified to his sobriety, and his usual correctness, having seen nothing about him indicating any mental disturbance. He had spoken of his family to them in the most pleasant manner, and had purchased several articles for his wife and children, that were found in the wagon on its return. Then suspicions, pointing in sundry directions, made the lives of several vagabonds in the vicinity uncomfortable; and some who were over-zealous made small scruple in stating their belief that So-and-so or So-and-so had a hand in it, as would eventually be found out. These were watched to see if they gave any evidence of possessing any more money than usual; but no signs were seen that denoted any change, and so suspicion banked its fires, but did not let them die out.

At length, when the zest of public feeling had worn off, some boys, at play in a distant wood by the side of a little pool, had found poor Wayne's coat that he had worn on the day of his disappearance, with its pockets unrifled of its money and papers, and still containing some trifling presents that he had purchased for his children at Centre Hebron. This was a vindication of those suspected; the spirit of search revived again; the pond was drained in expectation of finding the missing one; but all in vain. The secret was locked in the chamber of mysterious events, of which no one could find the key, and the excitement waned with nothing to feed it.

Mrs. Wayne and her two boys, George and Harry, — the former six and the latter four years old, — were objects of deep commiseration, and every aid was extended to them in settling the estate, which proved to be in a condition to place them beyond want. The boys were sent to school, and their mother, relinquishing all hope of hearing from her absent husband, settled down into a resigned state of widowhood. She was yet young, and very good looking, and, though she had loved Wayne very devotedly, her weeds soon grew tiresome. Her spirit was one that dwelt with the living more than with the dead; and when convinced that the dear departed had really gone, she listened to the blandishments of one more eloquent than the grave, and gave her hand to him for the sake of her children, who "needed a masculine hand to guide and correct them." Gossips condemned her for marrying again; but she knew best, of course. The care of the children decided it.

So time slipped by, and George Wayne was about as completely forgotten as though he had never existed. A new class succeeded him, and the world got along very well without him, as it will without us, when we, too, shall have passed on among the multitude that people the great Beyond. His children grew up to be industrious and worthy men, their father's name but a tradition to them; and their mother was again a widow, she having found, with her children, much more masculine guidance and direction than she had estimated when she married.

Of the two boys, Harry inherited his father's spirit, and became one of the best farmers in the country, showing by

27

his improvements and his sturdy crops what he knew about farming, supporting his mother, and proving by his public spirit that he was a worthy son of a worthy sire. Every one of those who could recall the father, though they were few, averred that Harry was like him as one pea is like another. George, like too many farmers' boys, took a distaste for the plodding life of the farm, and went to the city, where he embarked in trade with bright hopes of a fortune, with really but one chance in a thousand of its realization. Integrity and industry secured him friends, and his shrewdness and foresight won him position. He made money, and was on the high road to affluence at thirty.

Among his city friends was a family of elegant refinement by the name of Francis, the head of which, Solon Francis, Esq., had made his acquaintance in the walks of trade, and had invited him to his house through respect for his many virtues, introduced him to his family, and made him a welcome comer. He was quite good looking, very intelligent, could sing and play, was cheerful and happy, and the father's spirit of welcome became also that of the daughters, — three of them, — who looked upon him " as a brother." Ah, what a sweet illusion there is regarding this relation ! and, though "just like a brother" sounds perfectly rational and very harmless, there is too often a feeling mingling with the adopted relation that admits of a different, though not more tender, interpretation.

No one saw any danger, however; and the young people played, and sang, and laughed together, as happy and as unconcerned as birds. For months this continued, the old gentleman well pleased at their enjoyment. The mother of the young ladies, had she been alive, might have foreseen and told the danger; but she had been for some years dead. [I am sorry to introduce these mortuary episodes into a cheerful story, — first George Wayne, and then the mother of these charming girls, — but the exigency of the plot demands it. I have, however, done better than most tale-writers, who dismiss the mothers of their stories with but one pale-faced girl, to live in a state of uselessness, and make some spooney fellow "happy" in the future, for Mrs. Francis left three, and one son, who was a shipmaster, whom George Wayne had not seen.] She would have seen that all the charming Platonisms, which made the society of these young people so pleasant to each other, might one day harden into a sentiment more dangerous to their peace, which, if she could not thwart, she might control; but the singing, and playing, and laughing went on, all gliding along upon a summer tide, without a thought of danger beneath.

The names of the three Graces, which made George Wayne's life pass so blissfully, were Mary, Alice, and Jennie; but the introduction of all of them is merely a matter of courtesy, as my veracious story has to do with but one — Alice, the sweetest and most sparkling of them all. She was indeed a radiant creature, though to save my life I could not say whether her hair was "pale gold," which is flax color, or "tawny gold," which is copper color, or whether her eyes were like a pansy, or a tansy, or a violet, or her complexion like the bloom of an August peach in the sun, or a brunette, dusky, like the twilight. All I know about her is, that she was beautiful, vivacious, sensible; could converse, sing, play, and do housework; dressed in charming taste, and never broke her father's heart by any demand for extravagant trimmings, in which latter regard her daughters, in their day, follow her example. But I anticipate.

Dickens, commencing his story of the Cricket on the Hearth, says, "The kettle began it." I will not pretend to say on which side the "liking" began that settled the fate of George Wayne and Alice Francis; but by some means they soon found out that the "just like a brother" position was not tenable. Neither can I tell how it was discovered; but so it was, and the brotherly and sisterly delusion went down like unpopular stocks at the Brokers' Board. Why it was that Alice, and not all of the sisters, should fall in love with George, is another mystery, of which there are so many to bother one, and I refuse all further mention of them.

George's visits to the sisters soon had a different motive, and it was not disagreeable at all when the change came. Such of the facts as they had not guessed they got by inquiries from Alice; and she, not less communicative than the rest of her sex, had kept them posted regarding the progress of events. The father knew of it with much satisfaction, and George was installed in the family affections as the accredited lover of Miss Alice. He had also made his mother the recipient of the secret of his affections, so far as there was any secret about it, and she had breathed a blessing on the purposed union in eight long pages of note-paper. An interchange of visits had also taken place, and a mutual happiness was established that promised to be endless in duration. The wedding, however, was to be no hasty affair: eminent propriety forbade that: but it was an event for no very far distant day, as anybody reduced to half an eye could see. Congratulations were many, and the happy couple conceived themselves to be about the most favored of any since the primeval pair. The primeval pair had no period of courtship to endanger the union of the cup and the lip. They accepted the situation at once, and were true to it. There were no jealousies and heart-burnings to mar the peace of either; and so, maugre the trouble incurred because of that little episode about the apple, they lived happily on to the last. It is to be regretted that their example is not followed, in this respect, by their descendants.

It was in the midst of this heyday of blissful anticipation that one morning a carriage drove up to the door of the house, in which George Wayne was a partner, from which a gentleman and lady alighted, and were conducted to the counting-room, where sat the senior partner of the firm reading his newspaper. George saw, with a quick glance, as a playful breeze swept her veil aside, that she was very lovely, and though, just as she came in, he was thinking of selecting a pattern for a wedding coat, he wished heartily that he might be called in to consult with his senior on some matter, he cared not what, in order to get another glimpse of the beautiful stranger. Soon, much to his gratification, he heard his name called, and he obeyed the summons with alacrity.

"Wayne," said Mr. Simpson, of the firm of Simpson, Dodge & Co., "this is Miss Willison, daughter of our wine correspondent at Bordeaux — Mr. Wayne, Miss Willison; Mr. Clark, of Clark & Milton, Bordeaux, Mr. Wayne. Please be acquainted."

Wayne acknowledged the pleasure, and learned from the lady that she had been for some time in America, a guest of Mr. Clark, and was on the point of returning, when she heard the news of her father's illness, and had come to consult with the firm, of which he had long been a correspondent.

"Miss Willison," said Mr. Simpson, "represents her father, who, I am pained to hear, has been seized with a sudden illness, which renders his further attention to business impossible — a disease of the brain, and entire loss of memory. Some affairs, in which he was engaged at the

27*

time he was stricken, need adjusting: therefore it will be necessary for one who is competent to go on, and assume the charge of matters there until his recovery. Can you not go for a few months, and do this? — It will be very hard for him to go, I assure you, Miss Willison," — turning to her, — "for he has very strong ties to bind him here."

But Wayne at once, as Rebekah did when suddenly asked to go and be the wife of Isaac, said, "I'll go," and turned away, with a parting bow and smile to the visitors, to pack his trunk, and bid good by to Alice.

It was unfortunate that they could not have hurried things along a little, so that he could have taken Alice's trunks with his, and Alice, too; but the wedding was reserved for his return: and so, after a few days, he left, in the dangerous company of charming Miss Willison.

Dangerous, I mean, under the circumstances; for, though I firmly and fully believe that "the heart that once truly loves never forgets," still human nature is weak, and the heart may become etherized by passion, and all of human fealty be contravened in the heart's despite. Sea-sickness is a strong excitant of sympathy, and the charming Flo Willison — her name was Florinda Augusta, but there are no middle names in romance — was very sick, and George Wayne was not; so he sat by her, and soothed her, and dosed her with brandy and water, and carried her on deck, and acted anew the brotherly *rôle* he had lately assumed. "With the same result?" is asked. We shall see.

"Flo," as George had learned to call her already in the most brotherly way possible, was persistently sick, though the color returned to her cheeks and lips, and insisted on the attention that her invalid condition demanded; and at last, when she was able to eat a little something, he would go to the table, and select such delicacies as she liked, and they would eat them together in some quiet place, and desire no more society. All the young men on board, and, it must be confessed, many of the old ones, were eager to render service to the fair invalid; but she declined their attentions, as her "brother" was all that she desired. It was before the days of steamers, and the progress from New York to France was tedious; but to George and Flo it was like Juliet's "sweet sorrow" of the farewell, and they wished it might be extended, though Flo's sickness was of most alarming endurance.

I went to sea once with a captain who was seasick the first of every voyage, and who always laid in three gallons of gin as a remedy. I did not see that it did him any good, though he kept taking it till it was gone, and commenced his duties with the last dose, throwing the tin tumbler, from which he took it, at the steward's head, though I could not understand why.

Flo was sick every bit of the way across the ocean, but, on the principle of the captain's remedy, George's remedies were not exhausted, and so he kept on administering them, and she saw no necessity for getting well, and both regretted when the shores of France came in view, as they at last did.

George, when they left the ship, could not help admitting that the brotherly feeling for Flo was stronger than that which he had entertained for the sisters; but he supposed that it was owing to the fact of his having in that case to divide himself among three, while in this all was concentrated on one.

He rode with her in the carriage that bore her to her home in the suburbs of Bordeaux; but not wishing to interrupt the cordiality of meeting by the presence of a stranger, he bade her good by, with the promise of an immediate call, and gave her a chaste, brotherly kiss at parting, which she returned in a sisterly manner.

He drove to his hotel, thinking what a charming person she was, and was glad to think he had been instrumental in alleviating the pangs of her sea-sickness by his care.

He called upon her the next day, and found her equally charming. He saw her father, a perfect wreck of a man mentally, although his bodily health was good. He knew his daughter, but had no comprehension beyond the simplest facts. All business grasp was gone, and when she tried to introduce George as the companion of her voyage and her protector, he appeared to arouse at the mention of the name, rubbed his forehead thoughtfully, and then relapsed into indifference.

Flo was an only child, her mother having also, for the express benefit of my story, died when she was very young.

Wayne went immediately to work to adjust the business of the concern, but found affairs so complicated that months would be necessary to enable him to complete the work he had to do. In the mean time his correspondence with Alice had been prompt and glowing. But his letters, full of enthusiastic descriptions of his fair companion, did not elicit such cordial responses as he wished, and, greatly to his surprise, he found them growing colder with every mail. Strangely enough, he found himself making comparisons between Alice and Flo, with a large percentage in favor of the latter, and even questioned whether he had ever loved the former at all. His visits to Flo were frequent, and with every visit arose new doubts about the nature of the feeling towards Alice that had inspired him. The atmosphere of correspondence grew colder and colder, till it was almost icy, and then, without explanation, letters from Alice stopped coming altogether. Wayne thought himself a much injured man, but found a solace in the society of Flo that more than compensated him.

One night thereafter he and his fair patient were at the theatre, enjoying an opera, when he was attracted by a battery of lorgnettes aimed at him from a private box, and, turning his own glass in that direction, he encountered the stare of the whole Francis family, who indignantly repudiated him in the glance that they gave him. There was with them a tall, big-whiskered fellow, whom he did not like the appearance of, who made a motion as if to leave the box, but was held back by Alice, as though she would still show herself Wayne's good angel, maugre the hostility, if such it was, betwixt them. Before he could rightly decide how to act, the party had left the box, and, without explaining the motive that was evident in his conduct, he turned to admiring the opera with his fair companion, to whom he had never revealed the secret of his engagement —the ridiculous fellow!

He consulted the papers to learn the hotel where the Francis family were stopping, and went to find them ; but they had left for Germany. In the course of the day, however, as he was busied with his accounts, alone, a knock came upon the door, to which he responded, "Come in," when the same big-whiskered man of the theatre stood before him.

"Is your name George Wayne ?" he asked.

" It is."

"Then there is a card, which will tell you who I am, and you can guess the object of my visit. If you cannot, I will tell you."

The card bore the name of "Thomas Francis, New York."

"I suppose, by the card," said George, "that you must be Captain Francis, the brother of the Misses Francis, of New York, ladies for whom I entertain the profoundest affection and respect, one of whom, Miss Alice, was to have been my bride on my return."

"Yes," replied the captain, looking very savage; "and why isn't she to be your bride? Tell me that!"

"'Pon my honor," said George, "I know no earthly reason, except that she has stopped corresponding with me; and one would not wish to marry a person who is angry with him. Would you?"

"I don't know about that," said the captain; "but what do you mean, sir, by your infamous conduct in praising another in your letters to my sister? Is that the way you try to keep a young lady good-natured?"

"I certainly have," replied George, "praised a certain young lady passenger in the ship with me, who was sea-sick, and had no mother; but you know how it is yourself, and how natural attention at such a time would be. I would not have offended my dear Alice for any thing in the world; but as she has chosen silence as the bond of peace, I have nothing to say."

"But are you not going to marry her?" shouted the irate captain.

"I should not wish to do so against her will," said George; "but I stand ready to resume communications when the cable is fished up from the bottom of the ocean of doubt and jealousy, and re-united. Then, when I get a message from 'Heart's Content,' I shall know what to do."

The captain went out without another word, and Wayne resumed his figures. The captain did not put in another appearance; and in a short time George received a package containing all of his letters to Alice, and a note from Jennie regretting the disruption of the ties which they had all hoped were to last, and bidding him a sisterly farewell forever.

George dropped a tear or two upon the letter, with a real feeling of sadness at his heart, and went and made a confession of the whole matter to Flo, who shed sweet tears, and blamed him for not telling her before, which might have prevented her — Here she broke down, without explanation; but the meaning George guessed, for he clasped her in his arms, and was as much delighted as though she had spoken a whole chapter. In the midst of the scene, to the surprise of both, a door near them opened at this somewhat critical juncture, and her father stood before them, who, in a terrible voice, demanded to know what the scene he witnessed meant. That is what all enraged fathers say, as if they do not know very well what it means!

A great change had come over the old man. He stood before them in the strength of restored powers, his eyes clear and bright, with too much memory, if any thing, for the present comfort and peace of mind of those who stood before him.

"It means, sir," said George, taking Flo by the hand "that I love your daughter, and she has just avowed, by implication, a similar regard for me. We feel grateful, sir, that you have recovered, to consent to and bless our union."

"And what name does he bear who asks this?" replied Mr. Willison. "It is a modest request, truly, for a man to make whom I do not know!"

"True, I had forgotten, sir," said George, "that, though as the recent partner of Simpson, Dodge & Co., I was familiar with your name, you could not be with mine. My name, sir, is George Wayne."

The old man gave a start, as if electrified, and in a husky voice repeated the name. Seizing the young man by the arm, he turned him to the window, and gazed long and earnestly upon his features.

"Holy Heaven!" said he, smiting his forehead, while the tears poured from his eyes, "why was I waked to consciousness like this? And yet my returning saves us all from a great calamity. Flo, my child, leave — George Wayne" — speaking the name as if with difficulty — "with me."

She did as directed, casting a troubled look at George as she left the room, while he stood with all the active emotions visible on his face.

"You cannot marry her," said the old man, when they were alone.

"Why not?" asked George, in a tone of surprise, grief, and some vexation.

"Because," replied he, "she is your sister."

"It cannot be!" almost shrieked the lover, as he heard the words.

"Alas, it is too true, as I can convince you," said Mr. Willison — Willison no longer. "I, too, bear. or did bear, the name of George Wayne; but years ago I lost it, lost my identity, and, strange as it may seem, every thing by which I could know myself. In an oblivious state, I wandered away from home and friends, and awoke amid scenes that were new — to a new life. I did not know my name, the place I came from, the friends I had known, though I never forgot that I had a wife and children. These clung to me like a ray of sunlight in the gloom of a cavern; but I could get no clew to them. At last, in despair, I gave them up, hopeless of a re-union with them, married a worthy woman, the mother of Flo, and became Arthur Willison, correspondent of a respectable New York house, and made money, till the malady came that struck me down. I have had what seemed dreams of my early life — a misty memory of a ride in a blazing sun from a busy town to my own home, of being made partly unconscious, and leaving my cart in search of water in a wood, where all reason left me, until I came to myself here. I was told that I had shipped on a vessel at New York for this port; that I appeared in a state of bewilderment when asked to sign the shipping-papers, and made my mark, giving the name I bear. And now, tell me, is your mother yet alive?"

He watched eagerly for an answer.

"She is," replied George Wayne, the color of his hope all faded out, as it must necessarily have done, for did ever such a crushing weight obtrude itself upon "love's young dream" as a mutual father to interpose objections to the banns? Charles Reade, in his most artistic inspiration, I think, never conceived aught like this. I lead him here, though, in ordinary cases, he could give me eight points in ten, and beat me.

"Thank God for that!" said the old man; "and now, my son, show your manhood by endeavoring to overcome this hopeless passion, and give your mind to the re-union of your parents, and the reparation of past accidents, grateful for worse accidents just escaped."

George went to inform Flo, who received the announcement with astonishment, and some considerable regret that Fate had transformed a real nice lover into a very ordinary brother; but he consoled her, and kissed her tears away, as he had a right to do, and behaved so tenderly that Flo admitted that a brother was not so very much worse than a lover, after all.

Thus matters stood, when George wrote an urgent letter to his mother to come to France by the next packet, and, though it is very easy to state the fact, it took months for her to reach her destination. When she came, George carried her at once to Mr. Willison's residence, and told her she must not be surprised, though one came there as if from the dead to receive her. She looked on his face in great alarm, but his smile re-assured her.

"Suppose it should be father!"

"Oh, no; it can't be!" she said, wildly.

But the door was swung wide, and there stood the apparition of the former George Wayne, who came towards her with open arms, with the same look on his face, and she, simply murmuring, "My husband!" was enclosed in his embrace.

She had fainted, of course.

The morning journals announced the return from their travels of the Francis family, and to their hotel George Wayne went very early to propitiate the dark deities that at this time were brooding over both the houses. He found the captain in the reading-room, who received him, of course, very coolly; but upon his opening the discussion by an explanation of the new state of affairs, and lying a little about the new sister by suppressing the fact that he did not know she was such when he wrote about her, the captain was mollified, and he was sent aloft as an ambassador of peace, returning soon with an invitation to the prodigal to come up stairs, which he accepted; and there the inharmonies were adjusted, to the delight of all.

I might as well say here that George and Alice were married at the American consul's, and it was the greatest and grandest wedding celebrated in that city for many years, if I may except that of Captain Francis and Flo Willison soon after, which happened as a matter of course; anybody can see that it must have happened in such an atmosphere as surrounded them.

As soon as the business of his house was adjusted, which was now easily done with the help of the recovered George Wayne, all the parties returned to America, the old folks going by themselves to their first home, every scene of which was restored to the mind of the missing man. When they walked up the principal street of Elmwood, with Harry by their side, the astonishment of the people knew no bounds. The old hobbled out to receive their long-absent friend, while the young rushed in with wild curiosity. The bells were rung, and, when the people assembled on the village green, the old minister knelt down and devoutly thanked God, to which all responded AMEN.

MIGRATORY BONES,*

SHOWING THE VAGABONDISH TENDENCY OF BONES THAT ARE LOOSE.

WE all have heard of Dr. Redman,
The man in New York who deals with dead men,
    Who sits at a table,
    And straightway is able
To talk with the spirits of those who have fled, man !
    And gentles and ladies
    Located in Hades,
Through his miraculous mediation,
    Declare how they feel,
    And such things reveal
As suits their genius for impartation.
'Tis not with any irreverent spirit
I give the tale, or flout it, or jeer it;

---

* Dr. Redman, of New York, was a noted medium, and it was said that, for a while, wherever he might be, bones would be dropped all about him, to the confusion and wonder of everybody. These bones, he said, were brought him by a spirit, whose bones were of no further use to him.

For many good folk
Not subject to joke
Declare for the fact that they both see and hear it.
It comes from New York, though,
And it might be hard work, though,
To bring belief to any point near it.

Now this Dr. Redman,
Who deals with the dead men,
Once cut up a fellow whose spirit had fled, man,
Who (the fellow) perchance
Had indulged in that dance
Performed at the end of a hempen thread, man;
And the cut-up one,
(A son of a gun!)
Like Banquo, though he was dead, wasn't done,
Insisted in very positive tones
That he'd be ground to calcined manure,
Or any other evil endure,
Before he'd give up his right to his bones!
And then, through knocks, the resolute dead man
Gave his bones a bequest to Redman.
In Hartford, Conn.,
This matter was done,
And Redman the bones highly thought on,
When, changed to New York
Was the scene of his work,
In conjunction with Dr. Orton.

Now mark the wonder that here appears:
After a season of months and years,
Comes up again the dead man,
Who, in a very practical way,
Says he'll bring his bones some day,

And give them again to Redman.
When, sure enough
(Though some that are rough
Might call the narrative "devilish tough "),
One charming day
In the month of May,
As Orton and Redman walked the street
Through the severing air,
From they knew not where,
Came a positive bone, all bleached and bare,
That dropped at the doctor's wondering feet!

Then the sprightly dead man
Knocked out to Redman
The plan that lay in his ghostly head, man:
He'd carry the freight,
Unheeding its weight;
They needn't question how, or about it;
But they might be sure
The bones he'd procure,
And not make any great bones about it.
From that he made it a special point
Each day for their larder to furnish a joint!

From overhead, and from all around,
Upon the floor, and upon the ground,
Pell-mell,
Down fell
Low bones, and high bones,
Jaw bones, and thigh bones,
Until the doctors, beneath their power,
Ducked like ducks in a thunder-shower!
Armfuls of bones,
Bagfuls of bones,

28*

        Cartloads of bones,
        No end to the multitudinous bones,
Until, forsooth, this thought gained head, man,
That this invisible friend, the dead man,
        Had chartered a band
        From the shadowy land,
        Who had turned to work with a busy hand,
And boned all their bones for Dr. Redman!

Now, how to account for all the mystery
Of this same weird and fantastical history?
        That is the question
        For people's digestion,
And calls aloud for instant untwistery!
        Of this we are certain,
        By this lift of the curtain,
That still they're alive for work or enjoyment,
        Though I must confess
        That I scarcely can guess
Why they don't choose some useful employment.

A NEW YEAR'S REVERY.

Don't talk to me of waste-baskets for old letters;
even the insidious plea of eight cents per pound paid for
paper stock moves me not; they must be burned. As the
old Romans burned their dead, and preserved their ashes
in urns, cherishing them with religious reverence and affection, so old letters, embodying loves, and fears, and experiences, should be thus served, nor be allowed to pass to
baser uses. They have done their parts as ministers to

our pleasure or knowledge, and are deserving of the consecration of fire and preservation from ignoble purposes. There is a measure of pain in the consignment to ashes of that which has been a part of one's self, which has sounded the various chords of feeling, and drawn out by its subtile power the melody (or the discord) of our being — some of it that the world has not heard, which has but silently breathed and exhaled to harmonize with the music of the spheres. Letters, unless upon matters pertaining to history, or science, or the general welfare in other forms, should always be burned. Private joys and sorrows, that form the subject matter of ordinary letter-writing, should not be transmitted for the gratification of curious eyes, subject to invidious construction or the remark of the indifferent. They belong to me, and me alone, and they shall follow me, or lead me, to the bourne towards which we both tend.

I take from the receptacle where they have lain these many years the old soiled bundles, yellow with time, and the accretive dust, the hint of their own decay, gathered upon them. Here they are before me, pile upon pile, an incongruous collection, their contents long since forgotten, their writers dead or estranged, — which is worse, — or scattered to the ends of the earth. The old have passed away, the young become old, and mayhap all this living record of mind, that was, has not a recollection living in the breast of any. Yet here the thoughts, and hopes, and fears remain, and ere I consign them to the pyre, I will once again peruse them, and refresh my memory regarding their contents.

It is a befitting task for the close of a year, at a time when more serious reflections are awakened and retrospection finds exercise. Then the old forms come back to us, and the old scenes revive with wonderful vividness, needing but the voices of the past to give them vitality. In these soiled packages are the voices, still as eloquent with the thought that then filled them as the day they were written.

Here is one from Dartmouth College — scholarly, and imbued with the young ambition that was going to open the world like an oyster, and compel it to shell out. The writer is now an editor, the oyster but moderately seen in his life's results, but the old-time hope still remains, and the warm feeling displayed in his friendship still exists, revealed in a thousand domestic virtues and a geniality of life that renders him beloved. . . . This is a badly-spelled remembrance of a kind-hearted schoolmate in the Granite State, whose ideas of taste would hardly find echo in the modern saloons, but whose profanity would have done credit to to-day's greater experience. He was killed by a whale, it is supposed, up by the North Pole, and nothing but a spiritual communication, that spelled his name wrong, — the best proof in the world of his identity, — was heard from him afterwards. . . . This is from a pious adviser of my youth, long gone to his reward, counselling me to avoid the many temptations to be met with in the modern Babylon, as he regarded the Boston of that day — (what would he have said of this?) — and requesting me to send him, by stage, a pound of tobacco of a particular brand, the value of which he would remit, which he never did. . . . This is one of deeper interest, brimming with the fulness of a sister's love — unselfish, devoted, faithful. How pure such love seems, as we wake from our dream of passion and sin and hear its voice, speaking to us this time from the open heavens that bend as if beckoning our attention towards that sphere where such love alone is known, to be found " when corruption shall have put on incorruption," and the uses of passion, — the severest trial of love, — shall have been forgotten in the higher and brighter walks of the spiritual life! Burn, burn! the altar of sacrifice is greedy for the treasure that I fling upon it.

This soiled and crumpled paper recalls an incident of my early experience. Long ago I received this missive, directed in trembling and indecisive characters, requesting my aid in a very urgent matter. It gave an inkling of, what I fully guessed, one of those incidents in life that too often happen, which sink manhood and womanhood so low that we turn in disgust from contemplating them even while we stretch out our hands to save. My little playmate Mary, the letter told me, the widowed mother's youngest and fairest child, had been "lured by a villain from her native home," and was now, it was feared, in Boston. I subsequently learned that a young scamp from the metropolis had, during a month's sojourn in the vicinity of her home, won the affection of the too susceptible girl, and that, yielding to him, she had left her almost heart-broken mother, who, in this crumpled and faded letter, is again entreating me, by old companionship and old love, to save her dove from the hands of the spoiler.

Never did knight of old enter upon chivalric devoir with more enthusiasm than I did to find the whereabouts of the runaway. I walked through every street, scrutinized every carriage that passed by me, looked in at every window, attended upon all exhibitions that would excite female curiosity; but no clew could I obtain of the object of my search. My mission led me into some equivocal localities, subjecting me to many invidious shrugs and comments. Once or twice I was addressed by females of character far from snow-like, to whom I freely told my errand, and from whom I received an encouraging and even a kind word, leading me to look with different eyes upon a class so lowly sunk, but who yet retained enough of the divine to think with pity on a mother's grief and entertain a desire to save her daughter from a life of shame. Grave people shook their heads to see me in dangerous vicinities, which they knew better than I did; and some even went so far as to advise with me in the matter, repeating to me Solomon's words about the strange woman, whose steps take hold on the regions of darkness, and of the dart that pierces the liver. When I spoke to them, however, of the matter on which I was bent, they coolly told me that such a subterfuge was unworthy so well-seeming a young man, and turned away as if they were afraid I should prove that I was honest. This was a lesson I learned very early: That it is not alone to those who make the loudest professions we must look for genuine good; that even the poor outlawed girl may have more of the leaven of sympathy and love in her deeper nature than those who practise external righteousness to the last syllable of the mint and cumin, but who are sadly wanting in the weightier matter of the law. Poor, outcast, degraded, wretched, trodden under feet of men,—how much brighter this sweet flame of charity seems to glow when we see it kindle amid such surroundings! I went into obscure courts, and eyed all the windows with pertinacious impudence, as it must have appeared to the inmates, hoping to catch a glimpse of Mary. Sometimes. as my too bold glance compelled a hasty retreat of some fair one from a window, I would fancy that it must be she, and waited to see the face appear again, almost despairing with each disappointment.

The facilities for inquiry were not then as now, when the police system. like Argus, presents a hundred eyes through which to look. I enlisted the town police in the matter, and after a month's time, learned that one answering my description was living in a little cottage in Cambridge.

This intimation gave me great joy, and I resolved to go at once to see her, and entreat her to go back to the home she had left. Armed with this resolution, I went to Cambridge, and found the house described. Up to this moment I had formed no definite plan of operation. I knew nothing of the condition in which she was living, if found, beyond the mere suspicion of the moment — for which there were probabilities strong enough, but by no means proofs. I could make no charges, and my entreaties might be taken as insults, securing me a rapid passage to the door, and a swift ejectment through it. As I stood hesitating, a young man passed out of the house. He was just such a one as I should have selected for the person described, dressed according to the most tasteful fashion of the time, and wearing about him all the appearances of a scape-grace. He gave me a passing glance, without suspecting my errand, and vanished round the first corner.

Left to myself, and hesitating what to do, I was relieved by a voice uttering my name. I pretended some surprise, and went to the door, which was opened to me by Mary herself. She was as pretty as ever; but I fancied there was an expression of care on her face; though she gladly welcomed me, and smiled upon me with her early brightness.

"I am *so* glad to see you!" she said, shaking my hand; "and it is such a queer thing your finding me, — or rather my finding you, because I did!"

I assured her I was delighted to see her, spoke of the long time since we had met, and alluded to our former intimacy.

"And Mary," said I, "what a delightful home you have here! It realizes the old-time ideal of love in a cottage, with honeysuckled windows and all the romantic incident of young affection. I didn't hear of your marriage. He

is a fortunate man who has such a fairy to bless his bower.
I was in hopes, once, Mary, that I should share my fate
with you; but it was only a dream, and you are happy
with another. Well, be it so — that you are happy is
enough for me. Who is your husband?"

I looked in her face, and saw she was as pale as death,
though she tried to smile, as a rose strives to bloom with
the canker eating at its heart.

"What is the matter, Mary?" said I; "are you ill?"

"No, no," she replied, "not ill; but a chill came over
me, and "— She burst into tears.

"Dear Mary," I exclaimed, "something has happened
to you. Are you not happy? Does — does — he not treat
you kindly?"

"Yes, yes," said she, with a painful effort to look cheerful. "Oh! I am very happy, and — he — he couldn't treat
me better. See here; I have every thing to content me.
Here is my music, here my books, here my work."

"Yes," replied I, with a sublime attempt at Mentorship,
"every thing but one — peace of mind."

She placed her hand on her heart, as though I had
planted a dagger there, and almost screamed, as she exclaimed, —

"True, true, and without that all the rest is hideous;
but how did you suspect this?"

I told her that I had read it in her looks.

"Do my features indeed reveal this?" said she, sadly, and
going to a glass. "Has the poison done its work so soon?"

"Poison!" I exclaimed.

"No, no; what am I talking about?" she cried; "I am
wild to rave thus, and treat you so badly, who are my old
schoolmate and friend, — for you are my friend, and I have
few friends now. And now tell me every thing about —
about our *old* friends, you know. How long it is since I
have heard from them!"

She was now all attention, and I proceeded to recount the many things that had transpired since she left, speaking incidentally of her mother, and noting its effect upon her. She looked down and sighed, but asked no questions on those points that I saw she thought the most of. The scene was mutually painful — on my part to withhold my knowledge of her secret; on hers to keep me from knowing it. I parted from her without intimating that I knew aught about her, or that our meeting had been other than accidental, reserving my errand till the next time we should meet.

I resolved that but little time should elapse before this, and in about a week I went again, and was received with the same kindness. There was a deeper shadow on her brow, as I plainly saw; but her lips discoursed lightly, and a pleasant laugh frequently rippled upon the wave of our conversation. At last I spoke.

"Mary, I have heard from your mother since I was here last."

"The start that she gave, and the look that she turned on me! — saying, in an almost inaudible tone, —

"Have you?"

"Yes," I replied; "and she wants you to come home. She is very sad that you left her; your absence breaks her heart."

She saw that I knew all. Folding her face in her hands, she poured forth a torrent of self-crimination, regretting the misery she had inflicted, but not, through it all, implicating the one who had led her into trouble, ending by saying that she could never go home again. There was bitter sadness in the tone in which this was said; but when I attempted expostulation she repeated her words with more emphasis, thanking me for my effort in her behalf, and sending by me a blessing for her mother, whom she

29

did not dare to write to. I left her in a very sad frame of mind. A few days after I called again, but the bird had flown; the shutters were put up at the windows, and a placard, "To Let," was nailed on to the door. I immediately wrote to her mother of my discovery and disappointment; and though I had still my eyes open to see her, if possible, I hardly dared hope for it, deeming that she had been placed beyond the chance of my again troubling her.

Three years passed away, and the memory of Mary had become overwhelmed by the wave of passing events. I had received no tidings of her, and supposed she might have gone down beneath the tide, as so many had done, and left no trace by which to ascertain her fate. Passing along Washington Street hastily, one day, I saw a face that came across the disk of my vision like the memory of a painful dream — vague, ill-defined, with nothing tangible by which to locate or identify it.

I could not, for the life of me, recall the time or place where I had seen it, but it was a face that, once seen, was not to be forgotten. It was handsome, proud almost to insolence, and bore upon it a certain stamp of breeding that will always reveal itself. I turned to look upon it, but it had been swallowed up by the crowd, and blaming my treacherous memory, I gave it up as hopeless.

There was an exhibition of paintings at the old Athenæum in Pearl Street about this time. It was unusually fine, and comprised the works of many of the best native and foreign artists. Sauntering along and leisurely examining the collection, I at last stood before a portrait that I thought I recognized. Looking at the catalogue, I found it bore the simple title, "Portrait of a Gentleman." I tried to connect it with something outside — some incident or scene — but could not. Passing along, in the painful struggle to recollect, I was attracted by Duverne's great work, " Mary and the Master," when, like a flash of light, it came over me that the face which puzzled me was his that I had seen leave the cottage in Cambridge, three years before. I involuntarily said, " Mary."

I have lived long enough to discriminate between appointment and accident, as any one must who sees the wonderful phenomena imputed to accident take their part in the formation of fortune or character, or the coincidentals that astonish us by their frequency. Thus the simple name, " Mary," at this moment, breathed upon my memory the retrocast of years, and endowed it with form, and peopled it. I was almost startled by the suddenness and vividness of the recollection, when a hearty voice at my side said, —

" A fine picture, sir."

I turned to the speaker, and saw an elderly gentleman with his hand rolled up and held to his eye, looking through it earnestly at the painting. I saw that he had addressed me, and assented to the proposition that it was a fine painting.

" But who is Duverne ? " said he.

I assured him that I had never before heard of him, and indeed have never again heard of him to this day. After a few brief exchanges on art and artists, I related to him the reason of my ejaculation of the name that had attracted his attention, and asked him to look at the portrait that had provoked my curiosity.

" That ! " said he, in some surprise ; " that is my nephew, sir ; I may almost say my son, for he will possess what little I may have left when I pass from the stage. A well-looking young man, sir."

I assented very readily, as he really was, in appearance, all that could be wished.

"Is he married?" I inquired.

"Married!" he replied, almost angrily; "no, the dog, and that is what troubles me. If he would only marry and settle down into a steady-going citizen, I should feel some hope of him, and be better assured of his future happiness. He is a little wild, you know — the fault, as some deem it, of young people, though I am not a stickler for entire propriety at twenty-five. At any rate I can forgive a good deal in one at that age."

"Have you urged him to marry?" I asked, holding the great secret in my heart which made me bold.

"Certainly I have," he replied, shaking his cane threateningly, but fondly, at the picture; "certainly I have, but he pertinaciously laughs me to silence when I propose it; and I have such a match for him! — wealth and beauty, sir, waiting but the motion to fall into his arms. You know it is true, you rogue, you," said he, addressing the picture.

"Does he not love some one else, sir?" I ventured, but instantly saw that I had touched a tender point.

"He dare not," said the old gentleman, turning very red; "he dare not; for should he venture to bestow his affection where I did not wish him to, I would cut him off, sir, from all forgiveness, and not one of my dollars should he ever touch."

"Still human nature is weak," I urged; "and human love capricious; it will go where it is sent, like the measles. I know of no immunity that any of us possess."

"Nonsense!" he replied.

"He might do worse, even, than love without your consent," I said.

"How?" he asked.

I then drew for him a fancy picture of a young man who perhaps would do as I presumed he had done, telling Mary's story minutely as I had learned it, coloring it with the skill of an artist, and putting the color lavishly on the effective points. He listened very attentively, and sensibly assented to my proposition that this were worse than the crime of loving without his assent.

"This were an atrocity," said he, "that I would never overlook. I would disown him were he my son ten times over. But my boy is incapable of any thing of this kind. I have heard rumors of his indiscretion, but he has disavowed them to me, when accused of them, and I know him too well to doubt him. Besides, years and travel have tempered his youth, and the period of danger is passed. He has for three years been in Europe."

This accounted for my not having seen him. I thought I would here run the risk of speaking the thought that was in my mind.

"And yet," said I, very seriously, "I bring, here in the presence of his effigy, and of the affection that would shield him, the charge of having committed the very crime depicted in my sketch."

The old man almost shouted, "It can't be true."

"It is true, sir," I said; and proceeded to tell him my discovery of the cottage at Cambridge, the face momentarily seen and remembered, the recognition of it in the street, and the final identification of it in the gallery through the mnemotechnic hint of the associated "Mary." He listened attentively, and assured me he would sift the affair to the bottom. He wished me to be present at the interview with his nephew, and as the young man did not know me, he proposed that I should attend in the capacity of lawyer, to draw up some pretended marriage contract which he was going to insist upon having executed. Handing me his card in exchange for mine, the old gentleman left the gallery.

The time came sooner than I expected; for the next

day a note was brought me requesting my attendance
that evening in Blank Street — a street then "respectable,"
but now given over to desecrating uses, where washing is
done in consecrated halls, and tobacco and gingerbread
present temptation for old and young, from windows, then
rich with aristocratic hangings, now hung with onions.
Punctual to the time named, I presented myself, and was
at once ushered into a spacious and elegant parlor, in which
were my old friend and the original of the picture in the
Athenæum.   I was introduced as Mr. Trevor, and was
received with a seeming of shy reserve that promised little
for an extended acquaintance.

"I have sent for you, Mr. Trevor," said the old gentleman, "on a matter which concerns me and my nephew
very closely, though I have said nothing to him of my in-
tentions.   I have set my heart upon his marrying a lady,
young, rich, beautiful, and accomplished.   The act would
establish him for life in competency.   Many times I have
expressed my wish to see this, and as many times have
been denied; therefore I call upon you to prepare such
papers as may be necessary to secure the object."

I looked at the young man.   His face was deathly pale.
His lips were compressed, as though he were struggling to
repress the spirit of resistance that filled him.

"Uncle," said he, "I had hoped that this matter was
settled forever, and have, as you say, repeatedly declined
this union.   The lady is all you claim for her, but I never
can love her as a man should love a woman to marry her,
and I must again beg you to give up the hope you have
clung to.   Command me in any thing but that, and I will
obey you."

The old gentleman looked at him fiercely as he spoke,
and I saw the cloud gathering that suddenly burst upon
the victim.

"Suppose," replied he, "that I should tell you to give me an account of the last three years of your life, with all its duplicity and wickedness, counting in a broken-hearted mother's tears, a daughter's shame, a home deserted, and despair installed where peace had prevailed. Suppose I should demand this of you?"

"And if you should demand it," said the young man, proudly, "I should answer that the record would appear better than you believe, however much it might count against me in your esteem. The record is painful to me in some of its features, because of their concealment from you; but in the eye of conscience I am acquitted. The wrong I have done has proceeded from yourself. Dependent upon you, and knowing your feeling regarding my marriage, I had the fortune to fall in love with one in all ways deserving of it, but poor. In the fervency of young affection that saw only its own gratification, I induced her to leave her mother's house, under a promise of marriage, which promise was faithfully redeemed. I married her under a vow of secrecy, — fearing your anger, — and retiracy became necessary; and for years has the nest been hidden that holds my bird. She has suffered untold anguish from the concealment, bore shame and reproach for my sake; but from this hour she shall be free."

The vindication of Mary's honor gave me great happiness, and I saw that her confusion in the cottage might well have sprung from the embarrassment of her new position, self-exiled from home, giving up all ties for the new affection, which I was glad to learn had not been misplaced.

The old gentleman was livid with rage.

"This to me!" said he. "*I* the cause of *your* wrong doing! You have made your bed, and you must lie in it, though it prove of thorns. Leave me, sir; I wish to see you no more."

The young man went out sorrowfully. My feeling had changed to admiration for his honorable conduct, and following him to the door, I begged his address, that I might, if possible, reconcile the parties, requesting him to keep his secret until he heard from me. He gave me his address at once: "George Ulm, Hazel Street, Malden." Malden was at this time one of the inaccessible places. Isolated by toll-bridges, nothing but necessity ever brought its denizens in contact with city life, and one might well be considered secluded who took up a residence there!

As soon as he was gone I commenced the task of reconciliation, which I knew I could achieve. I pointed out the susceptibility of the young, the attractiveness of the object, the consciousness of dependence, the hope of favorable results, and more particularly I dwelt upon the honor of the young man through it all, so in keeping with the sentiment advanced by the old gentlemen himself at our first interview. My plea was effectual, and the old man relented. I asked his permission to manage a little surprise that I had a plot for, and *carte blanche* privilege was allowed me. I wrote immediately to Mary's mother, giving her the joyful news of her daughter's recovery, and the more joyful news of her vindicated fame, and requested her attendance in Boston by the next stage. She came immediately, and by the old gentleman's request, who entered with an excellent spirit into the business, made her home at his house.

Things were ripe for the dénoûment, and it was now the eve of New Year's Day. I prepared a note, written very hastily, thus: —

Mr. George Ulm.

Dear Sir: If you wish to see your uncle alive, come by the coach immediately, and bring your wife with you. Haste.

Yours truly,   A. Trevor.

Boston, December 31.

I gave the note to a careful driver with directions where to deliver it, and in about three hours, I heard a carriage drive up to the door, and hasty feet ascending the steps. The shutters had been closed, so that no light came through the windows, and the house looked dark from the outside. The parlor door was thrown open by a familiar hand, and a blaze of light burst upon George Ulm and Mary his wife, as they stood in the presence of the mollified uncle, the fond mother, and the diplomatic friend — meaning myself. Mary threw herself into her mother's arms, and begged her forgiveness, and George, after a moment's hesitation, stepped forward, and grasped his uncle's extended hand, saying, —

"Why, what means this? I was told to come if I wished to see you alive."

"Well, you didn't want to see me dead — did you?" said he; "and now where is the witch that has wrought this enchantment?"

"Here she is, uncle;" and, leading Mary before him, they both knelt at his feet.

"Get up, you deluders," said he, "and don't unman me. Preserve your homage for the King that holds our destiny in his hand, adjusting the balance by his will — whose great law is the law of love — eh, Trevor?"

It was the happiest scene I ever looked upon. It was a history I had helped make, of which I was glad. Mary afterwards confessed to me the misery she felt when I visited her in Cambridge — would have given the world to tell me all, but was restrained by her vow. Suffering rather than divulge a secret — a noble instance of reticence in a woman.

MY FAMILY.

BY PAUL SMUDGE, M. G. S.

I don't blame any one, who can boast of good blood, for occasionally alluding to it. I respect blood; it tells in the long run, though I do not think that a man who cannot boast of blood has any cause to despair. A man's blood becomes purified and ennobled by his aspirations, and a succession of good deeds will purify the blood, while a life of meanness will soon vitiate the finest toned fluid that ever coursed through blue veins. I never, to confess the honest truth, thought much about blood or family till I lived in the city of B——, in the year 18—, when a Genealogical Society was formed, and by some curious accident, I was elected a member. I never authorized any one to propose me for such an honor; I never asked who thrust the honor upon me; but I paid my admission fee, and assumed the responsibilities without attending the meetings.

The fact that I was a member of a Genealogical Society made an impression, and occasionally, when I shaved myself, I complimented the gentleman in the glass upon the important position he held. When I entered a crowded car and noticed no movement made to give me a place, I excused a lack of courtesy to a distinguished man on account of their ignorance of the position which I held; and once, when applying for a choice seat at the theatre, when there was a tremendous rush, I obtained precedence over other applicants, as I always supposed, by adding to my name the initials of M. G. S. But these emoluments of my position soon passed away, and my conscience began to intimate to me that I was rather unworthy of the honor I enjoyed. The inward monitor opened its port-holes and I felt pierced with a desire to do something which should make me indeed a valued member of society. I thought the matter over very seriously; and as I was putting on the member's boots one morning, the exertion started the perspiration, and at the same time an idea. The idea enlarged as I drew on the member's pants, it revolved itself into shape as I buttoned his suspenders, and when I had tied his cravat, the idea had become a part of my being. I resolved to prepare a Genealogical Tree of the Smudge family.

This was my resolution; but how to proceed was the question. I knew I had a father and mother, and a grandfather, perhaps two, though I could not remember — having left the family roof at an early age — any particular allusion to my paternal grandfather. The tree grew in my brain for at least three days, and having become finally rooted there, I was obliged to give it attention, or it might have proved injurious to my mental faculties. Uncertain whether to commence at the top branches and run the tree into the ground, or to start at the root and ascend skyward, I was forced to take advice; and in doing so I was told that in Shirley a family by the name of Smudge had long resided, who were reputed to have a vast amount of information in regard to the original stock. The key was thus obtained to my great work, and I resolved to trace back the race of Smudge till I reached the first one of that name. I therefore wrote to the town clerk of Shirley, asking for the address of the leading member of the Smudge family in that place. I waited for a reply. I waited two days — a week — a fortnight — a month, without evidence that the town clerk of Shirley was possessed of vitality. I wrote again, and the return mail brought me this reply : —

"When you address a town clerk, or any other man, on business of personal interest to you alone, you had better enclose postage stamps, for all mail matter must be pre-paid.   Yours, respectfully,

"P. SMUDGE."

This was tart, but I saw by the signature I had waked up one member of the family. I at once addressed him a very friendly epistle, and enclosed him a sheet of postage stamps, intimating to him that our correspondence might be frequent. In a day or two I received a very brief note from him, stating that he did not know who the leading member of the Smudge family was. One was a town pauper, two had long since lost all claims to respectability by their love of the ardent, and he added, " I am the only tax-payer by that name in this town, and hold the position of town clerk ; if you wish any more information I can copy from the records all that can be found concerning the family, for which I shall charge twenty-five dollars." I concluded to amputate the Shirley branch of the Genealogical Tree.

This dash of cold water rather retarded the growth of the tree for a month or more; but the idea of being an un-worthy member of the G. S. again stimulated me, and see-ing in the Coos County Republican that A. Smudge was a dealer in groceries, I addressed him a letter, stating my intention and soliciting his interest in the tree. I enclosed postage stamps. His reply came in due course of time. It was to the point, and read as follows : —

"Yours came to hand all right, but I haven't got time to bother my brain about my ancestors. It takes all my time to feed six hungry little Smudges. It is a pity you have such a quantity of idle time on your hands. You had better study to make yourself useful. Be virtuous and you will be happy. When your tree sprouts in our direction, let me know."

I called that impertinent. But was I to be discouraged? No. I remembered what Mr. What's-his-name said to Thing-embob about the impossibility of finding the word FAIL in his dictionary, and without replying to his interrogatories, I waited for more light, resolved to give the tree a fair start at the first favorable opportunity. I bethought me of the Press, and published, as a "feeler," a paragraph in my favorite paper to the effect that Paul Smudge, Esq., M. G. S., was about to trace back his lineage with the view to a general meeting of the Smudge family at some not far distant day, hoping that his fellow-citizens would sympathize with him in his commendable undertaking, and concluding, in the editor's own language, with the remark that the name of Smudge had become especially endeared to the community, in which it had got to be a household word, associated with many deeds of worth and usefulness. The compliment was agreeable, although I found some short time thereafter that he had charged me half a dollar a line for it, which I paid without a murmur. The result of the notice was, that letters began to come to me from all directions from individuals named Smudge, or those who had, by the accident of marriage, inherited any of its blood; so many indeed, that I had to hire a lock box in the post-office, which was not large enough to hold them. It was curious, too, how many laid claim to connection with the family on very small premises. There were the Smuggs of Boneboro', and the Smutches of Coalville, and the Smudgits of Hayfield, and the Smooges of Frog Meadow, and Heaven knows what; and all sorts
30

of questions were asked of me, pertinent and impertinent, concerning my family history: Had I a female cousin that married a Wiggin? did my grandmother by my mother's side have three or five husbands? was my great uncle hanged in Wales? and if I had not a cousin in the battle of Slievegamon? I answered them all, of course. A man came in one day, as I was waiting on a customer, and requested the loan of a few shillings on the ground that he was one of my family, and gave his card to assure me of the fact, which read "S. Mudge." I dismissed him, you may be assured, very summarily. I was annoyed for a while by the boys, who used to twit each other, within my hearing as I passed them, with having no family. But I was determined that my genealogical research should not be retarded by coarse and unappreciative remark.

One result of my newspaper notice was a long and bulky letter which I received from the venerable Professor Smudge, of Mung Institute, Vermont, who in many pages labored to give me light in my family research, but which left me in gross darkness at the end. He had traced the origin of the family as far back as the days of Abraham, and thought that I might, by proper application, extend it still farther, saying, however, that he thought it useless, as probably none of the original Smudges would be present at the contemplated gathering.

I answered this, delighted at having found one of kindred taste in genealogical matters, and our correspondence grew voluminous. So proud was I of my distinguished kinsman, that I resolved to attend the society meetings, and read one of his letters before it. I signified my intention at the next regular meeting, to the wonder of many members as to who I was. I made great preparations to do it and myself justice. I read it aloud to my wife several times, and she by frequent nods assented to the points made, though in some instances I fancied she grew somnolent; but, being a woman of many cares, I forgave the inattention. I forgave her the more readily because the calls upon my exchequer for postage had interfered materially with her supplies, at which she had never complained. (I must publish here, however, a qualification to the statement, that a woman failed to complain under such circumstances, the fact that, finding her supplies curtailed, she went very quietly and got trusted for what she wanted, leaving me thereafter to be surprised with many bills.) The eventful moment came, when I was to make my debut, — my first appearance upon any stage — before the august society. My friend, the Rev. Mr. Blow, had told me that to still the beating of my heart, which I found very turbulent, I must draw a long breath, and hold on a little before taking another. He explained the philosophy of it satisfactorily at the time, but though I tried it I couldn't still the tumult within. As I passed up the narrow stairs leading to the hall where the *savants* were assembled, before whom I was to speak, my knees smote together, and I was so weak that any one could have knocked me down with a slung shot. I entered the room, however, with some show of importance, not expecting applause, of course, but some little curious attention, and was surprised to find only the janitor present, and a venerable gentlemen with an ear-trumpet, who brought it round to me as though he expected I was going to put something into it. The janitor introduced me, loudly, —

"Mr. Smudge, this is the distinguished Dr. Grubb; Dr. Grubb, this is Mr. Smudge."

"Mr. Fudge," said the distinguished gentleman, "I am glad to see you."

"Smudge, sir," I corrected him.

"What?" he said, bringing the trumpet up under my nose.

"Smudge!" I yelled, in a tone that made the old gentleman start.

"Ah, yes," said he; and commenced turning over the leaves of a copious manuscript before him.

Where was the crowd I had expected? By and by they began to come in,— a few fussy-looking old men,— and then the president, looking very red, bustled in, about an hour behind time, took his seat, and rapped smartly on the table with his hammer.

"The first business before us," said he, "is the paper from Dr. Grubb, upon the probable origin, rise, and fall of the Simia race in Newfoundland."

Dr. Grubb shuffled together his papers, and commenced to bore, continuing the process through a two hours' effort, which nobody heard, the audience indulging in unrestricted conversation, in contempt of the trumpet which lay upon the table. At its close, one who had talked the loudest during its delivery made a motion that the venerable doctor be requested to have it published in some newspaper that might be induced to accept it, which was carried; and the president called upon me by name— "Paul Smudge, Esq."

The members raised their eyes as I stood upon my feet, and with assumed unconcern, proceeded to unfold the manuscript of my respected relative.

"Mr. President," said a member, rising, "Mr. Spudge will excuse me for interrupting him; but, as the hour is late, I will make a motion that the paper about to be submitted to us be read by its title."

He smiled amiably upon me as he spoke, and for the life of me I could not blame him after the infliction of Grubb's. The president looked at me inquiringly; I nodded, and smiled back. The motion was put and carried, and I read as follows:—

"Some Particulars of the Family of Smudge, by Dionysius Smudge, LL.D., Professor of Ethnology and the Learned Sciences in Mung Institute, Vermont."

The meeting adjourned; family pride succumbed to circumstances, and I went home, to be questioned by Mrs. Smudge, and dream of a genealogical tree as large as those big trees in California. The next morning, taking up my paper, I was surprised to see an account of the doings of the society the evening previous. "Large and enthusiastic," "highly respectable," "learned and refined," . . . "among whom our neighbor Smudge, whose modesty has too long kept him in the background, was conspicuous, who read an eloquent and able paper upon the ancient family he represents, which sparkled with wit, that gracefully embellished the sound philosophy and profound research of the production, the fine delivery of which elicited unbounded applause. Among those most delighted was the venerable Dr. Grubb, who waived the reading of an interesting paper of his own to accommodate his young friend."

Could I be dreaming? and did I really "speak my piece?" were questions I asked myself; but the editor was a truthful man, and would not deceive the world; therefore I let the world believe it. I received many compliments on my success, and the same week had twenty invitations to address kindred societies in different parts of the country, which I declined.

My family ambition increased. I nearly gave up business in order to answer my letters. I relinquished all interest in the great family of the world to look after my individual portion of it. On my return home one evening, after a hard day's work, I found Mrs. Smudge in a state of undue excitement. At first I could not tell whether she were most disposed to laugh or cry. There was no anger in her look, but it seemed as if mortification were struggling with merriment in her mind. She pointed to my reception-room. As I entered it, my eyes rested upon a most singular figure. It was that of a man of sixty, in a dress that dated at least forty years back — short-waisted coat, high collar, long skirts, puckered shoulders, brass buttons; long red vest, with glass buttons, single-breasted; pants tight, terminating just below the calf, gathered on the hips; blue woollen stockings; large, peaked-toed shoes. He held a hat in his hand, very tall, approaching the steeple-shape, very seedy, with evident marks of ink, put on to hide the brown spots.

"Good evening, sir," the figure said, smiling, and extending a large and bony hand to me, which I took instinctively. "You may not," he continued, "guess who I am that thus intrudes upon you; but I am your relative, of Mung Institute."

"The deuse you are!" thought I; but changed the form of the reply to, "Glad to see you" — a lie so frequently uttered, and by so many, that the virtue of it is all lost.

"Well," said he, "I thought you would be; and so I have improved my vacation season, and come down here to aid you in your researches into our family history. We must devote a month to it. That box you see there" — pointing to a chest about three by six — " is full of papers relating to the subject, which I shall be delighted to read you. Is smoking offensive to you?" — taking a pipe from his pocket, and lighting a match on the sole of his shoe. I told him no, — another lie, — and in a moment more the smoke ascended as a sacrifice upon the altar of my Penates, much to my wife's merriment and disgust, as she stood looking at us through the crack in the door.

My respected relative staid his month out, read all his papers, smoked all his tobacco, and then went back to Vermont, satisfied that he had conferred infinite benefit upon me, while I entertained the opinion that a more infernal bore I had never seen than my relative; that to employ him, Artesian wells might be made very plenty in Vermont; and that, if the tracing of blood subjected one to such annoyances, it were better to be nobody, with no more attainment of notoriety than the mere mention of an obituary at the end.

The gathering of the Smudge family never took place, and the world lost thereby much eloquence, and poetry, and wit; and the Genealogical Society lost a member, who felt that he had not sufficient heart in the work to bear him on triumphantly over the sea of troubles that lay in his path in establishing the fact that he had a family, leaving that to prove itself in the family record and the registry of marriages and births.

DRUMMING.

EVERYBODY knows that mercantile drumming is practised in Boston, as well as in other places. The performers will hang around the hotels for customers, and drum like partridges to secure their prey. The caution of traders is excited by a knowledge of their tricks, who either go in to enjoy the music, or meet the advances of the drummers with a little counter performance of their own. The former course was pursued by a merchant from the West, who came to Boston recently for the first time. He had heard of the drummers, and of their attention to visitors, — showing them the lions about their respective places, and treating them like princes, — and being endowed with a considerable capacity for a good time, and with not much power of resistance, he thought he would, if he fell in with any, let them have their own way. He accordingly came, and stopped at the American House, where his jolly face and laughing eyes were soon conspicuous. Several well-dressed young men at once attached themselves to him, and commenced talking about the West. "Drummers," thought the merchant; "not a doubt about it."

They were soon very well acquainted, and sipped a glass of wine together, or something stronger, as an oblation to the new bond between them. The stranger was surprised to hear from them no mention of business, and, after warming up a little with sundry more libations, he determined to touch upon trade.

"How are Hamiltons now?" said he, breaking the ice by a direct push.

"Hamiltons!" replied one. "Oh! Hamiltons are tip-top — ain't they, Bob?"

"They were the last time I saw them," responded Bob.

They all laughed at this, in which the questioner joined, though he could not, for the soul of him, see what they were laughing at.

"They think I'm a little green," thought he; "but let them go it. They'll come to business soon enough, I dare say."

"How are Amoskeags going?" he asked, after a while.

"Well," was the reply, "I saw Amos last week, and he looked as if he was going to the devil very fast — didn't he, Bob?"

Bob affirmed, with an expression considerably emphatic, that he never saw one going faster.

"Speaking of going," said the principal spokesman, "suppose we show you our town. I should like to have you see some of our lions."

It was beyond the business part of the day, and no objection was made; so the party sallied out, the merchant making the remark that it would be time enough in the morning to look at the Hamiltons. It was a hard season of sprouts that the accommodating drummers put him through. He had never seen better fellows in his life; but they were very mysterious for business men. Several times in the course of their ramble he ventured to put in some word about cottons; but they, with a laugh that he joined in, asked him how whiskey was going at the West, and when he said the tendency was downward, they laughed the louder. He mentioned shoes; but he found that this also was bootless. At last he let the boys have their own way, and shut his mind against business, going in for the fun of the thing. The day closed in a very affectionate manner, the parties separating about midnight, mutually satisfied.

As for the drummers, they carried their mysterious manner throughout, and to his last remark about Hamiltons, as they bade him good night, a reply was made that to his confused hearing sounded somewhat like " Pickles ! "

" Good fellows ! " he thought. " They'll be round in the morning, I dare say."

Turning to the man in the office, he asked him what house those gentlemen who had been with him drummed for.

" Drum for ? " replied the clerk, in a tone of surprise.

" Yes, drum for," said the inquirer, a little indignant at having his question repeated.

" They are not drummers," replied the clerk, bowing politely, " but students of Harvard College."

. " The deuse they are ! " exclaimed the seeker after Hamiltons and Amoskeags. " Then I've been confoundedly sold — that's all."

He booked himself to be called early, and the next morning started for New York without making a purchase, not caring to meet again with his friends, the drummers.

PREACHING TO THE POOR.

Father Taylor once said, " 'Tis of no use to preach to empty
stomachs."

THE parson preached in solemn way,
— A well-clad man on ample pay, —
And told the poor they were sinners all,
Depraved and lost by Adam's fall;
That they must repent, and save their souls.
A hollow-eyed wretch cried, *" Give us coals !"*

Then he told of virtue's pleasant path,
And that of ruin and of wrath;
How the slipping feet of sinners fell
Quick on the downward road to h—,
To suffer for sins when they are dead;
And the hollow voice answered, *" Give us bread !"*

Then he spoke of a land of love and peace,
Where all of pain and woe shall cease,
Where celestial flowers bloom by the way,
Where the light is brighter than solar day,
And there's no cold nor hunger there.
" Oh," says the voice, *" Give us clothes to wear !"*

Then the good man sighed, and turned away,
For such depravity to pray,
That had cast aside the heavenly worth
For the transient and fleeting things of earth !
And his church that night, to his content,
Raised his salary fifty per cent.

THE COURTS.

THE courts are great institutions. We always take our hats off in a court-room, partly from reverence for the law, partly from respect for the custom of the place, and partly from fear of having it knocked from our own poll by the pole of a constable. What a dignity — awful and sublime — seems embodied in the justice who figures in the reports as the alphabetical and familiar "J." We hear him addressed "yer honor," and the spirit prostrates itself before the exponent of stern justice, while fancy draws an imaginary sword and a pair of huge scales in his hand — the latter of which are to be used in weighing the exactest awards, and the former to cut off from the side on which the surplusage remains, as a butcher would divide a piece of beef, or a grocer divide a cheese. We cannot divest ourselves of the idea that we have seen his honor eating a hearty dinner at Parker's, laughing like he'd die at a funny joke, and telling many himself with infinite gusto; "dipping his nose in the Gascon wine" with stupendous relish, as though he were an excellent judge of such things. The judicial ermine becomes in the light of reality a genteel black coat, and the conventional sword and scales fade away like mystic things seen in dreams. What a subject for contemplation is the jury — that "palladium of our liberty," as some one has called it — which stands between the law and trembling rascality, in dignified impartiality to listen to the evidence, the pleadings, and the charge, and remember enough of the combined stupidity, if they are capable of remembering it, to say which side shall win.

We love to look upon those devoted conscripts of the state with their minds made up to one point before they begin, that they are *bored*. The sheriff's wand and the sword, that fearful implement, ready to impale any one who may transgress, are fearful things to contemplate, and we turn to listen to the oath so solemnly administered to the trembling witnesses, who hold up their right hands and bow when the sound of the clerk's voice has ceased, just as if they had understood what he said. But a sublime spectacle to be met with in court is the examination of witnesses in order to arrive at the truth of a case. Had this not been so faithfully described in the report of the case of Bardell *vs.* Pickwick, it would be well to speak of it at this time. Of course every one who goes on the stand is a conspirator on one side or the other, and is disposed — so great is the depravity of the human heart — to lie; hence it is necessary for counsellors, who are dear lovers of the truth, to browbeat and harass them by a thousand impertinent questions, in order to worry the scoundrels into truthfulness by making what they say sound as little like the truth as possible. A man goes upon the stand with an idea that he is, like Hamlet, indifferent honest; but leaves it with a strong impression that he combines in himself the qualities of all the great liars that ever lived, from Ananias to Munchausen, has robbed a graveyard, passed counterfeit money, spent ten years in state prison, and deserves to go there again. Great is Justice, and her courts are sacred. We take our shoes off, figuratively, in reverence, and move out, shutting the door quickly, lest any of the atmosphere of the precinct be displaced by the obtrusion of unsanctified air.

www.ingramcontent.com/pod-product-compliance
Lightning Source LLC
Chambersburg PA
CBHW032006120726

47902CB00014B/1361